Allen Ginsberg

Titles in the series Critical Lives present the work of leading cultural figures of the modern period. Each book explores the life of the artist, writer, philosopher or architect in question and relates it to their major works.

Allen Ginsberg

Steve Finbow

REAKTION BOOKS

Published by Reaktion Books Ltd
33 Great Sutton Street
London EC1V 0DX, UK

www.reaktionbooks.co.uk

First published 2012

Printed and bound in Great Britain
by TJ International, Padstow, Cornwall

'Death of an Irishwoman' from *Collected Poems* (2001) by kind permission of the Estate
of Michael Hartnett and The Gallery Press www.gallerypress.com

Excerpts taken from *Collected Poems 1947–1997* by Allen Ginsberg. Copyright © 2006,
Allen Ginsberg Estate, used by permission.

Excerpts by Allen Ginsberg. Copyright © 2006, Allen Ginsberg Estate, used by permission of The Wylie Agency (UK) Limited.

Excerpts taken from *Collected Poems 1947–1980* by Allen Ginsberg, copyright © 1984 by
Allen Ginsberg. Reprinted by permission of HarperCollins Publishers.

British Library Cataloguing in Publication Data
 Finbow, Steve.
    Allen Ginsberg.– (Critical lives)
    1. Ginsberg, Allen, 1926–1997. 2. Poets, American – 20th
    century – Biography.
     I. Title II. Series
    811.5'4-dc23

ISBN 978 1 78023 017 7

Contents

Introduction

This is Allen / the voice says / Allen Ginsberg calling[1]

In response to a question about an author's typical day, Paul Auster replied, 'That's about as exciting a life as it is for a writer: You write sentences, and you cross out sentences.'[2] If that statement were true of all writers, then the biographer's task would be at once simple and impossible. What we know of a writer's life we gather from interviews, letters, notebooks, journals and diaries. If Auster's assertion is true and writers live a sedentary life, then what in that life could be of interest to a reader? We could start with the facts: genealogy, birth date and place, first words, school, those tentative scrawls in a journal. However, as Philip Roth states in a book sub-titled 'A Novelist's Autobiography',

> obviously the facts are never just coming at you but are incorpo-rated by an imagination that is formed by your previous experience. Memories of the past are not memories of facts but memories of your imaginings of the facts.[3]

Maybe that is all we can do when approaching a writer's life – re-imagine the facts.

If most writers' lives are maps with hazy borders and smudged directions, then Allen Ginsberg provides his readers with a compass and detailed instructions in the form of poems, prose, journals, interviews, recordings and photographs. These documents chronicle his life from the first journal entry in June 1937, until his final poem – 'Things I'll Not Do (Nostalgias)' – on 30 March 1997. He would even show us the x-rays, if he could. In a sense, Ginsberg – born in the years between those two most famous writer-recluses – was the anti-Salinger, the counter-Pynchon.

In his essay 'The Death of the Author', Roland Barthes argues that 'it is language which speaks, not the author: to write is to reach, through a pre-existing impersonality . . . that point where language alone acts, "performs," and not "oneself."'[4] In 1967, the year Barthes' essay saw its first publication in English, Allen Ginsberg had just returned from The Congress of the Dialectics of Liberation in London, taken LSD on a hillside in Wales, composed the text for a Pentagon exorcism, met Ezra Pound, participated in the first Human Be-in, testified for the legalization of psychedelic drugs in a US Senate hearing, and been arrested with Dr Benjamin Spock and Susan Sontag during an anti-draft demonstration; events which appear in 'Wales Visitation', 'Pentagon Exorcism', 'Elegy Che Guevara' and 'War Profit Litany'. For Ginsberg, language speaks only of him, the poet Allen Ginsberg. His poems are autobiographical confessions in which 'Allen' performs, their form driven by self-referential content. Ginsberg's poetics comprise the liberation and revelation of the author in the very act of living. As far as analysis of Ginsberg's poetry goes, the death of this author has been 'greatly exaggerated'.[5]

Ginsberg's archive, sold to Stanford University in October 1994, contains journals, manuscripts, letters, photographs, and school records, badges, T-shirts, calendars, even bus tickets. The archive boxes stretch for 1,000 feet. It is as if Allen, from an early age, knew that one day he'd be famous. From the early poems in *Empty Mirror* and *Gates of Wrath* through to *Death & Fame: Last Poems 1993–1997*, Ginsberg charted his life, his thoughts, experiences, friends and lovers in a mix of raw, honest, egotistical and vulnerable poems. Without Ginsberg, there would have been no Beat Generation: Jack

Kerouac, William S. Burroughs and Gregory Corso would have struggled to find publishers. Without Ginsberg's trips to Morocco and India, his immersion in the Buddhist and Hindu religions, and his early experiments with LSD, the look and philosophy of the 1960s (and today) would have been very different. He gave his time and advice to younger poets, championed radical political causes, and spent half a century looking for someone to share his life. His rampant ego sometimes overshadowed his compassion; his honesty often resulted in contradiction and controversy.

During the summer of 2005, I visited the Allen Ginsberg Trust in New York City. Bob Rosenthal, secretary and friend of Ginsberg for twenty years, as generous as Allen, loaded me with books, CDs and DVDs. As I was leaving, Bob said, 'You know, Steven, since Allen died, the world's gone to shit.' I knew exactly what he meant. What would Allen have said about Live 8 concerts, George W. Bush's second inauguration, North Korea's nuclear weapons, and America's failure to sign the Kyoto Protocol? What would he say today about WikiLeaks, the 'Don't ask, don't tell' policy, the politics of the Tarnac Nine, the Invisible Committee's *The Coming Insurrection*, and Tiqqun?

In this cynical era 'in which "cosmopolitan fingering", a detached spectorialism, replaces engagement and involvement',[6] Ginsberg's immersion in politics, poetics, policies and causes; his participation in the social and the academic; the use of his writing and personality as tools to fight oppression and injustice; his obsession with ecology, insanity, drugs and sexual openness, make him still one of the prophets of the age and an indefatigable champion of the marginalized. In the words of Tiqqun's *Introduction to Civil War*, Ginsberg took '[h]is own presence to self as a source of energy for his revolt'.[7]

Allen Ginsberg's main biographers – Barry Miles, Michael Schumacher, Ed Sanders and Bill Morgan – provide a distillation and analysis of Ginsberg's life and work; all knew Ginsberg personally and approach his life from varying standpoints and gradations of intimacy. Outside of Ginsberg's poems, journals, letters, prose and interviews, it is to these four that I owe my biggest debt. This text is an amalgamation and agglomeration of the works, biographies, documentaries, secondary readings, correspondence and personal recollection. It is not a study of Ginsberg as Jewish poet, homosexual, Buddhist or psychedelic guru – comprehensive books, guides and essays on these subjects are listed in the bibliography. Nor does it use methodical criticism from any school of thought. I approached the writing 'with a sense of just having to go about and do it, without establishing first exactly what my theoretical position is'.[8] Rather than reach for my Penguin Freud, unless Ginsberg's texts prompted me in a speculative direction for which I already knew the coordinates, I reference what occurred to me at the time, be it Tintin or Foucault, Vonnegut or Wittgenstein. When critically referencing the texts, I refer to Allen as Ginsberg. When looking at the life so enwrapped and enraptured in the text, he is Allen – as he was to everyone. When I read the poems critically, they are living things in the present, not desiccated library husks yellowing in the past tense.

Ed Sanders writes that it 'might be interesting to do a Total Biography of Ginsberg . . . perhaps a day-to-day bio, maybe 25,000 pages long'.[9] Ginsberg's luminous traces certainly do not rob 'biographers of this material',[10] but in the belief that sometimes 'an eight-hundred-page biography is nothing more than dead conjecture',[11] I offer you one a quarter of that size in the hope of re-animating, for a time, a complicated, passionate and ebullient life.

Sketch for Presspop figurine, designed by Archer Prewitt, sculpted by Kei Hinotani.

1

'Hell on Earth', 1926–47

I dwelled in Hell on earth to write this rhyme[1]

Atlantic waves broke on the New Jersey shore: the place was Belmar in the summer of 1938 and a black-and-white home movie shows a skinny twelve-year-old boy in a bathing suit, bucktooth smile spread across his face, performing forward rolls on the beach. Cut to the boy and his seventeen-year-old brother as their father Louis douses them with seawater. The grinning boy shaking his skinny limbs looks like any other kid on the beach, dark mischievous eyes twinkling with thoughts of the nearby amusement park. However, if one were to sneak a look into his journal – the one he received the year before as a birthday gift – one would see two entries that mark out Allen Ginsberg as somewhat different from your average Jersey kid:

Tuesday. March 1, 1938. Nothing new today. Naomi is still in the sanitarium but will be out in about one month.[2]

September 10, 1938 – What fools these Nazis be. In later years I expect to use this book for history. The world is now in turmoil.[3]

Allen's mother, Naomi, had suffered from nervous breakdowns since 1919, the year she married Louis. These breakdowns took the form of visual and aural hypersensitivity, and their intensity forced her to relinquish her job as a teacher in a Newark grammar school. Allen enjoyed tales of his parents' backgrounds, like the one about how, in 1904, having fled pogroms and the Pale of Settlement in European Russia, eight-year-old Naomi Livergant's family eventually made their home in the mostly Jewish ghetto surrounding Orchard Street in Manhattan's Lower East Side. There, Naomi's mother and father invested their savings in a candy store and ice cream parlour:

> then struggling in the crowds of Orchard Street toward what?—
>   toward Newark?—
> toward candy store, first home-made sodas of the century,
>   hand-churned ice cream in backroom on musty brownfloor
>   boards—[4]

Or the one his father recounted where, in Newark, Allen's paternal grandfather Pinkus (Peter), having arrived in America from Pinsk in Belarus in the 1880s – but originally from Galicia on the borders of Poland and Ukraine – married Rebecca Schechtman. The couple put their savings into a laundry company and later ran a tobacco shop. Allen memorized such events and more. Born on 1 October 1895, his father Louis grew up an agnostic socialist. In 1912, Louis met Naomi at Newark's Barrington High School where, influenced by a teacher's class on Milton's 'L'Allegro', he wrote his first lyric poems. While dating, the young couple discussed poetry, played tennis and had vehement political arguments – Naomi was a member of the Communist Party.

By the time of the home movie, Naomi's mild schizophrenic episodes had become more frequent and intense. Although Louis tried to shield him from the worst of it, Allen found his mother's madness and suicide attempts both frightening and fascinating, recording and preserving the experiences in his notebooks:

Terror, that woke the neighbors—old ladies on the second
floor recovering from menopause—all those rags between
thighs, clean sheets, sorry over lost babies—husbands ashen—[5]

Foucault states that the madman (sic) 'crosses the frontiers of
bourgeois order of his own accord, and alienates himself outside the
sacred limits of its ethic'.[6] From the 1950s on, Ginsberg transformed
Naomi's insanity into a breaching of American morals, used it as a
basis for alienating himself from society, and to challenge the 'sacred
limits' of America's ethics. Living with madness created in Ginsberg
an anti-authoritarian stance, a protective and zealous regard for the
disenfranchised and oppressed.

If Allen's compassion and search for love stemmed from his
relationship with his mother then his interest in poetry came from
his father. Unfit for call-up during the First World War, Louis
entered Rutgers University, graduating in 1918 to become an
English teacher, his occupation for the next 40 years. He married
Naomi in 1919 and on 2 June 1921 Allen's brother Eugene Brooks
was born. Louis's poems appeared in *Poetry*, the *New Yorker*, the
New Masses and *New York Times* magazine, as well as anthologies.
In the 1969 preface to
his father's *Morning in Spring and Other Poems*, Allen confessed,
'Living a generation with lyrics wrought by my father, some stanzas
reflecting this eternal place settle in memory as perfected.'[7]

Irwin Allen Ginsberg was born at 2 a.m. on 3 June 1926. The
family, who lived in a cramped apartment at 163 Quitman Street,
Newark, were happy despite their debts, and Naomi doted on her
youngest son. When Allen was three years old, his mother had
major surgery on her pancreas and the family lodged with Allen's
Aunt Eleanor in the Bronx:

many-windowed apartments walled the crowded Bronx road-way
under old theater roofs, masses of poor women shopping

in black shawls past candy store news stands, children skipped
  beside
grandfathers bent tottering on their canes.[8]

The next year, the family moved to a rooming house at 83 Fair
Street, Paterson, closer to Louis's job at the city's Central High
School. In his new neighbourhood, the local kids nicknamed Allen
'The Professor'.[9] He sought acceptance throughout his life and,
knowing even at this early age that it wasn't always forthcoming,
found refuge in books and his father's recitations of Emily
Dickinson and Edgar Allan Poe. Future joys stirred – arguments
with his brother sparked his interest in debate; his favourite meal
of chicken fricassee became the main course of a lifelong love of
Eastern European food;[10] and when not at the Belmar beach he
spent summers at Communist Party-run camps singing Yiddish
folk songs and communist anthems. Madness, poetry, politics and
a longing for love – important elements of Allen's childhood –
obsessed him throughout his life and became the subject matter
of his greatest poems, 'Howl' and 'Kaddish'.

During the Depression, Louis took on additional teaching jobs
but still had to take Naomi out of private sanitariums and place her
in state hospitals. Eventually, in 1933, the financial difficulties
forced the Ginsbergs out of 83 Fair Street. Outwardly, things were
happy in the new house at 155 Haledon Avenue – Allen listened to
classical music and the radio serials *Flash Gordon* and *The Shadow* –
but bogeymen and bullies tormented him, and he would wet himself rather than visit the school's scary basement toilets. Allen
witnessed and participated in fellatio, watched older boys in acts
of sexual humiliation, exposed his genitals in public, and had
sexual dreams that involved spanking:

Last night I dreamt they blamed me again on the streetcorner
They got me bent over with my pants down and spanked my

behind I was ashamed

I was red faced my self was naked I got hot I had a hard on.[11]

Examining a troublesome appendix, a doctor probed Allen's anus, causing him to cry out in agony. Allen woke after the subsequent operation to find a nasty scar. He would write starkly confessional poems about his masochism and sexual preference for submissive intercourse, and would take as lovers men who mistreated him physically and mentally. Naomi, also scarred abdominally, was a naturist and vegetarian, and Allen later used nudity as a means of preventing aggression. His efforts at vegetarianism were not so successful.

In 1935, Louis committed Naomi to Greystone Park, the New Jersey State Hospital for the Insane, where she underwent insulin and Metrazol shock treatment. The Metrazol's side effects included gastro-intestinal bloating, nausea, vomiting, diarrhoea and depression. After returning home in 1936, Naomi's paranoia worsened and she believed doctors controlled her, having placed wires in her head during her treatment. With Louis at work and Eugene studying, Allen became Naomi's primary caregiver, missing school to nurse her through her paranoia and schizophrenia. If, as Foucault asserts, 'madness is childhood',[12] then Allen's was a happy one. In his spare time, he collected stamps and coins, and indulged his interests in astronomy and geology; his Aunt Hannah (Honey) and Uncle Leo remembered him excitedly racing his father around the block.[13]

In the journal he received for his eleventh birthday, Allen listed films he'd seen – *The Life of Emile Zola*, *Firefly*, *Saratoga* and *Hollywood Hotel*[14] – and books he'd read; he mused on politics and family life, and recorded his dreams, ambitions and fears. The journal opened: 'Don't mind my spelling, writing, or language.'[15] Three weeks later, on 24 June, after a party for Eugene's graduation, Allen's journal entry reported Naomi barricading herself in the bathroom and Louis smashing the glass-panelled door to find her covered in blood. Her latest suicide attempt – she tried to cut her wrists – meant a two-year incarceration in Greystone.

On 12 March 1938, Nazi Germany annexed Austria and Allen railed against Hitler and 'Mooselini'.[16] On 13 March, Clarence Darrow, one of Allen's heroes, died; his views on free speech and civil liberties inspired Allen's ambition to become a labour lawyer. After spending the summer of 1939 at Belmar, Allen started school at Central High, Paterson. He contributed to the yearbook, the newspaper *Criterion*, and became president of the dramatic club and debating society.

Even at the age of twelve, Allen understood his father's frustrations in caring for a schizophrenic wife while trying to raise two children. That sense of understanding was shattered when he discovered Louis's extramarital affairs. Louis and Naomi's marriage limped on with occasional times of lucidity and togetherness. The family visited the World's Fair at Flushing Meadows in 1940, but these happy episodes grew ever shorter. Later in the year, Naomi forced Allen to help her escape the Ginsberg home, taking buses across New Jersey in a nightmarish psychotic trip to a Lakewood rest home, culminating in a violent confrontation with the police, a desperate call to Louis, and what Allen believed was his mother's final descent into madness. In Naomi's mind, Allen turned from confidant to adversary: she denied her dependence on him, removed her trust, and withdrew what little remained of her maternal feelings. Out of these dynamics, Allen later created the poems 'Kaddish', 'White Shroud' and 'Black Shroud'. In his doomed love affairs, particularly in his relationship with Peter Orlovsky, he recreated his and Naomi's claustrophobic co-dependency.

Allen wrote articles for the school newspaper *Spectator* and a column for the local *Paterson Evening News*, stood unsuccessfully for class treasurer, and appeared in the school show. In September 1941, for his final two years of high school, he transferred to

Eastside High. There, his English Literature teacher, Mrs Francis Durbin, gave him Walt Whitman's 'Song of Myself' to read. Its impassioned declarative lines would become a seminal influence on his poetry:

> Earth of departed sunset—earth of the mountains misty-topt!
> Earth of the vitreous pour of the full moon just tinged with
>   blue![17]

Allen responded by writing his first poems. He also developed his first serious crush on a boy. The 'R——' in the passage below is Paul Roth:

> Went to bed exhausted, wanting to leave the world, (prob-
> ably that year newly in love with R—[18]

The love was one-sided – as were many of Allen's crushes – but the friendship remained strong enough for Roth, a Columbia freshman, to suggest that Allen send in an application to the Ivy League university.

Soon after Japan attacked Pearl Harbor on 7 December 1941, Eugene, studying to be a lawyer, received Air Force call-up papers and Allen threw himself into local Democratic Party politics. The war politicized Allen and he wrote passionate letters to the *New York Times* on American isolationism and failure to join the League of Nations.

To save money for Columbia, Allen stacked shelves in the Paterson Public Library during the winter of 1942–3. He read Havelock Ellis's sexual theories and Krafft-Ebing's *Psychopathia Sexualis*, looking for clues to his erotic dreams about his brother and father, and his homosexual, spanking, faecal and urophilia fantasies. With better than average marks, he graduated from Eastside High School on 24 June 1943. His fellow students chose one of his verses as class poem and it appeared in the school newspaper the *Senior Mirror*. A month earlier, a letter from Columbia University confirmed his acceptance and a scholarship of $300 per annum. Allen was set for college, determined to become a lawyer.

He admitted to his journal back in May 1941, that he 'began writing to (I suppose) satisfy my egotism', that he was 'capable of almost anything' and 'hasn't the time to be bored'.[19] The self-belief and inability to relax drove his literary ambition but had an adverse effect on his health. From the summer of 1943, the mentally precocious but still sexually naive seventeen-year-old Jersey kid would – after a few diversions – focus his energy, persuasive powers and ego on changing the course of American literature; after all, as he noted in his journal, 'finished Hamlet. I liked it, but I'd like to see it played before I pass judgment.'[20]

Galvanized by pre-law courses, economics, history, French and English literature, Allen joined the Columbia debating team and became editor of the *Jester* magazine and president of the Philolexian Society which strived to 'improve its members in oratory, composition, and forensic discussion'.[21] Sharing a suite of rooms on the top floor of the Union Theological Seminary on 122nd Street, Allen enjoyed the intellectual atmosphere and opportunities to discuss sexuality.

One night, during the winter recess of 1943, Allen walked the seventh-floor halls tracing the source of the dramatic music he heard playing. According to Bill Morgan in *I Celebrate Myself: The Somewhat Private Life of Allen Ginsberg*, without knocking, Allen opened a door and said: '"My name's Allen Ginsberg. Do you mind if I listen?" The blond, good-looking nineteen-year-old replied, "I'm Lucien Carr, and since you're in, you might as well sit down."'[22] Barry Miles in *Ginsberg: A Biography*, has it happening like this: '"I heard the music," explains Allen. "Did you like it?" asks Carr. "I thought it might be the Brahms Clarinet Quintet."

"Well, well! A little oasis in the wasteland," says Carr, inviting Ginsberg into his room.'[23] The music was Brahms's Piano Trio No. 1.

A year older than Allen, born in New York City on 1 March 1925, Lucien Carr grew up in St Louis. His parents divorced and, by the age of fourteen, Carr's rebelliousness led to his expulsion from various schools. While attending a Scout group in St Louis, he met 28-year-old David Kammerer, an English and physical education teacher. Fourteen years Carr's senior, Kammerer became sexually obsessed with him, following him to schools in Massachusetts and Maine and eventually to the University of Chicago. To outsiders, Carr and Kammerer seemed firm friends, living off a mix of alcohol, desire, repulsion and manipulation. During his time at the University of Chicago, Carr attempted to gas himself, his family blaming it on Kammerer. After committing him to two weeks in a psychiatric hospital, Carr's mother insisted he enrol at Columbia University. Inevitably, Kammerer followed, finding a job as a waiter in the Lion's Den, a campus cafe, and it was here that Allen met him.

Lucien, beautiful with a streak of insanity and a sophisticated taste in the arts, became the next impossible love of Allen's life. On 18 December, the three friends went drinking in the bars of Greenwich Village, Allen excited at the prospect of getting drunk and following in the footsteps of Walt Whitman who, with an earlier group of young bohemians interested in exploring different forms of consciousness and sexuality,[24] frequented Pfaff's beer cellar on Broadway.

Kammerer lived in a studio at 48 Morton Street, a one-block walk to 69 Bedford Street and an apartment rented by his childhood friend William S. Burroughs. Burroughs, twelve years Allen's senior, came from a privileged and once affluent background. His parents paid him a small allowance and he supplemented this with jobs tending bar, working for a detective agency and as an exterminator. Allen found the Harvard-educated Burroughs's intellectualism and outrageous behaviour fascinating: 'When I was 18, in college, and talking with Burroughs, he gave me Yeats' *Vision*, Spengler's *Decline of the West* and Blake's poems to read as well as Shakespeare's lines.'[25]

Situated on Broadway and 114th Street, the West End bar became the regular meeting place for the quartet. Allen had long dreamed about seduction by an intelligent, more experienced older man – in the wooden booths of the West End, he explored and developed these fantasies. It was also here that Carr met Edie Parker, a student at Barnard College, and dated her friend Celine Young. Celine Young's flatmate Joan Vollmer Adams once lived with John Kingsland, whom Allen knew from high school. Edie had taken over Kingsland's apartment on the sixth floor of a building at 421 West 118th Street and, although dating Henri Cru, she had fallen in love with his friend, a handsome, football-playing, Thomas Wolfe-obsessed writer. The Beat soap opera's pilot episode was about to go live.

By the time Allen met him in Edie's apartment, Jack Kerouac, born on 12 March 1922, in Lowell, Massachusetts, had spent a year at Horace Mann Preparatory School, played collegiate football, broken a leg in his Columbia freshman year, lost his scholarship, and left college. He had recently joined both the Merchant Marine and US Navy, and received an honourable discharge on psychiatric grounds, diagnosed as having an 'indifferent character' with a schizoid personality.[26] Kerouac's first impression of Allen was far from flattering: 'he was a lecher who wanted everybody in the world to take a bath in the same huge bathtub which would give him a chance to feel legs under the dirty water.'[27]

Within the circle of jazz-loving, poetry-quoting bohemians who hung out at the West End and at Edie's apartment, Jack and Allen recognized in each other a shared spirituality, sensitivity and literary ambition. Although he took classes with Lionel Trilling and Mark Van Doren, Allen's intellectual stimulation emanated from discussing Arthur Rimbaud's poetry and letters with Carr, Alfred Korzybski's philosophy of general semantics with Burroughs, and listening to Kerouac read from his early writings.

Allen cultivated a sexual interest in women, but his unspoken and unrequited love for Paul Roth, Carr and now Kerouac made him feel guilty about his homosexuality, as did the ongoing sexual dreams about his father. Arthur Rimbaud had similar erotic fantasies, the young Arthur listening to 'the dirty talk', feeling 'the strange stirrings', his 'fingers itching to undo the fly', to 'get at the big, dark, hard bit of my father'.[28]

In self-pity, on 3 August, Allen wrote a suicide note. Later that evening, walking along 115th Street between Columbia and Morningside Park, he had what Keroauc will later term a 'naked lunch' moment – 'a frozen moment when everyone sees what is on the end of every fork'.[29] In 1915, D. H. Lawrence had a similar experience, 'So vivid a vision, everything so visually poignant, it is like that concentrated moment when a drowning man sees all his past crystallized into one jewel of recollection.'[30] Likewise, Allen realized he was in the present, that raw existence and not the past was important, and he returned to his room believing, 'This is your single moment of life, Allen.'[31] Eleven days later, two blocks west, a single moment of violence would end a life.

On Monday 14 August, after drinking all night in the West End, Lucien Carr and David Kammerer staggered to Riverside Park. There, they quarrelled, the argument turned physical, and the two men wrestled in the damp grass. Friends would speculate on why the two men came to blows.[32] Did Kammerer insist on oral sex and Carr resist? Did they argue over Lucien's girlfriend? Whatever the reason, after years of stalking and obsession, Carr snapped, stabbed Kammerer twelve times with his Boy Scout knife, twice through the heart; then he gathered rocks, placed them in Kammerer's pockets, took out his shoelaces, tied his hands and rolled the body into the grey Hudson.

Drunk and bloodstained, Lucien made his way to Burroughs's apartment. Bill was having none of it and phlegmatically suggested Carr plead self-defence. Lucien turned to Kerouac, who helped dispose of the bloody clothing and knife. The two men spent the day at the cinema and drinking in bars mulling over what Lucien should do. With his mother, Carr visited the district attorney who advised him to go to the police in the hope that the court would consider this an 'honour killing' and be lenient. With the help of his parents' lawyer, and the payment of a $2,500 bond, Burroughs escaped prosecution as a material witness and returned to St Louis. Police arrested Kerouac and held him in jail; his father refused to pay bail. In order for Edie's parents to post bond, Kerouac and Edie married on 25 August, a police officer acting as best man.

When Allen heard the news, he called his father and asked Trilling and Van Doren for guidance. At court, Carr's legal team convinced the jury that Carr was an innocent victim of Kammerer's sexual predation. Convicted of first-degree manslaughter, the judge sent Carr to Elmira Reformatory, where he spent two years of a one-to-twenty-year sentence.

This event appeared in the fiction of William Gaddis, John Clellon Holmes, and in Kerouac's *The Town and the City* and *Vanity of Duluoz*. Written in 1945, Burroughs's and Kerouac's *And the Hippos were Boiled in Their Tanks* – the earliest extant collaboration between major Beat writers – is a fictionalized account of the slaying. James Grauerholz, Burroughs's literary executor, agreed to the manuscript's publication in 2008, three years after Carr's death.

The murder also inspired Allen to begin 'Bloodsong', a novel combining themes from Dostoevsky's *Crime and Punishment*, *Notes from Underground* and *The Idiot* (Allen's favourite novel) with others from André Gide's *The Counterfeiters*, *The Immoralist* and *The Vatican Cellars*; a fusion of existential and spiritual violence with the politics of homosexual repression and the problems of personal authenticity. He abandoned it after Columbia's Associate Professor Dean Nicholas

McKnight, wary of adverse publicity, read the manuscript and wrote to Allen asking him to rethink the project. Depressed, Allen wrote another suicide note and the poems 'Elegy on Cemetery Rosebush', 'Monologue on Deathbed' and 'Jupiter Symphony', evoking the melancholia of Romanticism, the image of the doomed poet – Allen Ginsberg as/is Thomas Chatterton.

Throughout his early college years, Allen attempted to shock his father by insisting the worldviews of Burroughs and Carr were more valid than his father's democratic socialism or his lecturers' academic conservatism. In a letter to his sister Hannah Litzky, Louis complained, 'Allen . . . is writing a novel whose hero is a fictionalized Lucien Carr, a twisted eccentric. In addition, Allen regards any protest against his use of vulgar words in a novel as questioning his artistic integrity.'[33] After an exchange of letters, Louis asked, 'What about a psychiatrist?'[34] Worried that his new friends and his extracurricular reading were becoming detrimental to Allen's studies, Louis visited McKnight and Trilling to ask if they could help Allen graduate.

Originally Carr's idea, 'the new vision' Allen promulgated in the early months of 1945 (and repeated to interviewers throughout his life) questioned established ethics and morals, promoted the

Allen Ginsberg, and brother Eugene Brooks (in uniform), photobooth 1944.

artist's role in society, prioritized the artist's honesty in self-expression, championed experimentation with new forms of consciousness, and called for transcendentalism through a Rimbaud-like derangement of the senses.[35] It was not dissimilar to many an undergraduate clique's pretentious manifesto, nor to André Breton's definition of Surrealism as 'psychic automatism in its pure state, by which one proposes to express – verbally, by means of the written word, or in any other manner – the actual functioning of thought. Dictated by thought, in the absence of any control exercised by reason, exempt from any aesthetic or moral concern.'[36]

Although banned from campus, on 16 March 1945, Kerouac surreptitiously visited Allen in his rooms. They talked up their theories on 'the new vision' and Kerouac stayed the night. Earlier that day, Allen and his roommate had drawn a penis, skull and crossbones and scrawled 'Fuck the Jews!' and 'Butler has no balls' on their dusty dorm window – Butler being Nicholas Murray Butler, President of Columbia. A cleaner found the graffiti and reported it. At 8 a.m. on 17 March, Assistant Dean Ralph Furey (one of Kerouac's football coaches) opened the door to Allen's room to find his ex-wingback in bed with Allen. Kerouac bolted from the room – maybe doing a version of his famous 'jack-off' style of running. The authorities fined Allen for Kerouac's overnight stay, told him to wipe off the graffiti and sent a letter to his father. Despite interventions by Trilling and Van Doren, Allen received a twelve-month suspension.

A Columbia University student from Denver, Hal Chase, took a room in Joan Vollmer's 115th Street apartment in September. Allen also moved in and developed a crush on the good-looking Chase. It was here that 'The Night of the Wolfeans and the Non-Wolfeans' occurred.[37] Fuelled by amphetamines and alcohol, Ginsberg and Burroughs championed European decadence while Chase and Kerouac advocated the American experience as found in Thomas Wolfe's *Look Homeward, Angel*. Not long after this legendary evening, a decadent angel made his own appearance on the scene.

Born in 1915, Herbert Huncke left Chicago in 1939 to hitchhike to New York City. He joined the Merchant Marine during the Second World War and became a hustler around Times Square and 42nd Street, selling his body to maintain his heroin addiction. Burroughs described him in *Junky* as 'small and very thin, his neck loose in the collar of his shirt . . . his mouth . . . drawn down at the corners in a grimace of petulant annoyance'.[38] Huncke introduced Allen to the criminal underworld of Times Square, male and female prostitutes, homosexuals, lesbians, gunrunners and drug pushers. When it came to narcotics, Allen's scientific approach meant consumption didn't become addiction – as it would with Burroughs and Kerouac – Allen viewed drug-taking as an experiment, not a lifestyle.

While suspended from college, Allen earned a spot-welder's certificate and enlisted in the Merchant Marine (the Military Sea Transportation Service) in June. He spent his days, when not cleaning out latrines, reading Hart Crane, Rimbaud, Tolstoy, Stendhal, *Batman* and *Superman* comics, swimming, sunbathing and going into the city dressed in navy uniform. He hoped to use the experience in novels or poems, a mildly heroic endeavour with hints of Herman Melville and Jack London.

The first two weeks of January 1946, Allen worked on the ss *Groveton*. While on board the tanker, he finished the poem 'Ode to Decadence', incorporating the 'jive talk' he had heard on board ship and while hanging out with Huncke.[39] He hadn't quite found the right tone, its language a hybrid of classicism and hipsterism, but he recognized this and knew he could cite Wordsworth's praxis of writing poems in a 'language really used by men'.[40] And nor had he found his sea legs – a crippling bout of seasickness brought on another depression.

Ginsberg in a photobooth shot taken during his six weeks Merchant Marine training, Sheepshead Bay, Brooklyn, August 1945.

For the next six months, Allen worked first on a ship carrying coal and then at a Bickford's cafeteria. Struggling with his poetry, he confided to Trilling that he might abandon the idea of becoming a writer. His formally composed poems hinted at the experimental, yet, according to Louis, they were 'a bit amorphous and not focused enough'.[41] However, 'Death in Violence', a more experimental poem with proto-'Howl' phrasing, won $150 for Columbia's George Edward Woodberry Prize:

O heroes, hipsters, humanists, Prometheans!
arrange your lives as best you can before the voyage—[42]

One night, Allen plucked up the courage to confess his love to Jack and attempted to seduce him. Kerouac mumbled a demurral and changed the subject. Frustrated and depressed because of his sexuality and low-paid jobs, Allen wrote to Dean McKnight requesting reinstatement. McKnight asked for reassurance that Allen would apply himself to his studies and requested a psychiatric evaluation before considering the matter. A Dr Hans Wassing obliged and Allen composed the letter (supposedly from the psychiatrist) outlining his renewed diligence. The re-application was successful and Allen returned to Columbia in September.

With Burroughs running a farm in Texas, Joan hospitalized in Bellevue's psychiatric ward, and Kerouac concentrating on his writing, Allen decided to move out of the 115th Street apartment and take a room on West 92nd Street. To escape the pressures of college and the confines of his new room, he frequented the bars in Greenwich Village and Times Square. One evening, Allen met a man in the Hotel Astor. They had rough sex, Allen passive, pushed down on to the mattress, the stench of shit pervading the room. In December, while having a drink with the newly released Lucien Carr, Allen admitted his homosexuality, and was relieved when Lucien listened without judgement. Despite Allen's tendency to fall in love, he was yet to have a homosexual relationship, the problem being – and this recurred throughout his life – that the men he fell in love with were mostly heterosexual.

Allen spent time with Huncke and Priscilla Arminger (aka Vicki Russell), a tall red-haired prostitute who showed the group how to swallow Benzedrine inhaler wads. Already experimenting with barbiturates and opiates – he first took heroin with Burroughs who was in the city for Joan's release from hospital – Allen asked Trilling's advice and was told, as Louis had suggested the year before, that Allen might want to undergo psychoanalysis and start acting his age.

In late October 1946, Neal Cassady stole some money, a few books, and a car in Nebraska. After dumping the car at the bus station, Neal and his sixteen-year-old wife LuAnne took a Greyhound to Manhattan. After lunch at Hector's Cafeteria on 44th Street, the couple rode the subway uptown to the West End to meet Neal's Denver friend Hal Chase. Chase had told Neal all about Allen, Kerouac and Huncke and, intrigued, Neal wanted to meet them. In Bill Morgan's version, Allen fell instantly in love with Neal.

Cassady's biographers assert that the meeting was not successful and that Allen made fun of LuAnne's name.[43] Whether sparked by love or sarcasm, subsequent meetings of Ginsberg, Kerouac and Cassady would, in different ways, change each of their lives.

Cassidy was born on 8 February 1926 in Salt Lake City. His parents separated after the family's Hollywood barbershop closed. From the age of six, Neal lived in cheap Denver hotel rooms with his alcoholic father. Highly promiscuous, he lost his virginity at the age of nine, sold his body for food and money from the age of twelve, boosted more than 500 cars to impress his many girlfriends, and spent fifteen months in correctional reformatories. He had a massive appetite for masturbation and sex of any kind.

Allen's dream of a loving sexual partner darkened somewhat when he met a sadist and a liar with whom he fell deeply and dangerously in love. Allen obsessed over Neal and, fearing rejection, considered suicide. But Neal rarely spurned anyone's advances and so Allen embarked on his first serious sexual relationship. Neal could do no wrong; Allen naively believed Neal's claim to be able to experience and process sixteen simultaneous cognitive strata, which allowed him, so he boasted, to conduct multiple concurrent conversations, and his boast that he had read all of Kant by the age of twelve. In the letters they shared over the first three months of the relationship, it is obvious that Allen was gushingly smitten; whereas Neal demanded things (books, addresses, suitcases, trousers). Maybe Neal had read Kant, even Heidegger, as his insistence and demand for Allen 'being-present-at-hand' goes along with the understanding that the 'being of objects is given immediately only in the way it is related to [Neal's] drive and [Neal's] will'.[44] Allen confided to his journal, Neal 'will do no wrong. I trust him.'[45]

On 4 March 1947, Neal left New York for Denver via Kansas City. Allen and Kerouac saw him off at the bus station. Returning to his room, Allen spent the next few weeks brooding over Neal (unaware Cassady had seduced two women on the bus to Kansas City), and writing poems imitative of Donne, Marvell and Hart Crane. One of these poems, 'A Lover's Garden', won Allen second prize in the Columbia Philolexian Society poetry contest and the *Columbia Review* published it in August:

> That all men may, as I, arrange
> A love as simple, sweet, and strange
> As few men know; nor can I tell,
> But only imitate farewell.[46]

In this poem, Ginsberg camouflages his homosexuality in imitative verse; however much 'the new vision' called for honest self-expression, in their writing, both he and Kerouac hid the true extent of their homosexual experiences. Ginsberg's poetic language here and in the Neal-inspired 'The Denver Doldrums', 'disguises thought. So much so, that from the outward form of the clothing it is impossible to infer the form of the thought beneath it, because the outward form of the clothing is not designed to reveal the form of the body, but for entirely different purposes'[47] – and he did this mainly to not upset his father.

Neal's departure and Joan's move to Texas to join Burroughs and Huncke exacerbated Allen's fragile state of mind and he sought counselling from various psychoanalysts, including Wilhelm Reich, to whom he sent a letter confessing his drug use, criminal friends, homosexuality, masochism, heterosexual impotence, depression and Kafkaesque sordidness.

During the summer, Allen decided to make his first cross-country journey to meet Neal at Burroughs's farm in New Waverly, Texas, and reignite their sexual relationship, the two having spent the spring exchanging love letters. Allen arrived to find the tumbledown farm manned by a morphine-addicted Burroughs, Joan seven months pregnant on a continual

Benzedrine rush and Huncke travelling to Houston and back to buy alcohol and marijuana seeds. Allen enjoyed himself on the farm, tending plants, learning to drive and listening to music. The main reason he was there was to see Cassady, but Neal was involved with a 'new interest'[48] – Carolyn Robinson – and wrote to Allen explaining that he was at his capacity sexually and that Allen should make a trip to Denver where, possibly, he, his girlfriend and Allen could live together – as long as Allen brought some of Bill's 'tea' with him.

After promising to return for the marijuana harvest, Allen spent the remainder of his cash on a bus ticket to Denver. When he arrived, Cassady told Allen he could not room with him. Burroughs mailed Allen $10 to tide him over until he found work vacuuming carpets in a department store. Allen and Carolyn became awkward friends, spending Neal-less time together while Cassady tended to his wife and other lovers. Neal was a sexual sadist and Allen a willing yet guilt-ridden masochist. One night, he lay awake listening to Neal have sex with Carolyn in the hotel room the three were sharing.

These two months of solitary longing, sexual experimentation, self-analysis and self-delusion inspired two of Ginsberg's earliest poems in which the later honest voice is evident, although the explicit sex and language remain absent:

> I ate a sandwich of pure meat; an
> enormous sandwich of human flesh,
> I noticed, when I was chewing on it,
> it also included a dirty asshole.[49]

'In Society' and 'The Bricklayer's Lunch Hour' move away from obfuscation towards a poetics of observation, analysis and confession. The world of 'In Society' is nightmarish – the claustrophobic hotel room mirrors Ginsberg's relationship with Cassady, his anger at Neal's behaviour, his separation from 'queer' society in pursuit of

Cassady, the triple-decker bed of Neal/Allen/LuAnne or Carolyn, makes him feel guilty and impotent. These masochistic tropes contrast with the need for protection in 'The Bricklayer's Lunch Hour'; the builders of houses, resting, sheltering kittens, a soft sexuality, a hope of respite against gathering madness and desire:

> A small cat walks to him
> along the top of the wall. He picks
> it up, takes off his cap, and puts it
> over the kitten's body for a moment.[50]

In these poems, a slow awareness that 'The world is my world: this is manifest in the fact that the limits of *language* (of that language which alone I understand) means the limits of my world', is apparent.[51] The subsequent openness about his sexuality, his politics, his illnesses and his impending death would create a confessional poetics sometimes shocking in its veracity, sometimes embarrassing in its neediness.

Passing through Denver on his way to San Francisco, Kerouac visited but left soon after, tired of Allen's romantic wallowing and delusional dreams. Cassady used Allen's passive masochism as a fallback for sex when none of his women were available. So blind was Allen to Cassady's true feelings that some of his friends called the affair 'Allen in Wonderland'.[52]

During the early hours of 24 August, Allen and Cassady hitchhiked to Burroughs's farm. While waiting for a ride, they knelt at a crossroads (or parking lot) and pledged their spiritual and physical love. Until his death, Allen considered this 'vow' a momentous occasion in his life, poeticizing the event in his tribute poem to Neal – 'The Green Automobile'. Cassady failed to mention the 'vow' in any of his writings.

They arrived on 29 August, and Allen and Huncke unsuccessfully tried to make a bed for Neal and Allen to share. With Burroughs and

Joan deep into drugs, and Huncke and Cassady wanting to go to Houston, Allen became depressed and felt rejected. There followed a week of slapstick sex-and-drug-fuelled days in Houston. Neal brought a beautiful 'mad woman' back to their hotel room and fucked her while Allen and Huncke listened in the adjoining room.[53] This made Huncke mad with Neal because he had brought a boy up to the room for the same purpose. With Neal unconscious, Allen threw the woman out of the room. He lost the job he had found on a freighter going to Marseille by showing up late on the day it was to sail. All three forgot to buy ice for Burroughs's icebox, the main reason for their trip, which meant Burroughs's food had spoiled by the time they got back to New Waverly. The atmosphere on the farm darkened and the group decided to split; Allen signed on to a collier bound for Dakar in French Equatorial Africa and Cassady returned to Denver.

Allen wrote to his father about finishing college 'unlike all the stupid Yiddish boys of yore',[54] but needed a break (as in his poetry, he disguised the truth of his relationship with Cassady) and asked Louis to contact the Dean to apply for a sabbatical. The college agreed and Allen set sail on ss *John Blair* from Freeport, Texas for Dakar. The trip took 50 days with Allen trading his Denver doldrums for the actual Doldrums of the Atlantic. Like his hero (and fellow masochist) Hart Crane, Allen considered killing himself at sea. Taking out his notebook, he began a suicide note that turned into a metaphysical poem:

> . . . I, for the sake
> Of little but my causelessness of soul,
> Am carried out my chill hemisphere
> > To unfamiliar summer on the earth.
> > I spend my days to meditate a fear;
> > Each day I give the sea is one of death.[55]

Allen took to the sea when confronted with problems; his running away was a type of madness in which 'confined on the ship, from which there is no escape, the madman is delivered to the . . . sea with its thousand roads, to the great uncertainty eternal to everything'.[56]

'Writers were rich and famous. They lounged around Singapore and Rangoon smoking opium in a yellow pongee silk suit . . . they penetrated forbidden swamps with a faithful native boy and lived in the native quarter of Tangier smoking hashish and languidly caressing a pet gazelle.'[57] Allen spent days ashore smoking marijuana and looking for sex, but was frustrated in his search for an opium den and a boy to share his bed. On the return journey, he completed the short story 'The Monster of Dakar', and composed the series of short poems that would become 'Dakar Doldrums'.

Back in New York, Cassady continued to ignore Allen's entreaties, love letters and ultimatums. However, Allen had a more pressing matter. As 1948 approached, a letter arrived from Pilgrim State Psychiatric Hospital asking his consent for doctors to perform a prefrontal lobotomy on his mother. Louis and Naomi separated in 1943 and had since divorced, and Eugene refused to get involved in Naomi's affairs, so Allen agreed to the procedure. In the years to follow, wracked with guilt, he would never forgive himself.

Depressed and unable to afford therapy, he spent the rest of the year smoking marijuana and studying the paintings of Klee, Cézanne and Rembrandt. To alleviate the depression, usually fuelled by Benzedrine, he gave Kerouac the occasional blowjob. Cassady's continuing rejection of him, his sexual passivity and masochism, his guilt about his mother's lobotomy and his continuing incestuous fantasies and dreams about his father and brother all caused Allen to theorize (despite his having read Havelock Ellis) that his homosexuality was a sign of insanity.

2

'The Lost America of Love', 1948–57

Will we stroll dreaming of the lost America of love[1]

In a photograph taken on 30 October 1947, a thin young man sits on a capstan, left foot resting on the rail while the right balances him on the capstan peg just above the deck. He wears a white vest, button-down front-flap bell-bottomed sailor's trousers, has a full head of dark curly hair and stares into the camera, serious, contemplative, New York harbour in the background. He was returning from Dakar. Allen Ginsberg, utility man on the fantail of the ss *John Blair*, could be the skinny geekier younger brother of Brad Davis's Georges in Rainer Werner Fassbinder's movie of Jean Genet's *Querelle of Brest*. He wished.

Allen shared his West 27th Street apartment with Herbert Huncke, despite Herbert stealing and pawning his possessions (this parasitic relationship continued for the rest of their lives). Allen's friendships and love affairs centred on responsibility: responsibility to others and their responsibility to him. Huncke used and abused Allen's generosity, but Allen offered it up as a means of caring. Derrida argues that,

I am responsible to anyone (that is to say, to any other) only by failing in my responsibility to all the others, to the ethical or political generality. And I can never justify this sacrifice; I must always hold my peace about it ... What binds me to this one or that one, remains finally unjustifiable.[2]

Ginsberg as a utilityman sailor aboard the ss John Blair in New York Harbor, c. 30 October 1947.

Throughout his life, Allen vacillated between the responsibility of the personal – Naomi, Huncke, Orlovsky – and the wider political and social responsibility of gay rights, nuclear disarmament and free speech. Feeling that he was never giving enough, he invariably went too far.

By February 1948, Allen had had enough of Huncke's antics and rented a room at 536 West 114th Street. He read Kerouac's *The Town and the City* manuscript and recommended it to Lionel Trilling, for the first time becoming his friend's de facto agent. In April, Allen and Jack discovered that Neal had divorced LuAnne and married Carolyn (ten days after a four-way orgy with a 'mad nymph' called Susie and another couple[3]). Devastated, Allen thought once again about suicide and on 17 April visited an unsympathetic Kerouac:

> Ginsberg went mad and begged me to hit him – which spells the end as far as I'm concerned, since it's hard enough to keep sane without visiting the asylum every week. He wanted to know 'what else' I had to do in the world that didn't include him. I told him I did have an unconscious desire to hit him but he would be glad later on that I did not.[4]

Spiralling down into depression, Allen moved into an apartment at 321 East 121st Street with fellow student Russell Durgin.

Inspired by and yet jealous of Kerouac finishing *The Town and the City*, Allen put together a collection of poems for publication, admitting, 'I am learning by the week, but my poesy is still not my own. New rhyme new me me me in words. I am not all this carven rhetoric';[5] but his studies and part-time job as an office clerk hindered his progress as a writer. In July, he confessed his sexuality to his father and received the curt response, 'Exorcise Neal.'[6] Allen wrote to Neal grudgingly congratulating him on his marriage and, through gritted teeth, claimed he was able to 'accept you for yourself (whatever that is) without hassles & tension & competition for power'.[7] Neal replied, telling Allen he was 'way, way, way off base' and wasting his time and love.[8]

Lovelorn and struggling to graduate, Allen wandered the streets of Harlem on a warm July night. After returning to his sweltering apartment, he stretched out on his bed masturbating while thumbing through his *Blake Reader*. As he climaxed, he heard the voice of William Blake reciting 'Ah! Sunflower!' Tender and resonating, the eighteenth-century poet's voice was as real as anything else in the room. Allen looked out of the window at the Spanish Harlem skyline and heard the voice recite 'The Sick Rose'.

During the 'vision', Allen witnessed the interconnectedness of the world, not just between humanity and nature, but between things, inanimate and animate, between poets through the ages. The spark that would become 'Howl' is evident in the poem he wrote about the event, 'Vision 1948', in which 'the spiritual scream' is heard 'as me in madness called thee from the deep'.[9] Allen encountered a visionary world divulging its secrets to the poet interpreter, the doors of perception thrown wide open, the universe apparent. As a means of recapturing and understanding these visions and translating them into poetry, Allen read Blake, Plato, Dante, Yeats and *The Mystical Doctrine of St John of the Cross*. A few days after the initial vision, Allen experienced a 'great unconscious' existing within and connecting all humanity and realized that most people wear masks that hide and repress this mystical gift.[10] Allen's 'moment of vision', his ecstasis, carried him away to 'whatever possibilities and circumstances are encountered in the Situation as possible objects of concern', a 'resolute rapture', a 'moment of vision' permitting him *'to encounter for the first time* what can be "in a time" as ready-to-hand or present-at-hand'.[11]

These hallucinatory experiences were vitally important to Allen, but others (including friends and psychiatrists) rejected them as meaningless. Allen's father (in a relationship with Edith Cohen), because of or despite the similarity to the visual and auditory hallucinations Naomi experienced, also dismissed the visions.

Allen moved to an apartment at 1401 York Avenue, from where he walked downtown to Rockefeller Plaza to start his new job as a night shift copy-boy for the Associated Press Radio News Service. After five years at Columbia, he had completed his coursework and would graduate in June 1949. He still dreamed of writing fiction, having spent the last months of 1948 planning and writing a 'naturalistic-symbolistic novel'.[12]

Allen's reading list for January 1949 contained a mix of Blake, Yeats, Lawrence, Melville's short stories and Geoffrey Household's existential thriller *Rogue Male*. The 'hunted man' scenario of Household's novel would resonate eerily in the months to come. Allen spent the holiday period going to parties and sharing his apartment with the visiting Cassady and Al Hinkle. In February, Huncke, released from Rikers Island after a 60-day sentence for marijuana possession, and as 'beat' as Allen had seen him, turned up at the apartment destitute and hungry. Allen, against his earlier determination and advice from friends and family, pitied the Benzedrine-addled man, took him in, cleaned and fed him. Huncke remained ungrateful and complaining on Allen's sofa for a few weeks, telling him tales of crime, the navy and his various addictions. Allen couldn't 'respond to the call, the request, the obligation, or even the love of another, without sacrificing the other other, the other others',[13] the 'other other' being Huncke, and the 'other others' being people who gave Allen advice. In later life, he attempted to balance these architectures of responsibility by becoming a Buddhist and a provider, blithely unaware of his own debt and physical deterioration.

Having Huncke as a guest meant Herbert's friends dropped by. Among them were Vicki Russell and 'Little Jack' Melody (Melodia) – a not very successful Long Island mobster – and the group sat around listening to jazz and smoking pot. Slowly, Vicki and Little Jack took over the apartment, using it to stash stolen goods. Earlier in the year, Allen had had an idea for a 'psychological portrait of young me spiritual man caught for robbery by the police'.[14]

Allen and Kerouac collaborated during this time, writing alternate lines to what were essentially nonsense poems; one of them – 'Pull My Daisy' – provided the title to the film Robert Frank and Alfred Leslie would direct in 1959. Allen gave Van Doren a manuscript copy of Kerouac's *The Town and the City*. Impressed, Van Doren contacted Harcourt Brace who snapped up the novel, paying Kerouac $1,000.

Ginsberg in a photobooth
photo, 1949.

Police arrested Burroughs on 6 April for possession of narcotics
and found letters from Allen containing details of a drugs deal.
Taking Lucien's advice, Allen asked Huncke, Vicki and Little Jack to
remove all stolen items from the apartment, but they ignored him.
On Thursday 21 April, Vicki and Little Jack drove Allen to his brother Eugene's apartment where he planned to stash his potentially
incriminating notebooks. After unloading some of the stolen goods
at Jack's mother's house on Long Island, they drove along Northern
Boulevard just after midday. Little Jack turned illegally (according to
newspaper reports, the car was driving the wrong way along a one-
way street) and police officer George McClancy stopped them to
issue a ticket. Little Jack – disqualified from driving and on parole –
gunned the car. The police gave chase. Jack swerved taking a corner,
hit the curb at speed, and the car somersaulted twice before landing
on its roof. Dizzy, without his glasses, Allen staggered away from
the crash, trying to gather his scattered manuscripts.

Police arrested Little Jack. Vicki and Allen escaped into the
streets of Flushing, Queens. Penniless, Allen made his way home

on foot. Not long after, two detectives arrived, the apartment still full of contraband. Allen spent the night in the Long Island House of Detention until Louis arrived to post bail. With the help and support of his father, Van Doren and Trilling, Allen agreed to a course of psychological treatment.

From 29 June 1949 until 24 February 1950, Allen was an inpatient at the New York State Psychiatric Institute. On his first day there, he met 21-year-old Carl Solomon. Regaining consciousness from a coma induced by insulin shock therapy, Solomon asked, 'Who are you?' Allen replied, 'I'm Myshkin', and Solomon said, 'I'm Kirilov.'[15] The famous opening lines to 'Howl' stem from the day the suicidal absurdist nihilist of Dostoevsky's *The Possessed* met Myshkin, the haplessly flawed innocent from *The Idiot*.

On his earlier travels, Solomon had known André Breton, witnessed an Antonin Artaud reading, became a disciple of Isidore Isou – the founder of Lettrism –and attended the 1947 production of Jean Genet's *The Maids* at Théâtre de l'Athénée, Paris. Influenced by Dadaism, Jacques Vaché and Arthur Cravan, Solomon had thrown potato salad at the stage during a lecture on Stéphane Mallarmé. After a number of similar absurdist acts, he had voluntarily started psychiatric evaluation. Taking on some of the mental aspects of his hero Artaud, Solomon had threatened to smear his room with faeces and had asked to be lobotomized; eventually, like Artaud, he underwent insulin and electro-shock therapy.

Solomon gave Allen Jean Genet's novels to read and Allen began to see himself as an outlaw – an insane queer poet fighting the system, Solomon explaining that madness in itself was rebellion against the hegemony of the doctors and the institution. Allen compared the characters in Genet's *Miracle of the Rose* to his friends – Neal as a rather more heterosexual Harcomone. With the influence of Genet's erotica and Kerouac's self-mythologizing, Allen combined autobiography, fantasy and psychosexuality in poems such as 'The Shrouded Stranger' (the title of three different poems written during this period). Yet he had doubts about his writing and believed these poems – and his homosexuality – stemmed from 'impulses reverse of normalcy'.[16] However much he wanted to explore these secret fantasies, he denied them in himself, but they began to percolate through into his slowly forming poetics, a 'Future Verse' incorporating 'sentence structure and thought determining stanza, each stanza a statement, each line in reference to the others, Pound's paragraph stanzas'.[17]

After refusing him mescaline treatment, dismissing his 'Blake visions', and noting that he risked becoming schizophrenic, the doctors persuaded Allen that he should try to live as a heterosexual, despite him confiding to his journal the previous December that his homosexuality was not something he could 'simply give up by holding my cock tight so that I don't come'.[18] On 24 February 1950, the institute released him into the care of his father and new stepmother Edith. Determined to conform, he found clerical work at the *New Jersey Labor Herald* and dated a number of women, including Helen Parker, confessing to Kerouac:

> we screw, and I am all man and full of love . . . The first days after I lost my cherry – does everybody feel like that? I wandered around in the most benign and courteous stupor of delight at the perfection of nature . . .[19]

But the reality of having a day job, the three-times-a-week psychiatric outpatient care and the presence of Neal in the city meant the love affair and 'perfection of nature' was shortlived, and would end in October after Allen became possessive:

> He gets in bed with her
>   and performs

as what in his mind
would be his usual
 okay job,
which should be solid
 as a rock but isn't.[20]

Echoes maybe of Henry James: 'The sign was that – though it was her own affair – he understood; the sign would be that – though it was her own affair – she was free to clutch. Since she took him for a firm object – much as he might to his own sense appear at times to rock – he would do his best to BE one.'[21]

On 18 March, Allen attended a William Carlos Williams reading and, after sending Williams letters, visited the poet at his Rutherford home. Allen had been experimenting with form, metre and rhythm, and Williams advised him to write using American speech patterns. Allen used his journals as source material and Williams liked the results, suggesting he continue in this mode, the manifesto ringing in Allen's newly tuned ears – 'No ideas but in things.'[22] Allen fused this materialist approach with his 'moment of vision' transcendentalism, generating a poetics of the American Spirit – similar to Kerouac's prose experimentations, but with Whitman, Williams and Pound as inspiration rather than Thomas Wolfe.

William Cannastra – Bill Finistra in Kerouac's *Visions of Cody* and *Book of Dreams*, Bill Agatson in John Clellon Holmes' *Go* and *Get Home Free* – found his way into Beat infamy alongside Kammerer, Cassady and Carr. On 12 October, after leaving his loft at 125 21st Street, Cannastra and fellow drinkers rode the subway. At Bleecker Street, as a prank, shouting that he wanted another drink, he climbed on to the seat and tried to get out of the window but became stuck. As the train pulled out, his friends tried unsuccessfully to drag him back in. As the train accelerated, the tunnel walls ripped Cannastra's body from the carriage. Allen believed the act to be a suicide: Cannastra, the ex-New York attorney and friend of Tennessee Williams turned alcoholic wild man, driven to reckless acts because of his closeted homosexuality.

Suffering with his own suicidal tendencies, Allen persisted with analysis. Terminated from a number of jobs, he looked for someone to take care of him sexually and financially. Jack, looking for the same thing, asked Allen to be his best man at his marriage on 17 November to Joan Haverty (they'd known each other just over a week), an ex-girlfriend of Cannastra's now living in the 21st Street loft.

A month later, Neal Cassady sat at the typewriter at his home at 29 Russell Street, San Francisco, composing the seventeen-page 'Joan Anderson Letter'. Sent to Kerouac on 22 December, the 13,000-word text contained autobiographical sketches written in a fast-paced, oral-narrative style. This spontaneous prose exerted a major influence on both Kerouac and Ginsberg's writing. Four months later, Kerouac, inspired by Cassady's breakneck verbal narrative, would take only three weeks to type up a new version of *On the Road* incorporating some of Neal's letters literatim into the scrolled text.[23]

Allen spent the first half of 1951 reading and critiquing *On the Road*, trying without much success to apply Williams's poetics to 'The Shroudy Stranger' and – despite being embroiled in Jack and Neal's domestic problems – dating Dusty Moreland in the pretence that he was heterosexual, writing to Jack and Neal in February, 'Dusty won't marry me, I asked her? What can I do?'[24]

In August, Allen and Lucien Carr travelled to Mexico City for a wedding; they planned to visit Burroughs, unaware that he was in South America. They spent time with Joan sightseeing and getting drunk, and returned to the US on 5 September. Strangely, Burroughs returned to Mexico City the day after.

On 6 September, in an apartment above The Bounty bar, Burroughs was trying to set up a gun deal. Facts are hazy but James

Grauerholz's exhaustive study 'The Death of Joan Vollmer Burroughs: What Really Happened?' synthesizes the known details.[25] Joan questioned Burroughs's marksmanship, placed a glass of water on her head and dared him to fire. Burroughs did, the bullet missed the glass and entered Joan's forehead. She died a few hours later in the Cruz Roja hospital. Charged with culpable homicide, Burroughs spent thirteen days in the Panopticon-style Black Palace of Lecumberri before his brother Mortimer bribed officials to release him on bail. The date for the trial kept changing, so, after two months, Burroughs's attorney suggested he skip the country. The court sentenced him in absentia to a two-year suspended sentence for homicide. In his introduction to *Queer*, Burroughs admits he would have never become a writer if it were not for the accidental killing of Joan; her death was the palimpsest over which he would write his future works.

Later in the year, while in a lesbian bar called the Pony Stable Inn, near Washington Square, Allen met Gregory Corso. Born in 1930, Corso had spent his childhood in foster homes and on the streets of Greenwich Village and Little Italy. By the age of thirteen, he had been incarcerated in New York's notorious Tombs for petty larceny and breaking and entry, and had been hospitalized in the psychiatric ward of Bellevue. Sentenced to three years in Clinton Correctional Facility, Corso had studied classical literature and had written his first poems. Gregory and Allen became close friends, discussing poetry and sharing women, including Dusty Moreland.

Allen spent the autumn working as a market researcher and living at 346 West 15th Street:

Walking home at night,
   reaching my own block
      I saw the Port Authority
   Building hovering over
      the old ghetto side

of the street I tenement
in company with obscure
Bartlebys and Judes . . .[26]

In December, John Clellon Holmes, who worked for the same
market research company as Allen, had his novel *Go* accepted
by Scribner's. *Go* portrays Holmes as Paul Hobbes, Kerouac as
Gene Pasternak, Cassady as Hart Kennedy, Burroughs as Will
Dennison, Cannastra as Bill Agatson, Huncke as Albert Ancke
and Allen as David Stofsky. A little jealous of Holmes's success,
Allen wrote to Kerouac, 'John Holmes' novel is no good, I
believe. I was shocked when I got his eyedea of me.'[27] Kerouac
agreed, 'And the smell of his work is the smell of death . . .
Everybody knows he has no talent . . .'.[28] Holmes characterized
Allen as sad and mad, continually talking about his Blakean hallucinations.

As the year ended, and the realization sank in that Lucien 'his
old dear eldest love' was to get married in the New Year,[29] Allen
became suicidal, fantasizing about slashing his wrists with a knife
he had bought in Mexico. He confessed his thoughts to his journal
and then transformed the prose into poetry:

Last attempts at speech.
And the carved
serpentine knife of Mexico,
with the childish
eagle head in the hand.[30]

The influence of Williams is apparent in the speech rhythms, the
short lines, the materialist-imagist view of the world, the edict to
'make a start, / out of particulars',[31] incorporating the this-ness of
things, a move away from transference and metaphoric nebulous-
ness. He would do this to great effect in 'Howl', replacing the

abstract 'anarchy' of the first draft with the site(cite)-specific 'Arkansas'.[32]

The New York doldrums hung over Allen for the first part of 1952. He guiltily seduced Corso, Dusty rejected his marriage proposal, and he failed to find an escape ship. To take his mind off his depression, he acted as agent for Burroughs's *Junk* and Kerouac's *On the Road*, sending the manuscripts to various publishers. Kerouac rejected a contract and $250 advance with A. A. Wyn's Ace Books. Carl Solomon – nephew of the publisher and working as an editor for the company – accepted *Junk*, publishing it in 1953 as *Junkie: Confessions of an Unredeemed Drug Addict* by 'William Lee'. Inspired by his success, Allen imagined himself, Burroughs and Kerouac as the nucleus of a literary movement that included Corso and the yet-to-be-memoirists Cassady and Huncke. Solomon wrote to Neal in March with the advice, 'I feel you would profit greatly from taking and then transcending a creative writing course . . . (Don't listen to Kerouac, he knows nothing.)'[33] As with Peter Orlovsky later in life, Allen pressured people to write even though they were far from comfortable putting pen to paper. Kerouac's new version of *On the Road* (published as *Visions of Cody* in 1973) became Allen's next publishing project despite finding it 'crazy in a bad way'.[34]

On February 26, Allen made a list of 50 subjects and scenes he could use in his writing, but most of the early poems were exercises concerned with the stratification of his depression.[35] The clichéd themes, the imitative imagery, the obvious rhymes, the simple rhythms, all point to a poet yet to find a style and voice. Solomon advised him to burn them as 'suffering of this self-pity type is worthless'.[36] Lines such as 'like a green / hairy protuberance' in 1948's 'Trembling of the Veil' point to the surreal imagery of 'a cloud of sexless hydrogen' in 'Howl', but the majority of the poems were derivative and conservative. The early collections *Empty Mirror* and *Gates of Wrath* were sketches of Allen's state of mind, his struggle to match form and content. Taking Williams's advice to stop using rhyme and metre, Allen found a more confident and personal voice in the 1952 poems 'An Atypical Affair', 'A Crazy Spiritual', and 'Wild Orphan', incorporating subjects that became mainstays of his later poetics – failed love affairs, driving across America, his mother and madness. Allen perfected his skill for networking – he attended a party in Rutherford with Williams, visited W. H. Auden, talked to Dylan Thomas in the San Remo bar and met the surrealist poet Philip Lamantia who put him in touch with poet and artist Charles Henri Ford and San Francisco Renaissance poet Kenneth Rexroth. Despite the contacts, publishers were not interested in a collection of Ginsberg's poetry.

Depressed, Allen turned to peyote and meaningless affairs with men to save himself from falling into madness: 'How like к's situation. Last night slept with . . . Why? Sheer easy sex – I sleep with creeps now. How like Kafka, we desire nothing.'[37] Unloved, he wrote a suicide letter willing his writings to Kerouac and his money and personal effects to his father and brother. For Allen, Nietzsche's maxim 'The thought of suicide is a powerful comfort' held true, and more so that 'it helps one through many a dreadful night'.[38] In May, he rejected an offer to go to Mexico City to stay with Kerouac and Burroughs, writing, 'I don't want to feel alone in the dark at the mercy of you and Bill – for I have no money of my own – traveling deeper and far away from world I know and love a little.'[39] And five days later, he declined an invitation from Cassady to visit him in California. The next few months he spent writing in his journals, noting ideas for novels and poems, and documenting the continuing struggle with his sexuality.

Allen found a cheap attic apartment at 206 East 7th Street in October. With friends visiting and Dusty back in his life, he was happy for a short while but when Dusty disappeared without leaving a note, he felt he was destined to lead a solitary life in small apartments, jobless, friendless and without love. In the poem 'In a Red Bar', Ginsberg sums up his feelings:

I need a haircut and look
Seedy—in late twenties,
shadows under my mouth,
too informally dressed,
heavy eyebrowed, sadistic,
too mental and lonely.[40]

Donning his agent's hat, he read Kerouac's autobiographic-phantasmagorical novel *Doctor Sax*, and, even though he felt Jack 'shat on me the last time I tried to help', wrote, 'The structure of reality and myth – shuttling back and forth, is a stroke of genius: casting the myth within the frame of childish fantasy, so giving it reality (?) in terms of its frame.'[41]

On a cold Sunday in mid-January 1953, Allen travelled out to Long Island to visit his mother in Pilgrim State Hospital and was shocked to see the extent of Naomi's physical and mental degeneration; strokes had made her weak and the lobotomy had increased rather than diminished her paranoia. Feeling guilty, Allen burst into tears believing that rather than alleviate her torment he had increased it. Depressed about his mother's plight, he escaped into the energy of involvement in other people's causes and needs.

Ace Books rejected Kerouac's *Maggie Cassidy* – an autobiographical novel about a teenage love affair – and Kerouac responded angrily, distancing himself from any publicity for Burroughs's soon-to-be-published *Junkie*. Allen responded with a sarcastic letter. But, fired from a number of jobs, he continued to promote his friends. *Junkie* earned Burroughs $270 and Allen a $30 agent's fee.

Carl Solomon, New York City, 1953.

Later in the year, Allen collated letters Burroughs sent him from South America, where he was searching for the hallucinatory drug yagé. Alene Lee – Mardou Fox in Kerouac's *The Subterraneans* – typed up the letters, and the manuscript eventually became part of *The Yage Letters*.

In 'Green Automobile', written between 22 and 25 May, Ginsberg rethinks his poetics, using Kerouac's new-found Buddhist idea of *satori* (understanding or awakening) and the driven-ness of Cassady's Joan Anderson letter. In doing so, he overcomes the constrictions of metre and rhyme, the clichés banished by vibrant spontaneous thought. This shifting of register, mixed with his sexual longings and the Beat writers' method of re-inventing themselves as 'legends', creates an experiential intensity, an honest transcription of sexual desire and dependence:

> and on an asphalt crossroad,
>> deal with each other in princely
>> gentleness once more, recalling
>>> famous dead talks of other cities.[42]

On his return to New York from South America at the end of August, Burroughs visited Allen at his East 7th Street apartment. Allen agreed to Burroughs moving in and the two men spent the next three months sharing the small space – made smaller by Burroughs's hand-built orgone accumulator. Corso also crashed at the apartment but a machete-wielding Burroughs proved too much even for Gregory and he soon moved out. As Cassady rejected Allen's love, so Allen rejected Burroughs's advances. Burroughs, deeply in love and insistent in his demands for sex, was devastated when Allen cruelly told Bill that he didn't want his ugly old cock[43] – a riposte that Allen could never take back, instantly transforming Burroughs from alien praying mantis to quivering greyhound puppy. The strange and strained relationship became fuel for Burroughs's routines in *Naked Lunch* and *Interzone*, the streets of the Lower East Side transmogrified into nightmarish tenements full of death-spurting executioners and their jizz-pumping victims.

When Burroughs decided to move to Tangier where he had heard boys and drugs were readily available, Allen accepted an invitation from Neal and Carolyn to join them in San Jose where Neal had found Allen and Jack jobs as parking-lot managers. Allen wanted to make the journey via Florida, Cuba and Mexico, before reaching California where he planned to study Buddhism and edit the draft of Burroughs's *The Yage Letters*. He left New York on 19 December to hitchhike via Washington, DC, Palm Beach and

William S. Burroughs and Jack Kerouac in Ginsberg's 206 East 7th Street apartment, Manahatta, autumn 1953.

Miami, to Key West where he took a boat to Cuba and spent a disappointing three days in Havana, eventually leaving for Mexico by plane – he had never flown before. He arrived on New Year's Eve and spent the evening at a country club in Mérida listening to the band and enjoying the food.

Pretending to be an archaeology student, he found cheap lodgings when he visited the Mayan buildings, temples and observatory at Chichén-Itzá on 1 January 1954. He stayed a few days, exploring, fantasizing that his mother was well and young again, dreaming of labyrinths in which enemy agents pursued a ghostly Burroughs. He then caught a train to see the Mayan ruins at Valladolid, Uxmal and the festival at Tizimín where a priest put him up for the night.

In the third week of January, in Palenque, a lost Mayan city swallowed by the jungle, Allen met a retired actor, Karena Shields.

Ginsberg's caption to this photograph taken in his New York apartment: 'Bill Burroughs at typewriter at which he fixed up 'In Search of Yage' at 206 E. 7 Street N.Y. 1953 Iris Brady's painting of Jackson Mac Low on wall, kitchen table with toaster, salt and a glass. My bedroom with sandstone Carib statue on wardrobe against striped wallpaper thru door.'

Running out of money, bothered by insects, suffering from dysentery – and 'beginning to really hate Mexico'[44] – Allen accepted an invitation to stay at her *finca*. The pair journeyed by horse into the jungle, which Shields knew well having grown up in the area, swam in the nearby mountain pools, drank rum and fished. Allen read, recorded his dreams in his journal, grew a beard for the first time, occasionally worked in the banana plantation, and posted letters to Cassady and Kerouac deferring his arrival in California. Meanwhile, Burroughs, not hearing from him, fretted over Allen's whereabouts, fired off letters of dread and horror from Tangier, still obsessed with the thought of Allen as his psychic partner: 'I have to have receiver for routine. If there is no one there to receive it, routine turns back on me and tears me apart . . .'.[45]

Ginsberg in a photobooth photo, 1954.

After an expedition to find the source of a series of earthquakes, which he hoped to write a story about in order to raise cash, Allen began work on 'Siesta in Xbalba', which he later dedicated to Karena Shields:

—One could pass valuable months
and years perhaps a lifetime
doing nothing but lying in a hammock
reading prose with white doves
     copulating underneath . . .[46]

With a loan from Shields, in mid-May, he finally headed for Mexico City. There, he hoped to stay with Burroughs's friend Bill Garver but the old junkie had gone missing, so Allen moved on to the artist colony of San Miguel de Allende. In the first week of June, after a few weeks of sightseeing, he arrived in Mexicali, spent the night and the next day, crossed the border into Calexico and caught a Greyhound bus to Los Angeles. After staying with his cousin for a week while writing the 'Return to the States' section of 'Siesta in Xbalba', Allen took the train to San Jose and made his way to the Cassady house.

His most ambitious poem to date, 'Siesta in Xbalba' describes a Burroughsian nightmare of evil spirits, vampires and mind control set against a backdrop of Allen's memories of friends in New York. He equates the deliquescing images of the jungle with his 'Blake visions', using the surreal couplings 'future blue saloons' to describe Mexico as America's hallucinatory underworld, bubbling darkly beneath the US's war machine. The place he describes – a mixture of Mexico, dream visions, reports from Tangier and the horrorscape of a rotting New York City – corresponds to and pre-empts Burroughs's satirical 'Interzone' (December 1954) and Kerouac's sci-fi 'cityCityCITY' (May 1955) – composite places where nothing is real and everything is permitted:

Pale Uxmal,
    unhistoric, like a dream,
Tulum shimmering on the coast in ruins;
Chichén Itzá naked
    constructed on a plain . . .[47]

This beseeching is echoed in Burroughs's 'Invocation' from *Cities of the Red Night*:

> to *Itzamna*, Spirit of Early Mists and Showers, to *Ix Chel*, the Spider-Web-that-Catches-the-Dew-of-Morning, to *Zuhuy Kak*, Virgin Fire, to *Ah Dziz*, the Master of Cold, to *Kak U Pacat*, who works in fire, to *Ix Tab*, Goddess of Ropes and Snares.[48]

Allen continued his Buddhist studies at the San Jose Public Library, reading books Kerouac had recommended to him. Neal and Carolyn, who were heavily into the mystic writings of Edgar Cayce, sat up all night discussing religion, literature and philosophy. Allen and Neal continued to have sex, with Allen giving Neal blowjobs whenever Carolyn was out of the house, Allen fantasizing about humiliation and submission at the hands (and cock) of Cassady:

> I will go into the bedroom silently and lie down between the bridegroom and the bride,
> those bodies fallen from heaven stretched out waiting naked and restless,
> arms resting over their eyes in the darkness . . .[49]

This idealistic portrait disguised the fact that, both jealous of the other's desire for Neal, Allen and Carolyn barely spoke to each other. Allen was in love (again) but slowly awakened to the reality of this 'artificial situation', this 'mad triangle'[50] – confessing to

Ginsberg in Mexico, 1954.

his journal that Cassady was a manipulative bastard, a boring manipulative bastard, who used him and used him again.

True to form, on 19 August, Allen was on his knees blowing Neal, when Carolyn walked in on them. It is unclear whether Cassady engineered this in order to upset Carolyn – or to alienate Allen – but, whatever the motive, Carolyn blamed Allen. Cassady disappeared, leaving Allen to deal with the problem as Carolyn's 'face waxe(d) green with evil'.[51] On his return, Neal ordered Allen to leave. Two days later, Carolyn drove him to San Francisco, gave him $20 and left him in North Beach. Allen took a room in the run-down Hotel Marconi at 554 Broadway and looked for work. Allen met Kenneth Patchen who lent him a copy of Blaise Cendrars' *La Prose du Transsibérien et de la Petite Jehanne de France*. The 420-line poem charts the young Cendrars's journey from Moscow to Manchuria after the 1905 Revolution and Sino-Russian War, accompanied by a young woman who might be a prostitute. Conflating time, memory and observation, this prototypical 'road' piece – 'the first simultaneous poem'[52] – had a profound effect on Allen's later poetry and journals.

On 13 September, Allen, dressed in suit and tie, started work as a market researcher for Towne-Oller earning $55 a week. He also moved into the apartment of Sheila Williams Boucher – a jazz singer he had half fallen in love with. The would-be radical visionary poet was now a salary man with thoughts of promotion, a ready-made family (Sheila had a four-year-old son), a cat and a cosy apartment in Nob Hill.

One night, after taking peyote with Sheila, Allen looked out of the window at the fog-shrouded buildings and hotels. Before him, the neon signs and lighted windows transmogrified into a monstrous face, eyes blazing. He saw 'Golgotha-robot—eternal—smoking machine crowned visage',[53] the embodiment of Moloch, Milton's 'horrid King besmear'd with blood / Of human sacrifice, and parents' tears' from *Paradise Lost*. On 17 October, Allen noted the vision of the hallucinatory Sir Francis Drake Hotel in his journal, thinking he might one day use it in a poem.

He soon became bored, writing to Kerouac that he would 'move in a month or so and get a secret nice pad'.[54] He took to walking the streets to escape the apartment, most nights visiting Foster's Cafeteria under the Hotel Wentley. One evening, Allen started a conversation with the artist Robert LaVigne. The two men met regularly, drinking coffee while discussing Cézanne and abstract expressionism. Allen visited LaVigne's studio with thoughts of buying a painting but had not reckoned on seeing one which would change his life – the canvas in the entranceway, a large

Bonnard-like painting called *Nude with Onions*, portrayed a naked young man reclining.

Smitten, Allen asked LaVigne the identity of the model, and LaVigne answered, 'Oh, that's Peter; he's here', and introduced Allen to Peter Orlovsky.[55] In a letter to Kerouac, Allen described the event, 'Then in walked the boy his model, who painter made it with too, gentle souled tall Russian red Kafka, respectful, silent.'[56]

Born on the Lower East Side on 8 July 1933, Peter, his sister Marie, and brothers Lafcadio, Julius and Nick, all suffered from a variety of mental illnesses. His parents were from a poor Russian background and Peter had spent his childhood shuffling between institutions and family slum housing in Long Island and Queens. After working at Creedmore State Mental Hospital, Peter had joined the army in 1953 as a hospital orderly in San Francisco. He met LaVigne in Foster's Cafeteria. Although Peter was predominantly heterosexual, LaVigne had seduced him and they had become lovers. When the army found out, they sent Peter for psychiatric tests; the doctors diagnosed schizophrenia and honourably discharged him.

Allen and Peter spent a night together in LaVigne's apartment/ studio on Gough Street – for once, Allen the dominant partner. Afterwards, Peter cried and LaVigne rushed in; a jealous scuffle ensued, after which matters became complicated in Gough Street – Allen had also been having sex with LaVigne. To make things simpler, Allen moved out of Sheila's apartment and in with LaVigne and Orlovsky, confiding to Kerouac that Peter was 'meanwhile promised to me, promise fades, we finally all three meet in kitchen and evil hate scenes . . . I can't stand it as he thinks I'm being dirty toward Peter, but I love.'[57] When Neal began an affair with Natalie Jackson, another of LaVigne's models, engineering a threesome with Natalie and Peter while Allen was at his brother's wedding, the soap-like saga became a sexual farce. Soon, LaVigne left for Mexico, and Peter and Allen agreed to go their separate ways. Allen moved into the Hotel Young opposite Foster's Cafeteria, while Peter rented a room in the Hotel Wentley.

Allen felt guilty about seducing Peter but wrote obsessively about the fantasy sex life they could have had. His psychotherapist advised Allen to do whatever he wanted, so he set targets to leave his job, concentrate on poetry, find an apartment and persuade Peter to move in. On 3 February 1954, he rented a two-bedroom apartment at 1010 Montgomery Street. After an all-night discussion, he and Peter made a lifelong commitment to each other and Peter, somewhat reluctantly, agreed to live with Allen.

Amid the sexual dynamics – Allen was still fucking Sheila and had one-off sex with Natalie Jackson – the Allen and Peter 'love affair' wasn't quite what Allen envisioned. Peter became depressed, locked himself in his room, spurning Allen's approaches. Rather than spend time making things work with Peter, Allen agreed that Neal and Natalie move in at the end of February. Unhappy, Allen studied Buddhism in the hope of any kind of enlightenment, but there was no *satori* in San Francisco. He left Towne-Oller on 1 May, and lived for the next few months on the $30-a-week unemployment payments. At 29, Allen was a mess; with no job, suffering from writer's block, Peter ignoring his advances, Neal spiralling down into priapic madness, Allen begged Kerouac to come to San Francisco to relieve his depression.

Meanwhile, Peter, fearing his mother would commit his fifteen-year-old brother to a psychiatric hospital, returned to New York to collect Lafcadio. Neal and Natalie moved out and Allen considered becoming a teaching assistant at Berkeley. Inspired by Gregory Corso's first collection of poetry, *The Vestal Lady on Brattle and Other Poems*, which Kerouac sent him on 14 July, Allen started to write again, editing poems he wrote through 1952–5:

Blessed be the Muses
  for their descent

dancing around my desk,
crowning my balding head
   with Laurel.[58]

Replying to Kerouac, he wrote, 'reading Corso's original good book I see what good verbal imagination he has and how beautiful it can be and how I have neglected that I realize.'[59]

With Corso's inspirational collection and Kerouac's spontaneous style in mind, in early August, Allen sat at his desk for marathon sessions writing the first draft of something he titled 'Strophes'. 'I saw the best mind of my generation destroyed by madness, starving, hysterical, naked.'[60] The singular 'mind' transformed into the plural 'minds' in the final document, Carl Solomon the metonym for the many tortured souls in Allen's life and imagination. On 14 August, in a letter to Eugene, Ginsberg admitted that the new style of writing was 'sort of surrealist' and 'more or less Kerouac's rhythmic style of prose'.[61] He acknowledged his debt to Kerouac – 'I need years of isolation and constant everyday writing to attain your volume and freedom and knowledge of the form'[62] – and took Jack's advice to change the title of the poem to 'Howl'. By 30 August, he told Kerouac that Lawrence Ferlinghetti 'will put out *Howl* (under that title) next year, one booklet for that poem, nothing else – it will fill a booklet'.[63]

Allen moved to a small cottage at 1624 Milvia Street, close to the Berkeley campus, on 1 September. There, at $35 a week and secluded, he concentrated on his writing, studied for his MA in English Literature, and was close enough to San Francisco to visit Neal and Peter. With the help of lecturer Thomas Parkinson, Allen began a close study of Walt Whitman's poetry and read *Jubilate Agno* by the eighteenth-century poet Christopher Smart:

For I bless God in the libraries of the learned and for all the
   booksellers in the world.

> For I bless God in the strength of my loins and for the voice
> which he hath made sonorous.[64]

Unbelievably, Allen had never performed in public. He did so for the first time at a Fisherman's Wharf festival, reading 'A Supermarket in California'. Allen – ever-networking – told Six Gallery founder Wally Hedrick that he could put together a one-off event involving Kerouac and Cassady, but Kerouac was too shy to read and Cassady wasn't interested. So, taking Rexroth's advice, Allen and Michael McClure (whom Allen met in 1954 at a party for W. H. Auden) contacted local poets.

Billed as 'all sharp new straightforward writing – remarkable collection of angels on one stage reading their poetry. No charge, small collection for wine, and postcards. Charming event',[65] the reading at the Six Gallery, at 8 p.m. on Friday 7 October, became a defining moment in Beat history, changed the public's idea of poets and poetry, ignited discussion in universities, bars and newspapers, and pinpointed San Francisco as the capital of counterculture. Kerouac handed out jugs of California Burgundy to the hundred or so audience; Kenneth Rexroth introduced the poets seated in a semi-circle on a podium; Philip Lamantia read poems by his friend John Hoffman who had recently died in Mexico of a peyote overdose. Next, Michael McClure read 'Point Lobos: Animism' and 'For the Death of 100 Whales', an apocalyptic ecological poem about Earth's future. Philip Whalen followed with his humorous 'If You're So Smart, Why Ain't You Rich' and his dramatic 'Plus Ça Change' – a poem which shifts the emphasis from the William Carlos Williams-influenced poetics grounded in American speech onto a more Buddhist (or even Heideggeran) object-oriented encounter with words, the lines becoming sound sculptures of observation: 'Well, save your breath you need to cool / Will you please shove the cuttlebone a little closer?'[66] Gary Snyder read last; his poem 'A Berry Feast' celebrates ritual and peace and warns of ecological disaster.

Between Whalen and Snyder, Allen, a little drunk, took the stage and began in a low yet clear voice to read the first part of 'Howl, for Carl Solomon'. As the reading progressed and he became more confident, Kerouac drumming on a wine bottle, spurring him on, Allen gave a reading full of emotion, the audience joining in, 'everybody . . . yelling "Go! Go! Go!"'[67]

In the years to follow, 'Howl' would produce more analysis, history, conjecture, tribute and scorn than any other poem of the late twentieth century. Its opening lines would be copied and parodied in films, on television and in print. The poem itself, in three parts with a footnote as a coda, uses parallel repetition, anaphoric phrasing, incantatory declamations, and mixes a trochaic rhythm section with softer anapests to control the headlong surge of the long-breath lines. The poem evolves from an imbrication and transposition of Whitman's long lines, Smart's mystical madness, Williams's American speech, Surrealist poetry and Kerouac's spontaneous prose. Its progenitors – besides the above – range from Blake and Shelley to Schwitters, Mayakovsky, Tzara, Apollinaire, Lorca, Hart Crane, Eliot and Dylan Thomas. An Imagist/Romantic piece of late-Modernism, it fuses the prophetic spirit of Shelley and Blake with the urban visions of Lorca and Crane, channelling the sound-poem experiments of the early twentieth-century Futurists, Cubists, Dadaists and Surrealists, while incorporating Charles Olson's theories of Projective Verse, 'ONE PERCEPTION MUST IMMEDIATELY AND DIRECTLY LEAD TO A FURTHER PERCEPTION', and Robert Creeley's dictum, 'FORM IS NEVER MORE THAN AN EXTENSION OF CONTENT.'[68]

If the form renders 'Howl' memorable, the content makes it shocking. Ginsberg uses repetition in a similar way to Smart and Eliot and incorporates surreal language couplings in the manner of Apollinaire and Thomas, but few poets in 1955 were writing about being 'fucked in the ass'. It would be a year before Yale University Press published John Ashbery's *Some Trees*, making possible postmodernism's entrance into American poetics. But before that, 'Howl' introduced new poetic subject matter, challenged societal status quo, and thrust the poet into the spotlight of social and sexual comment and change, revolutionarily extending what Deleuze characterizes as Whitman's convulsive and fragmentary spontaneity.[69]

Part I uses Poundian paragraphic stanzas with a Gertrude Stein-like dictum – 'A Sentence is not emotional a paragraph is'[70] – to list the experiential biographies of his fellow travellers (Huncke, Lamantia, Solomon, Kerouac, Cassady, Burroughs, Cannastra), while referencing heroes (Hart Crane, Marlon Brando and W. B. Yeats, among others). Rimbaud also stalks these lines; his 'Who hid their skinny yellow fingers, dark with mud, / In hand-me-downs smelling of shit'[71] (from 'Seven-Year-Old Poets') could slip easily into the anaphoric lines beginning 'who'. Likewise, Artaud's 'Fragmentations', written in March–April 1946 during the final months he spent at the asylum of Rodez and published in a French literary journal the year Solomon was in Paris, may have influenced the opening lines of 'Howl':

> I saw Yvonne's swollen sac, I saw the sac puffed up with the dregs of Yvonne's blistered soul, I saw that hideous soft sac of Yvonne's buggered soul, I saw Yvonne's ballooning heart punctured like an enormous sac of pus . . .[72]

Part II invokes Moloch, a Semitic god (idol) associated with child sacrifice, and in Ginsberg's mind with the materialist and military excesses of America and the West, materialism winning the battle with spirituality, sacrificing the best minds. If, as Stephen Greenblatt states, 'Capitalism is built into the poetics of everyday behaviour in America',[73] then Ginsberg takes the behaviour of the dispossessed and with it questions materialism's alienatory structure.

Howl (1956), Ginsberg's first book.

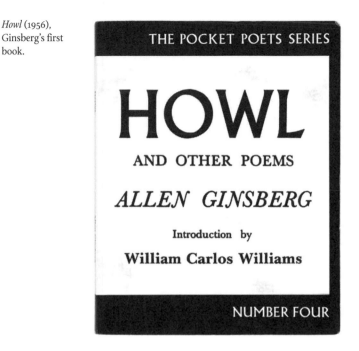

THE POCKET POETS SERIES

HOWL

AND OTHER POEMS

ALLEN GINSBERG

Introduction by

William Carlos Williams

NUMBER FOUR

Part III calls to a friend who suffers more than the author, a man that society wants to shock into sanity, torture into an acceptance of its 'reality'. Ginsberg – and the others who populate Part I – form a hipster rearguard against American hegemony. The 'Footnote' explains how we are to battle this raging, unrelenting capitalist machine with the 'kindness of our soul', for everything – even the excremental vision of the asshole – is holy.

Back in Beat soap-opera land, Cassady attempted a get-rich-quick scam. With Natalie pretending to be Carolyn, he withdrew $2,500 from his and Carolyn's joint account and bet it on a horse. The horse lost. Natalie became paranoid about her role in this and on 30 November, while Neal was at work, with Kerouac supposedly looking after her, she slashed her throat and fell to her death from the roof of 1051 Franklin Street, San Francisco.

In January 1956 Gary Snyder, preparing to enter a Zen monastery in Kyoto, and Philip Whalen invited Allen on a camping trip to the Pacific Northwest. Allen wrote 'Afternoon Seattle' about the trip, a long-line, spontaneous description of what he saw and experienced. The three poets walked in the mountains and gave readings at the University of Washington and at Reed College.

Incrementally, Ginsberg was writing himself as a book, using the page as mirror, proclaiming as Pessoa did that:

> I am, in large measure, the selfsame prose [poetry] I write . . . I've made myself into the character of a book, a life one reads. Whatever I feel is felt (against my will) so that I can write that I felt it. Whatever I think is promptly put into words, mixed with images that undo it, cast into rhythms that are something else altogether.[74]

The Town Hall Theater in Berkeley staged a reprisal of the Six Gallery reading on 18 March. This time, the poets sat on thrones, Rexroth again presided, and Allen read a longer version of 'Howl' and a new poem called 'America', which concludes with the line 'America I'm putting my queer shoulder to the wheel'.[75] Allen agreed to run a discussion group on poetics at the Poetry Center, San Francisco State College. With the help of poet Robert Creeley and Rexroth's wife Marthe (with whom Creeley was having an affair), Allen put together a mimeographed edition of 'Howl', which he sent out to writers including T. S. Eliot, Ezra Pound and William Faulkner.

In a letter to his father in April, Allen apologized for not writing in a while, explaining he had found work as a baggage handler at the Greyhound Bus Terminal. Bored by menial jobs and depressed, Allen considered a dramatic suicide, fantasizing that Louis would find his dead body in the Berkeley cottage. Inevitably, he found work as yeoman-storekeeper on the cargo ship USNS *Sgt Jack. J. Pendleton* and waited to ship out to the Arctic Circle.

A telegram arrived for Allen at Peter's apartment on the evening of 9 June and Peter delivered it to the Berkeley cottage. Naomi had died from a stroke that afternoon. Allen fell to his knees and sobbed. Because of commitments to the maritime service, he was unable to attend the funeral, but a few days after the service – conducted without saying Kaddish – Allen received a post-dated letter from Naomi in which she stated, 'I still have the wire in my head. The doctors know about it. They are still cutting the flesh & bone.'[76]

A week later, Allen shipped out. For the first few weeks, the ship plied its trade between Oregon and Los Angeles and he spent his time aboard trying to mollify and understand his grief by reading the Old Testament and the lives of the saints. He also wrote to Corso, LaVigne and Kerouac, worked on proofs of *Howl and Other Poems*, put together a self-printed edition of 'Siesta in Xbalba' and wrote lines that would become part of 'Kaddish', a personal lament for his mother.

Having saved $1,000 from his pay and adding it to the same amount Naomi left him in her will, he decided to end the relationship with Peter, visit Europe and Morocco, and set up a small press to publish Burroughs's manuscripts. Lawrence Ferlinghetti agreed to publish Corso's *Gasoline* for the Pocket Poets Series, so Allen joined Gregory at the Poetry Center in October and read 'Many Loves' about his sadomasochistic desire for Neal.

With Corso, Allen hitchhiked to Los Angeles to give a reading for *Coastlines* magazine. A drunk heckled Gregory, and Allen came to Corso's aid, stripping naked and confronting the man, daring him to take off his clothes. A few days later, Allen, Gregory, Peter and Lafcadio arrived at Burroughs's old address, 212 Orizaba Street, Mexico City, where Kerouac was staying in a rooftop cell working on *Tristessa* and having sex with fifteen-year-old prostitutes. The group went sightseeing, Jack took Peter to the local brothel, and Allen caught gonorrhoea from Peter. Gregory, staying in a tourist hotel, soon became bored with the bohemian scene and planned to fly to Washington, DC as soon as money arrived for his ticket. Finally tired of Mexico, Allen, the Orlovskys and Kerouac paid $135 for a five-day alcohol-and-speed-fuelled share-ride back to New York.

Viking bought the rights to *On the Road* in January 1957, paying Kerouac a healthy advance. Allen saw it as a sign that the group were finally becoming important and sent out his friends' work to Ferlinghetti, James Laughlin and Barney Rosset. When Lucien Carr insisted his name be removed from the dedication page of *Howl and Other Poems*, Allen agreed and later wrote that Carr 'preferred his name to be dropped lest it cause his life to cast a shadow beyond its actuality'.[77]

With a $225 loan from Allen, Kerouac left New York on 15 February for Tangier to visit Burroughs and help type the *Naked Lunch* manuscript. Allen and Peter planned to join him and travel around Europe, but Orlovsky's family commitments and a dock strike delayed their departure until 10 March, when they eventually left for the nine-day journey to Casablanca on the Yugoslavian freighter *Hrvatska*. For the first few months of the year, Allen, Peter, Elise Cowen – whom Allen had known since 1953 – and her girlfriend Carol engaged in threesomes and group sex; Peter preferred it this way and Allen was able to control the situation if they all had sex together. The sexual tension spilled over on the voyage and, between blowjobs, Allen and Peter argued about sexual need and control. Visiting Burroughs might not have been the best idea.

After a stopover in Casablanca, they arrived by bus in Tangier. Burroughs lived in a ground-floor garden room at the Hotel Villa Muniria (Villa Delirium as it was known) at 1 calle Magallanes, situated in the old French Quarter. Allen and Peter explored the city's international sectors, the Medina, the Kasbah; they walked along the shit-strewn beach, and shopped in the

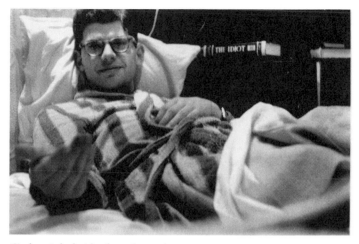

Ginsberg in bed with a favourite novel, 1957.

souqs. After a 'cure' in London in 1956, Burroughs was in better health than he had been in years and was using only *majoun* and marijuana. He composed his routines on a typewriter, scribbled annotations and then left the pages on the floor. Although he thought them nightmarish and unpublishable, Kerouac typed them and Allen set to work editing the 'word hoard' in the hope of finding a publisher.

Still in love with Allen, Burroughs sulked and disappeared on solitary walks, or to pick up boys, armed with his knives and cloaked in his 'hombre invisible' persona. With Kerouac planning to go to France, sick from tainted hashish and an opium overdose, Allen disappointed with Burroughs's chaotic texts and his rude treatment of Peter, it wasn't exactly the halcyon days of the West End revisited.

Peter soon tired of Tangier, the heat, his illnesses; he found the women unavailable or too expensive and Burroughs offhand and aloof; he started taking opium, spending the day reading, drawing or dreaming of taking a boat to Spain. After Kerouac left for

Marseilles, Allen wrote to him, 'Bill quieter lately, had liver trouble so no eat majoun nor drink so much, easier to live with. We don't know where we're going for sure. Peter unhappy here, wants to get on with girls and Europe – soon, soon.'[78]

Allen received a letter from Ferlinghetti on 27 March, informing him that San Francisco Customs had seized 520 editions of *Howl and Other Poems* under the obscene publications act, and that City Lights had contacted the American Civil Liberties Union for help if the charge went to trial. On 3 June, two plainclothes police officers purchased *Howl and Other Poems* along with the magazine *Miscellaneous Men* from City Lights Bookstore. Police arrested store clerk Shigeyoshi Murao and later Lawrence Ferlinghetti for distributing obscene literature. Allen thought about sailing home but decided to support Ferlinghetti and City Lights from afar.

Alan Ansen had arrived in Tangier to finish editing Burroughs's manuscript, so on 11 June, Allen and Peter took the ferry across to Spain and travelled to Granada. There, they explored the Alhambra, then moved on to see the Catedral de Sevilla, and Córdoba's great mosque the Mezquita, before taking the night-train to Madrid. Peter picked up a stomach bug and stayed in the hotel while Allen visited museums to see works by Rubens, Goya, Poussin and El Greco, and Pieter Bruegel the Elder's *The Triumph of Death*. Before leaving Madrid, Allen and Peter went to but did not enjoy a bullfight; then they witnessed more cruelty in the streets, coming upon a butcher botching the slaughter of a cow. After sightseeing in Barcelona, they headed for Perpignan. Low on funds, they hitchhiked and caught trains to Montpellier, Marseilles and, finally, to Venice where they met up with the returned Alan Ansen.

A year earlier, Burroughs had stayed with Ansen in Venice. Invited to a party at Peggy Guggenheim's residence and counselled to kiss the wealthy benefactor's hand when meeting her, Burroughs, a little inebriated, had replied, 'I will be glad to kiss her cunt if that is the custom.'[79] Allen and Peter fared no better with the millionaire, who thought them uncouth. They smoked joints at the party, talked about sex and mopped themselves with a perspiration-drenched towel, nearly hitting their host in the face while throwing it to one another over lunch.

After touring the city, they visited Florence and Rome, Allen inspired by the works of Leonardo, Botticelli and Michelangelo and the frescoes of Giotto and Fra Angelico. Visiting the Non-Catholic Cemetery in Rome's Testaccio district, Allen wept at Keats's grave and took two clover leaves from the grass surrounding Shelley's tomb, one to send to his father and the other to Gregory Corso (whose own ashes were interred next to Shelley's after his death on 17 January 2001). On his last day in Rome, Allen visited the house in which Keats had succumbed to tuberculosis in 1821 but could not afford the entrance fee. Spending the last of their money on a train to Assisi, Allen and Peter stayed a troubled night and day begging for food in the hometown of St Francis, Allen arguing with the local priests about Papal censorship.

While Allen was on his not-so Grand Tour, on the other side of the world, the *Howl* court case was in session, presided over by born-again Christian Judge W. J. Clayton Horn. City Lights, charged with publishing obscene literature, was defended by the ACLU and had support from Donald Allen, Robert Duncan, James Laughlin and Kenneth Patchen. The prosecution's weak case meant that, on 3 October, the judge found in favour of City Lights, declaring that *Howl* had 'redeeming social value' and 'social importance' and therefore was not obscene.

Allen travelled south to Naples via Mount Vesuvius, Pompeii, Herculaneum, Capri and Ischia where, during a drunken lunch with W. H. Auden, he confessed a preference for Whitman's poetry over Auden's conservative modernism, writing to Louis a few days later, 'Auden is a great poet but he seems old in vain if he's learned no wildness from life – sort of a Wordsworthian camp.'[80] Allen and

Peter then headed to Paris by way of Vienna and Munich to meet up with Corso but Gregory had hotfooted it to Amsterdam after a little trouble with local criminals.

George Whitman, owner of the Le Mistral bookshop (later Shakespeare and Company) at 37 rue de la Bûcherie, let Allen and Peter sleep in the store for a few nights while they looked for an affordable hotel. With none available, they took the train to Amsterdam to stay with Gregory. While Peter combed the red-light district, Allen visited the museums. After three weeks in Amsterdam, Allen, Peter and Gregory returned to Paris to take room 32 for $35 a month in a hotel at 9 rue Git-le-Coeur (later christened by Corso 'The Beat Hotel'). The room was basic, tenants shared a bathroom on each landing, and Allen saved money by cooking on a small gas stove. The landlady, Madame Rachou, rented her rooms to artists and writers, and promised Allen she would find them a larger space when available, which Allen hoped to finance with royalties from the sales of *Howl and Other Poems*.

For a year, Allen's writing had suffered, his journal entries were patchy, but Europe inspired him and Paris excited him. He bought Olympia Press editions of Apollinaire's pornography from *Les Bouquinistes* (the bookstalls along the Seine); he also found a second-hand copy of Jean Genet's novel *The Thief's Journal*, unaware that Genet had once worked on one of these bookstalls. Taking notes in his journal about his experiences, the poems began to flow.

Even though the hotel was cheap, Allen struggled to pay the rent. Now in room 25 on the third floor, he and Peter lived on oatmeal, lentils and handouts from their neighbour. Peter, worried about the state of his family's mental health, started snorting heroin. Gregory also picked up a habit, and Allen, sick with the flu, sometimes took junk as an experiment and to supplement his sleeping tablets. The little money they had came from Gregory's rich girlfriend, Peter's disability check and sporadic royalty payments from Ferlinghetti.

While waiters bustled around the tables, Allen wrote to Kerouac, 'I sat weeping in Café Sélect, once haunted by Gide and Picasso and well dresst Jacob, last week writing first lines of great formal elegy for my mother—'.[81] These first lines – borrowing a poetic structure from André Breton's 'L'union Libre' – would appear in the opening to Part IV of 'Kaddish' as:

O mother
farewell
with a long black shoe
farewell
with Communist Party and a broken stocking
farewell
with six dark hairs on the wen of your breast
farewell
with your old dress and a long black beard around the vagina . . .[82]

With *Howl* and *On the Road* both published, Allen believed it time Burroughs's new work found a publisher; he took the manuscript of *Naked Lunch* to Mason Hoffenberg, who wrote for Olympia Press, but Maurice Girodias (the owner) rejected the novel arguing that it would never sell as straight pornography.

Allen and Peter visited Montparnasse and Père Lachaise cemeteries, where Allen left copies of *Howl and Other Poems* on the graves of Baudelaire and Apollinaire. By the end of 1957, Orlovsky was planning a trip back to New York and Allen, prompted by the visit of President Eisenhower to Paris to discuss the recent Sputnik launches by the Soviet Union, considered the future of America and the fate of the world:

I visited Père Lachaise to look for the remains of Apollinaire the day the US President appeared in France for the grand conference of heads of state . . .[83]

This tone, this leap forward to *The Fall of America*, set Allen's politics against those of the more conservative Kerouac. Allen envisioned an Eastern future, one of socialism and spirituality, whereas Kerouac believed in America's pioneer spirit, supported Eisenhower, Nixon and the incumbent Republican Party. Allen believed the GOP financed right-wing dictators and strove to increase military presence in Vietnam. Kerouac wrote, 'You didn't pick up on Americana till you read *Visions of Neal*, before that you were big Burroughsian putter-downer of Americana.'[84] In a political rekindling of 'The Night of the Wolfeans and Non-Wolfeans', tension between the two old friends intensified. Kerouac was also having problems with the Beatnik phenomenon and owed the destitute Ginsberg $225.

3

'Ugh!', 1958–67

Ugh! the planet screams[1]

Skip forward a year to early January 1959. In a scene from *Pull My Daisy*, Allen ('Alan' in the credits) and Gregory share a joint. Allen becomes agitated, re-enacting Apollinaire's supposed manic reaction on finding Balzac's grave; he falls to the floor, spins, waves his limbs in the air, speaks rapidly and rapturously – telling Corso, 'That's right. That's right. That's what I said.' The performance is part Groucho Marx part dead fly as Allen writhes around, much to Gregory's annoyance. Here we see Allen's exuberance when explaining theories alongside his occasional adolescent antics. In the next scene, he announces, 'The Lower East Side has produced all the strange gum chewing geniuses.' Spontaneity (whether on film, prose, poetry or photography), self-mythologizing and the belief in poetry as documentation, are important aspects of Ginsberg's work. The year leading up to the shooting of *Pull My Daisy* would see Allen produce some of his best poetry and make decisions about his life that transformed him from Allen Ginsberg struggling poet-poseur, to 'Allen Ginsberg', world-famous proto-hippie poet-provocateur.

On 17 January 1958, with emergency funding from the US Consul, Peter sailed on the RMS *Mauretania* for New York. With his usual occult timing, Burroughs arrived in Paris just as Peter left; Bill was in the city for psychoanalytical sessions and to clear the air with Allen after the jealousies of Tangier. Even though they had sex on a number of occasions, after a frank talk, Allen believed Burroughs's obsession was over, writing to Peter, 'I feel like a million doves – Bill is changed nature.'[2]

Allen took a ferry from Calais to Dover on 1 February to visit Thomas Parkinson. In England, he met Christopher Logue, Gael Turnbull, George Melly and Stephen Spender; made trips to Stratford-upon-Avon, Stonehenge, the National Gallery, the British Library and St Paul's Cathedral; read at Oxford University; and recorded 'Howl' and 'Supermarket in California' for BBC Radio. Back in Paris, a man he picked up robbed him, Burroughs was junk sick, and Ferlinghetti had written Allen a paranoid letter. Between journeys, Allen finished the long autobiographical poem 'The Names', a eulogy to his past, and a kind of coda to 'Howl':

> It's all lost we fall without glory to empty tomb comedown to
>   nothing but evil thinkless worm, but we know better
> merely by old heart hope, or merely Desire, or merely the love
>   whisper
> breathe in your ear on lawns of long gone by Denver . . .[3]

This poem extends the autobiographical thrust of Ginsberg's poetry and mythologizes his friends, using their experiences as reflections on his own sanity, sexuality and suicidal tendencies. In 'The Lion for Real' (March 1958) and 'At Apollinaire's Grave' (winter–spring 1958) Ginsberg incorporates surrealist motifs into long American voice/breath lines more successfully than he did in 'Howl', yet he continues to use that poem's poetic aura and formula in his compositions. Reluctant to move on poetically, his poems reflect themselves as they reflect Ginsberg's life. The poetic gravity of 'Howl' pulls in all around it, sucks the life out of the lesser poems, casts them aside as sketchy husks. Yet 'Howl' also creates a centrifugal force in which poems such as 'At Apollinaire's Grave',

'The Lion for Real' and 'To Aunt Rose' create their own atmospherics; energized with the glow of 'Howl', they appear as luminous cerebral objects in their own right, their own smaller yet infinitely dense systems.

With Cassady in jail on possession of marijuana charges, Kerouac struggling with fame, Burroughs obsessed with drug cures, Allen – although surrounded by people – felt lonely. In early May, he returned to England with Corso. At first, things didn't go as planned. A member of the Campaign for Nuclear Disarmament threw his shoe at Gregory during a reading of 'Bomb' at New College and the two poets left after shouting insults at the audience. They met Auden for tea in Oxford, Edith Sitwell for lunch at the Sesame Club in London, and visited Blake's grave in Bunhill Fields.

Back once more in Paris, pressure began to build. Although he thought it a substandard poem, Allen worried he would never better 'Howl'. He became paranoid about the absurdity of the Cold War and wondered whether, as a poet, he could influence international events. Most of all, he was homesick, and wrote to Peter asking him to find an apartment for them in New York. He then set out to meet as many of his heroes as possible and – despite 'no sign of Genet'[4] – at various cafes, bars and parties, managed to corner Tristan Tzara, Man Ray, Marcel Duchamp and Benjamin Péret. On 8 July, Allen and Burroughs visited Louis-Ferdinand Céline to pay their respects. The day before Allen sailed, the poet-painter Henri Michaux visited the hotel where he, Burroughs, Corso and Allen discussed mescaline, and Gregory chided the others because one of them had pissed in the sink.

On the morning of 17 July, with a loan from his father and royalty payments from City Lights, Allen paid $225 for a berth on the ss *United States* for the six-day voyage. On board, he wrote 'American Change', an affectionate, satirical ode to America, money and what he hoped would be a new beginning:

Money money, reminder, I might as well write poems to
you—dear
American money—O statue of Liberty I ride enfolded in money
in my mind to you—and last . . .[5]

Peter arrived at the docks on 23 July, but couldn't find Allen
among the disembarking passengers, so Allen made his way to
Elise Cowen's apartment on 87th Street and 1st Avenue. After
recovering from a kidney stone attack, he visited his father and
caught up with Lucien Carr. Kerouac, slipping into alcoholism,
shunned publicity and distanced himself from the 'beatnik' scene;
a now reactionary figure, Jack lived with his over-protective mother
in Northport, Long Island, and 'Memere' did whatever she could
to prevent him from seeing Allen.

Peter worked as an orderly in the New York State Psychiatric
Institute and Allen, refusing to accept money for readings, set out
to find a job to pay his share of the $60-a-week apartment at 170
East 2nd Street. The Lower East Side stimulated Allen, its history
recalled his mother's childhood and, in places such as the Five Spot
Café, he met people like Thelonious Monk and ethnomusicologist
Harry Smith.

During a check-up in August, his dentist cousin gave Allen
nitrous oxide. The effects inspired Allen to experiment with the gas
and he experienced a new form of consciousness in which he per-
ceived existence as a simulacrum – the universe wasn't real, it was
a 'cosmic cartoon'.[6] In a similar way to William James's experiments
with the drug, Allen experienced 'a togetherness of things in a common world, the law of sharing . . . a self-consuming process, passing
from the less to the more abstract, and terminating either in a laugh
at the ultimate nothingness, or in a mood of vertiginous amazement
at a meaningless infinity'.[7] Allen wanted to reach this state through
meditation and Buddhist study, and he confessed to Kerouac that
maybe Jack, Whalen and Snyder might have been on to something:

The many worlds that don't exist
all which seem real
all joke
all lost cartoon . . .[8]

Busy editing a poetry anthology for City Lights, acting as agent
for Snyder, Whalen and Corso, playing host to endless visitors and
drinking at the Cedar Bar with Kerouac, Larry Rivers, Frank
O'Hara, Kenneth Koch and Philip Guston, Allen didn't have much
time to write. In demand, he read at Hunter College, Yale, NYU, at a
benefit for the Living Theatre, and offered to go to Chicago to read
in a fundraiser for the *Chicago Review*. Before he could leave, the
Chicago University authorities quashed the winter 1958 issue, with-
drawing funds because they considered the journal's contents
obscene.

Rereading Naomi's last letter, Allen realized he had the makings
of a long poem. He would extend the breath lines he had used in
'Howl' Part III, use his journals, his family history, his mother's
paranoia and schizophrenia, and his own experiences in institutions. After listening to Ray Charles's records at his friend Zev
Putterman's apartment, taking morphine and methamphetamine,
Allen walked home through the Lower East Side and wrote for 40
hours, weeping as he worked – 'I gotta get a rhythm up to cry'[9] –
and chasing Dexedrine with coffee to keep him awake. Satisfied
he had a workable draft, he slept for 24 hours. When he woke, he
added Part IV – the lines he had written in the Café Select the
previous year.

Between 1955 and 1958, Robert Frank travelled across the US taking
over 28,000 photographs of its citizens, 83 of which he used in his
book *The Americans*. Frank met Kerouac at a party and asked Jack
if he could film his play *Beat Generation*. The shoot began on 2
January 1959, in co-director Arthur Leslie's 12th Street and 4th

Avenue studio loft, starring Ginsberg, Corso, Orlovsky, Larry Rivers, Alice Neel, David Amram, Richard Bellamy, Delphine Seyrig, Sally Gross and Robert Frank's son Pablo, with narration by Kerouac. Based on a true story from Neal Cassady's life, *Pull My Daisy* uncharacteristically fuses cinema-vérité techniques with a mostly improvised narrative similar to the spontaneous prose of Kerouac's novels and the incantatory thrust of 'Howl'. The underground New York film scene immediately claimed the film as groundbreaking and it inspired avant-garde directors Jonas Mekas, Ron Rice and Shirley Clarke. The vérité of the characterization is debatable, the public image of the Beats slowly taking over from their individual personas, Allen becoming the angel-headed hipster of his own poem, moving inexorably towards the mediatized figure of Allen Ginsberg. Allen shared with Frank a skewed vision, an 'ad hoc aesthetic', both artists conscious of how poetry and 'photography might be changed for the next twenty or thirty years'. Both now 'rooted in a tradition which they seemed, initially to flout, challenge or overthrow', they – like Thelonious Monk and Harry Smith – 'change[d] our perceptions of the work that ha[d] gone before'.[10] Allen earned $18 a day for five days of filming, which mostly meant sitting around drinking wine and getting naked. This money, and the increased royalties from the sale of 20,000 copies of *Howl and Other Poems*, helped him to write without having to look for work.

Irving Rosenthal and Paul Carroll, editors of *Big Table* (the uncensored successor to the *Chicago Review*), asked Allen, Gregory and Peter to come to Chicago to support and help raise funds for the magazine's first edition. On 29 January, the three read at the Sherman Hotel's Bal Tabarin Hall and at the folk-music club The Gate of Horn, attracting large audiences and publicity in the *Chicago Sun-Times*, *Chicago's American* and even *Time* magazine. The readings helped raise $2,900 towards the cost of printing and distribution for *Big Table*'s 17 March publication.

Ginsberg (top right) in a photobooth with Gregory Corso, Peter Orlovsky and Paul Carroll at the time of the Big Table benefit reading, Chicago, January 1959.

Invited by the John Dewey Society, Allen, Corso and Orlovsky read at the McMillin Theater of Columbia University on 5 February, Peter having written his first poems in Paris in November 1957. Over 1,400 people – including Louis – with a further 500 locked out, watched Allen tearfully read from the draft of 'Kaddish'. The reading polarized the critics. Norman Podhoretz, writing for the *Partisan Review*, dismissed Beat writing, stating 'worship of primitivism and spontaneity is more than a cover for hostility to intelligence; it arises from a pathetic poverty of feeling as well'.[11] Allen responded in a letter to John Hollander on 7 September, 'all these objections about juvenile delinquency, vulgarity, lack of basic education, bad taste, etc etc, no form, etc I mean it's impossible to discuss things like that – finally I get to see them as so basically wrong . . .'.[12] In the 30-page letter, Allen attacked the *Partisan Review*, Columbia University, reviewers of *Howl*, and defended Beat, San Francisco Renaissance and Black Mountain poets.

Allen embarked on a mini reading tour, recorded 'Howl' for the Library of Congress, then flew to California where he stayed with Philip Whalen and read at the San Francisco Poetry Center and at Berkeley. While in California, he visited Cassady, serving two counts of five years to life in San Quentin. In prison, Neal attended the Comparative Religion and Philosophy course run by the gay-liberation pioneer and astrologist Gavin Arthur. Grandson of President Chester Arthur, father-in-law of Buddhist philosopher Alan Watts, Arthur had had sex with the English writer and politician Edward Carpenter (author of *The Intermediate Sex*) who had had a sexual encounter with Walt Whitman. Inevitable, really, that Allen became part of this time-travelling circle-jerk – or literary 'gay apostolic' succession – he had had sex with Neal who had had sex with Arthur (later author of *The Circle of Sex*). Having written Neal into history in 'The Green Automobile', 'Love Poem on Theme by Whitman' and 'Many Loves', Allen felt he owed Neal support, so extended his stay in San Francisco hoping to have some influence on Neal's parole hearings scheduled for October.

Stanford's Mental Research Institute in Palo Alto were running trials on LSD-25 and Allen volunteered to participate. While tripping, he looked at artwork by Klee, Cézanne, Van Gogh and Picasso, and listened to music by Wagner, Bach and Charlie Parker in order to stimulate his LSD visions. He locked eyes with the 'multiple million-eyed monster', didn't blink and heralded its consciousness and life-changing properties – 'This is the Work! This is the Knowledge! This is the End of Man!'[13] He recommended the drug to his father and to Peter, proclaiming the effects superior to any other hallucinogen.

Back in New York, trying to finish 'Kaddish', Allen still had time to suggest writers for LeRoi Jones and Ted Wilentz's Totem/Corinth press, advise *Big Table*, *Evergreen Review*, *Yugen*, City Lights, Grove Press, Alexander Trocchi and Seymour Krim on contributors to journals and anthologies, find the newly released Huncke an apartment, and read at the Gaslight, Queens College and Fordham University. He lived with what John Cheever called 'the blessings of velocity',[14] a need to be constantly doing. But sometimes the blessing became a burden – to escape unwanted guests, Huncke's need for handouts, the increasingly drunk and mother-whipped Kerouac, Allen accepted, along with Ferlinghetti, an invitation to participate in the South American Conference of Leftist Writing in Chile.

This perpetual motion could also be a symptom of manic depression. Allen lived a life of excitable intoxication, particularly in the time surrounding the composition of 'Kaddish'. Could Allen's restlessness have been a sign of bipolar disorder? The irritability and euphoria, the self-loathing and inflated self-esteem, the suicidal tendencies and the sexual energy all point to a positive diagnosis: 'Freud's "economic" speculation is that the discharge of energy which is suddenly available and free in mania and experienced as exaltation and joy is the same energy that was bound and inhibited in melancholia', and so 'love can flip over into hate, sadism into masochism, voyeurism into exhibitionism'.[15] Allen experienced these 'bipolar' mood disorders and regularly wallowed in and proclaimed their hallucinatory opposition.

If 'the true life takes place when we are alone, thinking, feeling, lost in memory, dreamingly self-aware, the submicroscopic moments',[16] then Allen's life, increasingly under the media microscope, had very few moments of reflection. He spent very little time alone; his experiments with LSD, his desire to travel and his search for some kind of spiritual awakening were attempts to snatch moments of self-analysis, the 'small dull smears of meditative panic' we all need.[17]

Allen saw in the New Year of 1960 with Lucien, Peter, Lafcadio, a drunken Kerouac and a deranged John Wieners, who was committed to a psychiatric hospital later in the year. Two weeks later, Allen flew to Chile but soon found the University of Concepción conference tiresome. He read from works by Corso, Lamantia and Wieners, talked about drugs and jazz, and made friends with the

Chilean poet Nicanor Parra. On 27 January 1960, as soon as the conference finished, Allen caught a train to Pablo Neruda's childhood home of Temuco. From there, he travelled on to the Isla de Chiloé where he hoped to finish work on *Kaddish and Other Poems*.

With Burroughs's yagé letters from 1953 in mind, Allen searched for a similar hallucinatory drug on his journey. Burroughs had travelled for seven months around Central and South America looking for and sampling *ayahuasca* (yagé), a brew prepared from the *Banisteriopsis caapi* plant. Used in shamanistic rituals, Burroughs and others claimed the plant had telepathic properties. Struggling with a bad cold and diarrhoea, Allen made his way down the coast to the island of Calbuco. While there, he stayed with the poet Hugo Zambelli, tried sea urchin for the first time and watched penguins swim off the coast.

After cashing a royalty cheque from City Lights, Allen travelled from Santiago to La Paz to commence his search for yagé. Although suffering from altitude sickness, he toured the city, Lake Titicaca and the surrounding mountains. In La Paz, the antibiotic injection a doctor administered for a painful anal growth may have been the source of the hepatitis C doctors would diagnose thirteen years later. At the end of April, he spent a week exploring the pre-Columbian Inca city of Machu Picchu. In Lima, Peter Matthiessen – author of *The Snow Leopard* – acquired some yagé for Allen and he took it in his hotel room:

> I'm going to Pucallpa
> to have Visions.
>   Your clean sonnets?
> I want to read your dirtiest
>   secret scribblings,
>   your Hope,
> in His most Obscene Magnificence. My God![18]

During the two weeks he spent in Lima, he wrote 'To an Old Poet in Peru' and 'Aether'. Continuing his journey, he cadged a lift on the night of 3 June, his 34th birthday, to Pucallpa, a town Burroughs visited in 1953. There, he met a man who took him to see a *brujo* – or medicine man – called 'Maestro' who gave Allen a draught of *ayahuasca*. As the drug began to work, he experienced an overwhelming sensation of being consumed by a vacuum, a pure spiritual and creational consciousness; he witnessed the universe breaking loose around him, realized how much Peter needed him, and concluded that he wanted to have children, to start a family. Invoking 'Kaddish', he saw a vision of the 'Great Being' as a huge vagina ready to swallow him whole. Allen next took yagé with some of the townspeople, threw up the mixture and retired to a hut where he had waking nightmares of death and apocalypse:

—To be It, need to be
   also the mosquito
      that bites me
—I am also mosquito
   on the Great Being[19]

During his third and fourth experience with the drug, Allen came to an understanding of what his mother must have gone through during her schizophrenic episodes. He experienced multiple and simultaneous realities, discovered that life until the point of death was suffering, a suffering only understood through a shift in consciousness. He wrote to his father, 'It was like stepping into a voodoo movie & finding it was all *real*.'[20] As if chasing revelation, he journeyed further into the jungle, to Iquitos where another *brujo* initiated him into further yagé-ic mysteries. Eventually, he returned to Lima and flew back to New York with a Peruvian government-sanctioned gallon of *ayahuasca*. Back in New York after six months away, an idea was forming that India would be his next destination.

In August 1960, the Harvard psychologist Dr Timothy Leary flew to Cuernavaca, Mexico, where he and colleagues 'choke[d] down the black, moldy fungus' of the psychedelic mushroom *Psilocybe mexicana*.[21] The results were so spectacular that, on his return to Harvard, Leary and colleague Richard Alpert (later Ram Dass) initiated the Harvard Psilocybin Project to study the effects of the drug on mentally ill patients and convicts – Aldous Huxley was on the board of trustees. Finding the initial results unsatisfactory, the patients unable to communicate their experiences – how does one describe hallucinations? – Leary switched his attention to artists and writers. In mid-November, after Allen read 'Aether', 'Laughing Gas', 'Mescaline' and 'Lysergic Acid' at a meeting of the Group for the Advancement of Psychiatry at Harvard, Dr Humphrey Osmond, impressed with Allen's reports during the Palo Alto LSD-25 trials, acted as psilocybin matchmaker and introduced Allen to Leary.

Researching hallucinogens, Allen read William James, Robert de Ropp's *Drugs and the Mind*, Aldous Huxley's *Brave New World Revisited* and Weston La Barre's *The Peyote Cult*. On 26 November, Allen, Peter and Lafcadio arrived at Newton House for the tests. Leary gave each of them a 36-milligram dose in eighteen tablets. In his room, naked and nervous, not wanting a return of the nightmarish yagé visions and vomiting, Allen listened to Wagner's *Götterdämmerung* with Peter and Lafcadio, Leary reassuringly checking in on them every fifteen minutes. When the drug started to work, Allen witnessed a spiritual light, cosmic beckonings, felt an overwhelming experience of 'god' and 'creation' within everyone, and heard the universe call for a saviour. He and Peter walked naked through the house, proclaiming Allen to be the new messiah. After Leary (whom Allen failed to cure of deafness) and colleague Frank Barron talked Allen out of going into town to spread the word, Allen called Kerouac and demanded he come to Boston, telling the unimpressed Jack that everyone

The cover of *Kaddish*, 1961, in its enlarged 50th anniversary edition.

THE POCKET POETS SERIES

KADDISH

AND OTHER POEMS

1958–1960

Expanded 50th Anniversary Edition

★

ALLEN GINSBERG

NUMBER FOURTEEN

was god. Leary and Barron finally calmed Allen by playing him a recording of Joyce reading *Finnegans Wake*, and – once again – Allen decided it was time to start a family. The group met later in the kitchen; over warm milk, they made plans for the psychedelic revolution using Leary's stash of psilocybin and Allen's voluminous address book.

In the early 1950s, Humphrey Osmond theorized that the body secretes a surfeit of adrenalin creating schizophrenic effects similar to those experienced on mescaline and other hallucinogens. In his research, he self-administered mescaline and a synthesized drug called adrenochrome (decaying adrenalin) to replicate the symptoms of schizophrenia.[22] Allen, albeit in a less scientific manner, experimented with ether, laughing gas, mescaline, yagé, peyote, psilocybin, opium and LSD as a means to expand his consciousness, as a poetic muse and in an attempt to understand his mother's disengagement from reality.

At the end of 1960, Allen received an unexpected grant of $1,000 from The Poets Foundation. While preparing to leave the country, he devoted time to proselytizing Leary and psilocybin, giving the drug to Thelonious Monk, Charles Mingus, Willem de Kooning, Franz Kline, Charles Olson, Robert Lowell and Dizzy Gillespie. The 'La Guardia Report' (1944), prepared by the New York Academy of Medicine, studied the effects of smoking marijuana. Its findings contradicted claims by the us Treasury Department that marijuana was addictive, contributed to crime and encouraged further drug usage. Allen promoted this information, hoping to persuade the government to decriminalize drugs. Believing a conspiracy existed between government agencies and organized crime, he saw hypocrisy in the legalized sales of tobacco and alcohol. On 12 February 1961, Allen took part, alongside Norman Mailer and anthropologist Ashley Montagu, in a discussion on marijuana use on the John Crosby TV show. The guests concluded that the current laws were too extreme and that marijuana was harmless. The show aired live and the Federal Communications Commission (FCC), unable to cut provocative footage, considered legal action against the station. Allen accused the FCC of McCarthyist attacks on freedom and a war began between him and the regulator.

A month earlier, Allen had invited Kerouac to take psilocybin along with Peter, Leary and Bob Donlin. Kerouac, drunk and depressed, triggered a bad trip for Leary. Allen helped him out of it, and Leary and Kerouac eventually bonded playing football with a loaf of bread. Kerouac dismissed the psychedelic philoso-phizing with the quip, 'Walking on water wasn't built in a day.'[23] Despite Jack's refusal to see psilocybin as the answer to the prob-lems of ego, creativity and reality, this statement became a motto for Allen.

Having finished the manuscript of *Reality Sandwiches*, Allen prepared to travel to Paris to meet up with Corso before going to India.

In his journals, he wrote:

S.A. America
   O look!
Manhattan is gone—
  snows over the
   flats of Bklyn . . .[24]

As Louis, Eugene, Carl Solomon and LeRoi Jones waved farewell, on 23 March, Allen and Peter set out on the nine-day crossing to Le Havre. Allen hoped this new journey would enable him to 'enter the Soul on a personal level and *shake* the emotion with the image of some giant reality'.[25] However naive about politics, Allen didn't shy away from projects that, in a Marxian and Rimbaudean sense, attempted to transform the world and change life through poetry.

At the Beat Hotel, Brion Gysin hinted that Burroughs had left Paris because he didn't want to see Allen, but Burroughs had already told Allen that he'd grown tired of the city. Aloof and secretive, Gysin explained the cut-up method to Allen as if Allen were incapable of understanding its purpose. After a trip to the Cannes Film Festival, St Tropez, Marseilles and Aix-en-Provence to soak up Cézanne country, Allen, Peter and Gregory boarded the ss *Azemour* bound for Tangier. They arrived on 1 June, but Gregory's passport was out of date, so he and Allen travelled to Casablanca to renew it, leaving Peter to find accommodation. They returned a few days later to an unwelcoming Burroughs. Working on *The Ticket That Exploded* under the influence of Gysin, Bill spent most days in his room creating cut-ups of text, sound and film with the help of English acolytes Ian Sommerville and Michael Portman.

Ginsberg with Gregory Corso, Tangier, Morocco, July 1961.

Allen accepted an invitation from Paul Bowles to visit Marrakech in July. The two writers smoked *kif,* ate *majoun* and visited Djemaa el Fna with its 'acrobats, fortune tellers [and] snake charmers'.[26] On his return, Peter told Allen that he wanted to move on to Istanbul and, at the end of July, he finally escaped Tangier, Burroughs's cruelty, the bouts of jaundice, hepatitis and dysentery, and Allen's inability to see the contradictions in their relationship; he took a boat to Gibraltar and another to Piraeus in Greece, unsure of when or if he would see Allen again. 'Opium makes separate Identities bearable', Allen wrote in his journal.[27]

Visits by Leary and Ansen went some way to alleviate Allen's loneliness but when Leary agreed with Burroughs that poetry was an outmoded art form, Allen felt alienated. Burroughs, Kerouac, Orlovsky, even poetry, were turning against him, and he considered abandoning his homosexuality, admitting:

I will have to accept women
     if I want to continue the race,
   kiss breasts, accept
   strange hairy lips behind
         buttocks . . .[28]

Allen left Tangier on the ss *Vulcania* bound for Athens on 24 July. Once there, he visited the Parthenon and Acropolis, and frequented the tavernas where he wrote 'Seabattle of Salamis Took

Ginsberg's caption: 'Gregory Corso Tangier 1961 – Street near Bill B.'s gate.' The 'B' is Burroughs.

Place Off Perema'. *Show Business Illustrated* magazine paid him $450 for a report on the Cannes Film Festival. With some of the money, he treated himself to sex with one of the local street boys. Using Hachette's *World Guide to Greece*, *The Odyssey* and *The Iliad* as guides, he visited Delphi, climbed Mount Parnassus naked and ferry-hopped to Hydra, Mycenae, Phaestos, Epidauros and Crete. Back in Athens, he discovered Peter was in Beirut on his way to Jerusalem once he had sold enough blood to pay for the trip. Allen took a boat to Haifa to rendezvous with him and while in Israel visited family members and met the existentialist philosopher Martin Buber. After catching up with Peter in Tel Aviv, they visited the Dead Sea and the site of Sodom:

> Salt slagheaps move down to Sodom
> brackish water shifts, the slimy plain's cracked,
> arid mud pods & sunken clay beds slick the feet—[29]

After going through bureaucratic hell arranging visas for India, they set out on 28 December for the circuitous journey to Mombasa.

One of Allen's heroes, Arthur Rimbaud, having abandoned poetry for a life of adventure in Arabia and Africa, traded along the Djibouti coast in the 1880s. Allen and Peter came ashore at 7 a.m. on 3 January 1962 to look around Djibouti City for traces of the poet, but found none. They then took a boat to Dar es Salaam, on which Allen read *Hitler's Table Talk* and books on Buddha. After another boat journey to Mombasa, on 6 February, they boarded the ss *Amra* bound for India.

In his journals, Allen questioned the 'Beat' phenomenon and his feelings for Peter, asking, 'what is there to love in people, they're not really there to begin with.'[30] Frustrated with his sex life, the direction of his poetry, the control forces of politics and his impotency in facing them, Allen sought an Emersonian disengagement from society in a place – India – where he could become self-reliant.

In a similar way to Derrida, Ginsberg had an ambivalent attitude to his Jewish background. In Judith Butler's phrase regarding Kafka, Ginsberg was 'arguably Jewish'.[31] More interested in exploring the fragmented nature of self-referentiality – Jewish, Russian, American; Jewish, Hindu, Buddhist; Communist, Socialist, Anarchist; homosexual, bisexual, heterosexual – Allen created triumvirates of identity. His rejection of industrial-military capitalism, his disengagement from – yet constant need of – immersion in everyday life, reinforced a Derridean responsibility in deconstructing antitheses, a constant questioning in pursuit of an always deferred resolution. Allen hoped to regain some semblance of faith while in India; interested in Sikh, Jain, Buddhist, Hindu and Islamic teachings, he sought something non-Western, visionary, almost hallucinatory in its exaltation, a non-existential, and non-materialistic human experience.

On arrival in Bombay in the middle of February, Allen and Peter stayed two nights in a cheap hotel and then took an overnight train to Delhi where they found lodgings in the Jain Rest House on Lady Hardinge Road. With Gary Snyder and his wife Joanne Kyger they travelled to the Himalayas to visit Buddhist and Hindu places of worship. On their journey, they met the Dalai Lama. Snyder asked him questions about meditation techniques. Allen – more forthright – asked about Buddhist monks' use of psychoactive drugs and offered to arrange for Leary to send the Dalai Lama psilocybin. The disengagement from America and engagement with the East began as Allen studied yoga, wore Indian clothing and tried vegetarianism. Snyder and Kyger instructed Allen in Zen techniques and explained the intricacies of Buddhist and Hindu scriptures. India reminded Allen of Mexico, Morocco and South America but with a deeper and multilayered spirituality; and he thought he might have found the source of whatever it was he had been looking for. D. H. Lawrence had similar thoughts about Ceylon, writing, 'east, is the source: and America is the extreme periphery: Oh god, must one go to the extreme limit, then to come back?'[32]

Back in Delhi, Allen and Peter visited an opium den, the resultant dreams and highs being more to Allen's liking than the effects of heroin and morphine. On opium, he could write, experience new dimensions and, more importantly, remember them:

dreams spun of so fine a gossamer that the threads snapped ere I woke to fix them in notebook. Coleridge's milk of Paradise a description of interior microcosmic thoughtful organism in hypnogogic reverie—[33]

Approaching his 36th birthday, Allen listed his achievements, his possessions, drugs he'd taken, future trips he planned, his beliefs, and thoughts about Peter, Jack, Neal, Gregory and Bill.

Believing himself consumed by a 'slow-motion death' – Allen enjoyed suffering – he was aware that however much he thought his life meant nothing, the more he documented his every experience; however much he told himself he hadn't 'the energy to make a great passional autobiography of it all', the more he continued to write it.[34]

From Bombay, Allen and Peter made the two-day train journey to Calcutta and encountered Kafkaesque American bureaucracy – the Veterans Administration had decided Peter was well enough to work and so stopped his pension payments. While Allen visited the mountains, tea plantations and monasteries on the Nepal border, Peter remained in Calcutta taking tests to prove he wasn't sane enough to find a job. On his return, Allen found Peter sick with bronchitis and the pension problems unresolved. Allen had lost his passport while in Darjeeling, so had bureaucratic problems of his own. To save money, they found cheap accommodation in the Amjadia Hotel.

Peter turned 29 on 8 July, and Allen treated him to a Chinese meal, a trip to an opium den, and composed a poem 'To P.O.' that ends '"Did we take our pills / this week for malaria?" Happy birthday / Dear Peter, your 29th year'.[35] The medicinal reminder was necessary because of the ongoing colds, fevers, bronchitis, allergies, kidney stones, dysentery and an infection of worms. The VA reinstated Peter's pension and he bought a *sarod* (a stringed instrument) to play while Allen proofed the *Reality Sandwiches* manuscript and planned a trip to the holy city of Benares (Varanasi) on the banks of the Ganges.

On the day of Peter's birthday, Allen noted a shift, a realization of postmodernism's ascendancy, art that emphasized the work itself and not the artist, wilfully anathema to Ginsberg's living autobiography:

Composition in Void: Gertrude Stein
Association: Kerouac & Surrealism

Break up of syntax: Gertrude Stein
Arrangement of intuitive key words: John Ashbery's *Europe*.
Random juxtaposition: W. S. Burroughs
Boiling down elements of Sounds: Artaud, Lettrism, Tantric
Mantras
Record of Mind-flow: Kerouac.[36]

Ginsberg assimilated into his poetry Gertrude Stein's repetition, language as a means to alter consciousness, spontaneous composition and words grappling to pin down the very nature of thought.[37] His interest in Lettrism stemmed from earlier encounters with Carl Solomon. The Situationist theories of *détournement* and the *dérive* influenced Burroughs's random juxtapositions as much as the poetry of Tzara and Lautréamont's 'beautiful as the chance meeting on a dissection table of a sewing machine and an umbrella!'[38] Ashbery's 'Europe' used techniques derived from Raymond Roussel and the Nouveau Roman novelists, incorporating other texts, detective fiction and war novels in a poem that goes beyond Burroughs and Kerouac's literary experiments. Kerouac's 'Record of Mind-flow' merged bop improvization and the stream of consciousness techniques of Dorothy Richardson, James Joyce and Virginia Woolf. But Ginsberg was reluctant to take the new route, 'to write poetry about poetry', to use '[l]anguage, the prime material itself'. Regarding his poetry as 'habitual humanistic series of autobiographical photographs' and 'old abstract & tenuous sloppy political-sex-diatribes', he admitted, 'I really don't know what I'm doing now.'[39] This was not 'a primer in the building blocks of Language poetry',[40] nor a premonition of poetry to come, it was Ginsberg referencing poetic influences and potential directions that his poetry might have taken. Stephen Greenblatt provides a clue to Ginsberg's turning away, taking a path more linguistically conservative:

the new postmodern condition has obliterated all the place markers – inside and outside, culture and society, orthodoxy and subversion – that ma[k]e it possible to map the world and hence mount a critique of its power structures.[41]

Ginsberg (as subversive outsider) would have no longer been necessary, would have no longer existed, his view of himself would have disappeared in postmodern smoke and mirrors – he wrote about himself; he did not write about himself writing about himself.

In 1971, Robert Grenier proclaimed, 'I HATE SPEECH'.[42] American poetry continued its break from William Carlos Williams and the Beats to concentrate – in a similar manner to the 'linguistic turn' in philosophy – on language and the process of writing as the subject-matter of poetry. Ginsberg resisted the influence of Language poetry, preferring the Beat-inspired verse of Antler, Anne Waldman, Andy Clausen and David Cope to the post-avant-garde writings of P. Inman, Charles Bernstein, Bruce Andrews and Ron Silliman. Ginsberg's work – and that of Keroauc and Corso – remains the bright flare-out of Modernism, closer to the sincerity of the Objectivist poets, the phraseology of Imagism, and the psychological honesty of confessional poets Robert Lowell, John Berryman and Anne Sexton.[43]

While in Calcutta, Allen met Ashok Fakir, a holy conman, who took Allen to smoke local ganja and inhale air thick with the ash of burning bodies at the ghats along the Hooghly River. One day, Ashok showed Allen a letter he had received from Bertrand Russell and Allen, having read Russell's *History of Western Philosophy* in June 1954, wrote to the philosopher asking his opinion of William Blake. Russell replied, outlining his fear of a nuclear apocalypse. Allen responded, asking, 'How exact is your statement of statistical probability?'[44] and promised (once he had proof) to do what he could to stop the proliferation of missiles. The festival of Kali, the goddess of destruction, took place in Calcutta. No doubt Allen remembered the lines Robert Oppenheimer quoted from the Baghavad Gita, 'Now I am become Death, the destroyer of worlds.' Allen smoked ganja, listened to music, and watched the parades of puppets depicting Hindu gods carried down to the river and torched. Around the same time as the festival, the world lived with the possibility of Russell's nightmare scenario – President Kennedy having sent the US Navy to blockade Cuba until the Soviet Union removed its missiles from Cuban soil.

Allen, Ashok and a young poet, Shakti Chatterjee, travelled to Tarapith, a pilgrimage that included smoking ganja, attending cremations and Allen learning the basics of pranayama yoga. From Calcutta, he and Peter made visits to the Jagannath Temple in Puri and, after viewing the erotic sculpture in the Konark Temple, Peter took a photograph of Allen standing in front of one of the 24 giant chariot-wheel sundials.

Before moving to Benares, Allen visited the Nimtallah ghats for the last time and a *sadhu* presented him with a dedication to Kali Ma (mother of the universe) in the form of a third eye painted on his forehead. As he left in a cab, he saw

a few dancers & drummers & a fellow skipping backward showering small blossoms on the corpse path moving borne by group of friend bearers, and some few mourners behind, the whole Breughel Disney scene passing in an eyeglass . . .[45]

He and Peter left Calcutta on the Doon Express via the famous Howrah Bridge, which Allen sketched in his notepad.

Arriving in Benares on 11 December, Allen and Peter rented a cheap apartment close to the Dasaswamedh ghat. Each day, Allen walked along the river passing the many ghats, looking at the 'meat dolls' of bodies, 'their ivory-yellow pudding of brains blackening in flame'.[46] At night, he talked to the *sadhus* as they passed the ganja between them. From the room's windows, he watched the lepers,

'Peter Orlovsky on the Howrah Bridge that spans the River Hooghly (Ganges), Calcutta, summer 1962' – Ginsberg's caption to this photograph.

the sacred cows stealing vegetables and people taking flowers to the temples.

Allen befriended Shambhu Bharti Baba, a *sadhu* of the Manikarnika ghat – the oldest and most sacred cremation ghat of Benares – and took photographs of him naked and wearing a towel. Allen and Peter gave money to and took photographs of an old beggar woman they call Kali Ma. Because they dressed in *salwar kameez*, grew their hair long and lived on local foods, the police became suspicious and took them in for questioning but released them soon after.

Allen and Peter spent Christmas at the Taj Mahal, sleeping in the building and listening to the guests' improvised poetry. To Allen, the building was the most remarkable place on earth:

> Xmas even, raw Microphone Urdu voices
> in neon blue at the Door—we slept
> cold on a window ledge—
> dry but inside warm alcove marble—[47]

They toured the area, visited abandoned cities, and met two Bhakti yoginis, one of whom announced that Allen should adopt William Blake as his spiritual guide and devote his life to the right-eous path. Allen was still not sure what that was or where that path went, but he was interested in following it. Like Walter Percy's Binx Bolling from *The Moviegoer* published the previous year, for Allen,

> the search is what anyone would undertake if he were not sunk in the everydayness of his own life. This morning, for example, I felt as if I had come to myself on a strange island. And what does such a castaway do? Why, he pokes around the neighbour-hood and he doesn't miss a trick.[48]

Exactly.

After spending New Year of 1963 in Mathura, Krishna's birth-place, Allen and Peter returned to their Benares apartment where the Indian Central Intelligence Police called on them. They had enough money through Peter's pension and an advance from Ferlinghetti to show they were able to support themselves, and Allen, waiting for a ticket to Vancouver for the July Poetry Conference, could prove he had the means to leave the country.

On his return from a trip to witness the *kumbh mela* at Prayag (Allahabad) in which thousands of *sadhus* bathed in the river, Alice Glaser, an *Esquire* reporter, asked Allen if she could accompany him around the local area. This stirred local CID interest and an agent questioned Allen and Peter's neighbours. Allen read at Benares Hindu University and was condemned by the head of the English department because of the swear words and explicit sex in his poems. Peter had been seeing an Indian woman called Manjula and Allen worried that this – rather than the reaction to his read-ing – was the reason for the police questioning them.

The authorities rejected Allen's visa application and told him he had to leave the country by 15 February. After visiting the

American embassy and travelling to CID headquarters in Delhi, his visa was extended until June and Peter's until August. The communist students of Benares Hindu University had posted copies of *Howl* to the police, the obscene words marked, and they had enclosed a letter hinting that Allen was a CIA agent or a spy for the Chinese. Allen increased the hours he spent practising yoga; he also studied breathing exercises in order – among other things – to control his considerable temper.

William Carlos Williams died on 4 March. Allen received the news a few weeks later. Saddened at the death of his mentor and friend, he wrote 'Death News':

> Quietly unknown for three weeks; now I saw Passaic
> and Ganges one, consenting his devotion
> because he walked on the steely bank & prayed
> to a Goddess in the river, that he only invented . . .[49]

Allen left Peter in Benares while he travelled to Bodh Gaya where Gautama Buddha attained *bodhi* (enlightenment). Allen sat beneath the branches of the bodhi tree, a sacred fig in the grounds of Mahabodhi Temple. It was here that Allen discovered Buddha's footprint – the figure of three fish with one head – that became his motif.

While in Benares, Allen and Peter cared for a beggar who had had his tongue excised in the violence during India's partition. They found the skeletal man lying in a puddle of urine, covered in faeces and flies; they brought him pyjamas and a mattress, cleaned him, eventually secured him a bed in a charity hospital and contacted his family. They helped a number of beggars this way, Allen battling Indian bureaucracy and corruption to provide food, shelter and medicine. The police visits, travelling and near poverty put a strain on Allen and Peter's relationship. Peter decided that he wanted to live on his own, so Allen went to Calcutta to wait for the Vancouver Conference organizers to send him money.

On 26 May, ill from a kidney infection, bitter and sad at his parting from Peter, he boarded a plane to Thailand. Allen broke two abstinences while in Bangkok – sex was readily available, plus there were too many temptations for a reluctant vegetarian, all the 'Chinese meats hanging in shops'.[50] He stayed in the city of divine beings for five days before moving on to Saigon on 1 June.

While there, he met with US Embassy officials who denied any involvement in the civil war, while – conversely – journalists showed him evidence of America's military presence. On 5 June, a reporter from the *New York Times* wrote a piece on Allen, quoting a Buddhist spokesman saying,

> Well, he was tall and had a very long beard and his hair was very long in the back and curly . . . He said he was a poet and a little crazy and that he liked Buddhists. We didn't know what else he was so we decided he was a spy.[51]

He next visited Angkor Wat in Cambodia, where he cycled around the Hindu/Buddhist temple complex, taking notes for his next long poem. Written in shorter lines than 'Howl' or 'Kaddish', 'Angkor Wat' approximates the field or projective verse poetry of Charles Olson:

> As might be read for poesy by Olson
> At least moves from perception to obsession
>   according to waves of Me-ness
>   Still clinging to the Earthen straw
>   My eye . . .[52]

His eye integral to his reflexive vision, the me-ness radiating out – radar-like – detecting objects that interest him poetically, the 'words and propaganda' of Angkor's ruins, its vegetative abandoned libraries,[53] the residual elements of empire, reverberating contiguously through Allen's autobiography and world history. LeRoi Jones, Robert Creeley and Philip Lamantia are ghostly inhabitants of the ruined libraries as much as Shiva, Buddha and Pope John – they are avatars of a god conspicuous by his/her absence.

Allen flew to Tokyo and, finding the hotels too expensive, slept on cardboard in Tokyo station. The next morning, he road the train to Kyoto to stay with Gary Snyder and Joanne Kyger. With Snyder, he practised Japanese Buddhist breathing techniques and found Japan a welcome release from the poverty of India. In 'The Change: *Kyoto–Tokyo Express*', written on his return to Tokyo on 17 July, Ginsberg concentrates on the length of the line according to breath, honed from his breathing exercises with Snyder. He realizes in the poem that his obsession with death, the existential questioning of events and actions, his search for a hallucinatory reality outside of the everyday, are false preoccupations, and he confirms his imagist stance – his eyes locate the content, his breath dictates the form, the inspiration. He confided to Kerouac a few months later that, after having sex with Gary and Joanne, 'I want a woman wife lady, I want I want, want life not death.'[54] After spending a few days in Tokyo, he returned to the West with a positive outlook, a reaffirmation of his poetics, and a determination to take care of himself and others.

The 1963 Vancouver Poetry Conference from 24 July to 16 August at the University of British Columbia included lectures and readings from Ginsberg, Creeley, Olson, Duncan, Whalen, Donald Allen, Denise Levertov, Margaret Avison and Bobbie Louise Hawkins. Allen returned from Asia a hippie before his time, sporting traditional Indian clothing and beads, wearing his hair and beard long, advocating free love and nakedness, and singing the Hare Krishna mantra to whomever would listen. The conference became a prototype for the love-in, sex as much as poetry shared between teachers and students.

Whalen drove Allen to San Francisco where he worked on the final proofs of *Reality Sandwiches* and a script for a planned Robert

Ginsberg at the 1963 Vancouver Poets Conference, in a photograph he captioned:
'with Jerry Heiserman (later Sufi 'Hassan'), the late 'Red' a poet, Bobbie Louise
Hawkins Creeley, Warren Tallman, Robert Creeley above Charles Olson, left to
right top rows; seated left Thomas Jackrell then student poet, Philip Whalen
& Don Allen'. 'Red' (Dan McLeod) went on to edit *The Georgia Straight*; both
Creeleys, Olson and Whalen were writers, Tallman an academic and Allen
an anthologist.

Frank film of 'Kaddish' for which he received much-needed money.
On Gough Street, in the house in which he first saw the painting of
Peter, Allen shared accommodation with Cassady (Allen rented a
typewriter for Neal to capture his speech-patterns for an autobiography),[55] Michael McClure, and a new love interest in the poet/
collagist/filmmaker – and later Cherry Valley Editions publisher –
Charles Plymell. But Allen had changed and by the end of
November, sick of the noise and people in the Gough Street
apartment, missing Peter, and caught in an unhealthy lust
riangle with Plymell and his girlfriend, he returned to New
York for the first time in twenty months.

Allen asked Kerouac to help with the dialogue for Frank's *Kaddish*
but Jack remained distant, only calling Allen to abuse him and

voice his support for the growing military presence in Vietnam. The two old friends rarely saw each other, their correspondence dried up, and Allen's fame increased while Jack slipped into alcoholic obscurity.

Early January 1964, reconciled for now, Peter and Allen were living above Ted Wilentz's Eighth Street Bookstore, giving Allen opportunity to visit his old haunts and the newer places in the Village. It was here that Allen met Bob Dylan for the first time and the two men struck up an instant friendship. Peter and Allen soon moved to a rundown walk-up at 704 East 5th Street. Allen, ready to get back to serious work, wrote:

> Black smoke flowing on roofs, terrific
>   city coughing—
> garbage can lids music over
>   truck whine on E. 5th St.
> Ugh! I'm awake again—
>   dreary day ahead
> what to do?—Dull letters
>   to be answered . . .[56]

These views of the city, endless correspondence, requests for poems, obituaries, notes, recommendations, introductions, blurbs and the ceaseless ringing of the telephone remained the hectic background to Allen's mode of working.

Since he had been away, a new group of radical artists had come together in New York: artists/filmmakers Andy Warhol, Jonas Mekas, Stan Brakhage, musicians John Cage, La Monte Young, Lou Reed, and writers Tuli Kupferberg and Ed Sanders who were also members of rock band The Fugs. Sanders edited and published the mimeographed *Fuck You: A Magazine for the Arts*, and ran the Peace Eye Bookstore at 383 East 10th Street, which had become the focus of New York counterculture.

Allen became involved in political, literary and social causes –
campaigning on behalf of The Living Theatre, raising funds for
poetry coffeehouses and underground theatres threatened with
closure by city authorities. Allen and Sanders, with the help of Paul
Blackburn, Diane di Prima, Harry Fainlight and Jackson Mac Low,
formed a defence group called the Committee on Poetry (COP),
visiting politicians to put their case for free assemblage and free
speech. As a protest, Allen cut off his beard and hair and sent it to
Richard H. Kuh, the Assistant District Attorney for New York. On
3 April, the COP successfully challenged the authorities and the NYC
License Department allowed coffeehouses and theatres to operate
without having to pay expensive licences. Appearing in magazines,
on television and in films, Allen became promoter and representa-
tive of a new group of radical writers and artists.

Having crossed the country in a psychedelic bus driven by Neal
Cassady – its destination sign reading 'Further' (or 'Furthur') –
the Merry Pranksters, a group of artists, writers, musicians and
like-minded hangers on exploring the American countryside with
aid of psychedelic drugs and led by Ken Kesey, arrived in New
York in June. Allen, Cassady and Kesey attended a party on
Madison Avenue and 90th Street. Kerouac made an appearance
but felt uneasy in the proto-hippie, LSD-charged atmosphere,
chiding the Pranksters for covering a sofa with an American flag,
accusing them of being communists and calling Allen a 'fairy kike
pinko'.[57] Neal drove Jack home, whatever they discussed on the
journey to Northport lost forever – the two men would never
meet again.

The Ginsberg/Orlovsky apartment became headquarters for
the older Beats and the new avant-garde. The filmmaker Jonas
Mekas introduced Allen to Barbara Rubin, a young director from
Long Island, or as Allen described her 'a little 19 year old LSD
nymph moviemaker girl'.[58] Infatuated with Allen, Barbara moved
in and became his de facto girlfriend sharing threesomes with him

and Peter. Instrumental in organizing the Velvet Underground's first residency, Barbara took Allen along one night to mingle with the writers, filmmakers and musicians at the Café Bizarre. Allen spent weekend nights at The Dom – an old converted Polish dance hall on St Mark's Place – or at Café Metro with Bob Dylan.

Later that year, on 21 November, William Burroughs sent a postcard to the English poet Jeff Nuttall, informing him he would be sailing for New York City. Burroughs arrived on 8 December and, after customs officials searched his belongings, made his way to the Hotel Chelsea on 23rd Street. Allen hadn't seen Bill for over three years.

On 11 January 1965, Allen flew to Boston to testify in the *Naked Lunch* obscenity trial. Ed de Grazia, Grove Press's lawyer, questioned Allen, Norman Mailer and other 'experts' about the moral and literary worth of the novel. Allen gave an impassioned defence, arguing, 'it was an enormous breakthrough into truthful expression of exactly really what was going on inside his head, with no holds barred. He really confessed completely, put everything down so that anybody could see it.'[59] Despite the evidence, the court found against *Naked Lunch* and banned the book from the Boston district. On appeal, the Massachusetts Supreme Court overruled the decision on 7 July 1966.

Asked by Minister of Culture Haydée Santamaría to be a juror for the Casa de las Américas poetry prize in Cuba, Allen agreed but had to seek special dispensation from the State Department for the visit, receiving the permit on 7 January 1965, eight days before he was due to leave. After a brief flu-ridden stopover in Mexico City, he flew to Havana on 18 January. He planned to report on the Revolution and the Castro government to his father, friends and underground newspapers. After checking in to the Hotel Havana Riviera, he caught a bus from the Malecón to La Rampa where he met a group of young writers and poets formed around the literary magazine *El Puente*. Back in September 1960, despite Fidel Castro's record of imprisoning homosexuals and administering medical and political 're-education' as a 'cure', Allen had attended a reception for him at the Hotel Teresa in Harlem. In Havana, Allen listened to stories of homophobia, harassment, labour camps and capital punishment. Over the next few days, he worked on the jury along with Julio Cortázar, Miguel Grinberg (leader of the *Movimiento Nueva Solidaridad* alliance of poets[60]) and Mario Vargas Llosa. During a lecture on poetry, dreams, drugs, yoga and mantras, he talked about ways of combating dogmatism and brainwashing.

When the hotel denied José Mario Rodriguez and Manuel Ballagas access to his room, Allen became angry and complained to the International Cultural Exchange Program. A few weeks after their visit, the two young poets were leaving the Auditorium Theater when police took them in for interrogation. Allen's proselytizing of marijuana and homosexuality, rather than liberalizing

Ginsberg with the Argentinan poet Miguel Grinberg in Havana, Cuba, in February 1965. Photo by Ernesto Fernández, with Grinberg's camera.

Cuban government policy, provided the authorities with an excuse to imprison the *enfermitos*, a youth sub-culture who smoked marijuana and listened to jazz and rock music.[61]

> I clang my finger-cymbals in Havana, I lie
> with teenage boys afraid of the red police,
> I jack off in Cuban modern bathrooms . . .[62]

Allen curtailed interviews in fear of incriminating his young friends; in return, the organisers cancelled his lectures wary of Allen's controversial statements. Tired of bureaucracy and bored by academics, Allen hung out with members of *El Puente*, had sex with Manuel, and recorded erotic fantasies about Fidel Castro, Raúl Castro and Che Guevara in his journal.

Allen had a far from satisfactory meeting with Haydée Santamaría. The Minister of Culture agreed to look into the young poets' arrest only for Allen to slap her arse on her way out of the room. Nine months later, after Allen's trip to Czechoslovakia, Russia, and his involvement in peace protests, his father would chastise him, 'Your holier-than-thou-attitude, with your noble intentions, does not prove you have a Heavenly blueprint of the Truth!'[63]

After a drunken evening, Allen returned to his hotel at 5 a.m.; a few hours later, soldiers arrived to serve him with deportation papers – he would be leaving on the 10.30 a.m. flight to Prague. Relieved that the soldiers didn't confiscate his notebooks, he chanted his mantra quietly. Carlos Verona – head of Cuban Immigration – escorted him to the airport. Because of the complicated relationship between the US and Cuba, travellers were forced to enter through Mexico but could only fly back to the US via Czechoslovakia. That was no problem for Allen; he had always wanted to visit Eastern Europe.

The author Josef Škvorecký met Allen at Prague airport and took him to the Art Nouveau Ambassador Hotel. Consumed with ideas of totalitarianism, bureaucratic nightmares, and his own literary history, Allen visited Kafka sites including the author's grave in the New Jewish Cemetery. With money from Czech royalties, he toured the thawing city, met young men at the Turkish baths and frequented the Violacaff, a Beat/jazz cafe adorned with pictures of him and other Beat poets, where he listened to his poems recited in Czech and drank beer with underground writers such as Václav Havel.

On 20 March, Allen caught a train to Moscow, passing through Lvov and other Ukrainian towns that were once home to his grandparents. After checking in to the state-run Minsk Hotel and eating a Russian lunch, he visited the Kremlin, noting its strange concertination and concatenation of time, a sixteenth-century fortress home to the controllers of Soviet nuclear missiles. Allen's cousin Joe Levy and his wife Anne invited him to their apartment where Joe told the story of Naomi's life in Russia at the end of the nineteenth century. Allen listened to tales of his grandmother's mental illness, famine, war, pogroms, poverty and the Levy family's voyage to America. He found a photograph of himself as a skinny four-year-old, and ones of his parents in the 1920s and '30s. He talked to Joe about Stalin and Communism, chanted, and then Joe and Allen rode the subway back to his hotel.

After a visit to Leningrad to tour the Hermitage Museum, on his return to Moscow, he stayed at the Bucharest Hotel on historic Balchug Island, and witnessed a Red Square parade for returning cosmonauts. During a visit to Yevgeny Yevtushenko's apartment, they discussed homosexuality, drugs and Allen's 'Blake visions', but Yevtushenko dismissed these as juvenile interests compared with state censorship and Stalin's atrocities. Allen extended his stay in Moscow to meet Andrei Voznesensky.

The Polish Ministry of Culture hosted Allen's trip to Poland. While in the country, he visited the site of the Warsaw Ghetto – its monument bringing tears to his eyes – and spent a week in the ancient city of Krakow. He also made a surreal pilgrimage to

Auschwitz-Birkenau, driven there in a car 'with some boy scout leaders who were trying to pick up schoolboys hanging around the barbed wire gazing at tourists'.[64]

He returned to Prague on 30 April, in time for the May Day festival. Škvorecký, suffering from flu, telephoned Allen and asked him to deputize for the Engineering School's nomination for King of May (*Kral Majales*) contest. The next day, after watching the May Day parade, Allen returned to his room to rest. A few hours later, woken by students, he donned a gold cardboard crown, boarded a truck and sat on a homemade throne clinking his finger cymbals. While rock bands played and Allen chanted 'Om Sri Maitreya', the students voted him 1965's *Kral Majales*, the first since the Communists banned the celebrations in 1945. The authorities had other ideas. Not being a student and not being Czech, Allen was far from their ideal King of May. By midnight, the government had stripped him of his title.

While out walking with friends on 5 May, a man punched Allen: 'Once knocked down on the midnight pavement by a mustached agent who screamed out BOUZERANT'.[65] The man who shouted 'Faggot!' claimed he saw Allen exposing himself. Five police officers appeared and arrested Allen. In the scuffle, one of his notebooks (18 February–14 March) went missing. The police later visited Allen's hotel, escorted him to the station and asked him to sign for the return of his notebook. He did so and officers told Allen the public prosecutor would investigate the notebook's contents; however, the authorities confiscated it and Allen, despite his efforts to retrieve the journal, never saw it again. A few days later, due to his 'sexual theories', the police revoked Allen's visa and expelled him from the country. On 7 May, Allen left Czechoslovakia for London. As in Cuba his presence resulted in a government clampdown on underground culture. During the flight, he wrote the first draft of 'Kral Majales':

And *tho'* I am the King of May, the Marxists have beat me upon
 the street,
 kept me up all night in Police Station, followed me thru
 Springtime Prague, detained me in secret and deported me
 from our kingdom by airplane.[66]

Bob Dylan, in London preparing for a concert, introduced Allen
to The Beatles in his Savoy Hotel room, where they spent 'a drunk-
en night talking about pot and William Blake'.[67] The next day, in
an alley (Savoy Steps) behind the hotel, Bob Neuwirth and a rab-
binical Allen stood in the background while Dylan shucked cue
cards for the promo film for 'Subterranean Homesick Blues'. Two
months later, on 25 July, Dylan would shock the folk world by
playing electric guitar at the Newport Folk Festival.

If the revolutions in Russia and Cuba hadn't delivered on their
promises (or Allen's perception of them), then the artistic and
political revolutions fomenting in London, New York City and San
Francisco met with his approval. In his prison notebooks, Antonio
Gramsci commented, 'The crisis consists precisely in the fact that
the old is dying and the new cannot be born; in this interregnum a
great variety of morbid symptoms appears.'[68] The 1950s were finally over. Philip Larkin pinpointed the true start of the 1960s as 1963;
The Beatles first appeared on the Ed Sullivan Show in 1964; but
1965 saw the introduction of the mini dress, the beginning of the
Black Power movement, and the escalation of the Vietnam War.
Allen soaked up this cultural tension and became a conduit
between the disparate groups.

After visiting Tom Pickard and Basil Bunting at the end of May,
Allen travelled to Liverpool to take in the new Merseybeat groups and
poets, the city reminding him of San Francisco. Back in London, he
stayed in Primrose Hill with Jonathan Cape editor Tom Maschler,
then with Barry Miles – writer and manager of Better Books – in his
Fitzrovia home. Better Books, frequented by writers Bob Cobbing,

Alexander Trocchi, Jeff Nuttall, Iain Sinclair and Tom McGrath, was London's equivalent to Ed Sanders's Peace Eye bookstore and centre of the new British poetry scene. Allen read there in May, enjoying his celebrity status. For Allen's 39th birthday, Miles threw a party and invited The Beatles. Allen drank too much, stripped naked and passed out on the sofa where someone tied a 'Do Not Disturb' sign to his penis. Allen complained to Nicanor Parra that The Beatles 'got scared and ran away laughing over their reputations'.[69]

New Zealand poet John Esam and Barbara Rubin hired the Royal Albert Hall for one of the formative events of the UK underground. Six thousand people listened to Allen, Corso, Ferlinghetti, Adrian Mitchell, Alexander Trocchi and other poets read at The International Poetry Incarnation on 11 June. Peter Whitehead filmed the performances and released *Wholly Communion*, a 33-minute documentary of the event.

After a visit to the Fitzwilliam Museum in Cambridge to study Blake's manuscripts, Allen travelled to Paris with Corso and stayed once more in George Whitman's bookstore before returning to New York happy, exhausted and broke. Customs officials detained Allen and strip-searched him, looking for illegal narcotics. Finding him clean, they released him and he arrived home to discover the new apartment at 408 East 10th Street had been burgled and his new typewriter and Peter's harmonium stolen.

Allen returned to Berkeley on 12 July for a conference with Duncan, Spicer, Olson, Snyder, Creeley, Wieners, Kyger and others. During the fortnight-long event, the poets voted Charles Olson President of Poets and Allen Secretary of State for Poetry. Anne Waldman had called Allen a number of times since 1963, asking him to read at Bennington Women's College, Vermont, but missed his Berkeley reading on 21 July, unable 'to get over the bridge' from San Francisco because she had been tripping on LSD.[70] Anne met Allen during the Berkeley seminars, but it was the Olson reading that changed her life, influencing her to become an experimental performance poet and political/ecological activist. While in Berkeley, Allen supported the Free Speech Movement, a group of students protesting against the university's ban on political activity.

With $2,000 from a timely Guggenheim Award, Allen purchased a second-hand Volkswagen camper and – having never taken his driver's test – asked Snyder to accompany him on a trip to Oregon. On 22 August, in Portland, they watched The Beatles, John Lennon addressing Allen from the stage. From the 150 people at the Six Gallery to the 6,000 at the Poetry Incarnation, Allen fantasized about having the pulling power – both sexually and numerically – of a rock star. Two of Allen's obsessions were apparent here and strangely connected. Nicholson Baker notes that fame also fascinated Walt Whitman. The writer Edmund Gosse once found Whitman in his Camden, New Jersey, home surrounded by reviews of *Leaves of Grass*, which he would snatch from the piles and read to whoever would listen.[71] Allen also obsessed about the fame of others; it captivated him as much if not more than his own fame, and he cultivated the friendships of Dylan, Lennon, McCartney, and later Bono, Joe Strummer and Johnny Depp.

Back in San Francisco, Allen moved out of Shig Murao's apartment near City Lights and into a larger space near Golden Gate Park. On 6 September, the *San Francisco Examiner* ran the article 'A New Haven for Beatniks' about the Blue Unicorn coffeehouse in Haight-Ashbury, and the author Michael Fallon used the term 'hippie' to differentiate the younger 'hipsters' from their older beatnik counterparts. Allen was now a major figure in the hippie movement, connecting Kerouac's wanderlust and Burroughs's anti-authoritarianism with Eastern religion and the music of Bob Dylan and The Beatles.

At Ferlinghetti's Bixby Canyon cabin at the beginning of October, Allen and Peter took LSD, relaxed on the beach and walked in the woods. With McClure and Ferlinghetti, on 15 October, Allen read at the Vietnam Day Committee's teach-in before taking part in a protest march on an army induction centre in Oakland. Threatened with violence by Hells Angels, the march turned back. The following day, with Allen leading, the protest marchers reached Oakland where the Angels were waiting to tear down peace banners. The marchers staged a sit-in in the street until the police took control.

Allen became the facilitator of the hippie movement, introducing the San Francisco poets to Dylan and Joan Baez, inviting Ken Kesey and his Merry Pranksters to a Robert LaVigne party, and mediating between the peace movement and the motorcycle gangs. With Cassady and Kesey he met Hells Angel leader Sonny Barger. They argued about Communist plots and Vietnam, Allen told Barger he loved him, while Barger admitted a liking for Bob Dylan and Joan Baez. Allen even persuaded the Angels to chant the Mahaprajnaparamita Sutra. Barger agreed not to attack the 20 November peace march. A few weeks later, the Angles attended a party at Ken Kesey's La Honda cabin. They all took LSD, Allen danced naked, and he and Hunter S. Thompson questioned the police waiting outside the gates to arrest partygoers. The Angels thought Allen 'the greatest straightest unstraight guy they ever met'.[72] Allen recorded the events in 'First Party at Ken Kesey's with Hell's Angels'.

Prompted by the enforced closure of the Peace Eye Bookstore, Allen had the idea of making the Committee on Poetry a non-profit organization to 'gather money from those who have it in amounts excess to their needs and disburse it among poets and philosophers who lack personal finance or wherewithal to accomplish small projects in the society at large'.[73] Money raised by or donated would be used to 'promote freedom of expression where such expression is threatened by social prejudice', 'aid sick, wounded or nervous creative souls', 'participate in projects for altering consciousness' and 'help unlucky poets and painters avoid confinements in jails and madhouses or ease their turn to free-dom'.[74] Any payment due to Allen for readings went directly into COP funds.

On the day LSD became illegal – 1 February 1966 – Allen, Peter and Peter's older brother Julius drove to New Mexico to see Creeley and then to Kansas where Charles Plymell had arranged readings. The police stopped the VW a number of times looking for illegal narcotics. In Kansas City, Robert Frank shot footage of Allen, Peter and Julius for his film *Me and My Brother*; on his return to New York, Frank enlisted Sam Shepard to help with the script. Travelling in the VW across California, Arizona, New Mexico, Texas, Oklahoma, and into Kansas, Allen worked on 'Hiway Poesy: L.A.–Albuquerque–Texas–Wichita' and 'Wichita Vortex Sutra', a visceral anti-war poem with its:

> bomb blast terrific in skull & belly, shrapneled throbbing meat
> While the American nation argues war . . .[75]

Ginsberg channels the thoughts of a changing nation, the slow recognition that, as Norman Mailer highlighted back in 1957, peo-ple not only fear an 'instant death by atomic war' but live in terror at the thought of a 'slow death by conformity with every creative and rebellious instinct stifled'.[76]

While at an immigration checkpoint in Laredo, Texas, on 22 December 1965, officials had arrested Timothy Leary and his wife Rosemary and charged them with tax evasion, marijuana posses-sion and attempting to transport half an ounce of the drug across the border. On 11 March 1966, Judge Ben Connally sentenced Leary to 30 years in prison and fined him $30,000. His lawyers launched an appeal but Leary was almost bankrupt. Allen agreed to read at a benefit for him on 5 April. A month later, District Attorney G. Gordon Liddy and members of the Sheriff's Office arrested Leary for possession of drugs at his Millbrook home.

Allen continued to raise funds for Leary's defence, appearing at a number of benefits.

Allen read his 'First Manifesto to End the Bringdown', extolling the advantages of marijuana use to a huge audience at a peace demonstration in Central Park and planned to use his fame and oratorical experience to question the government's stand on narcotics. In May, the US Senate invited him to address a sub-committee and, Allen, dressed in a suit, gave what he calls 'a paper, which has been very long' on LSD,[77] providing medical data, personal experience and statistics, in a well-argued and well-presented statement.

A few weeks after his fortieth birthday, Allen and Ferlinghetti stayed at the Bixby Canyon cabin. They took LSD, discussed his new collection *The Fall of America*, and the publishing deals offered by Random House, Doubleday and Grove Press. Although loyal to City Lights, Allen wanted better distribution for his books. On his return to San Francisco, he worked on the Sanders and Leary legal cases and an article on drug use – 'A National Hallucination' – for the *Washington Bulletin*.

For all his pro-drug writing and speechmaking – he gave a talk in November at the nineteenth-century Unitarian Universalism Arlington Street Church urging everyone healthy and over fourteen to take LSD at least once – Allen tried to keep his apartment free of narcotics. With Peter using heavily, and the likes of Huncke and Corso regular visitors, it wasn't easy.

He continued his interest in Hinduism, meeting Abhay Charanaravinda Bhaktivedanta Swami Prabhupada, founder of the International Society for Krishna Consciousness. Looking for sex as well as enlightenment, Allen summed up 1966 in a poem he wrote on 14 December:

Done, finished, with the biggest cock you ever saw.
3 A.M., living room filled with quiet yellow electric,
curtains hanging on New York, one window lit

in unfinished skyscraper.

Swami White Beard
Being-Consciousness-Delight's photo's tacked
to bookshelf . . .[78]

A few lines later, he questions the energy he expends on demonstrations and lobbying, once again desiring a permanent love, still
hoping for a family and all the 'inconceived babies'.[79]

In 'Bayonne Turnpike to Tuscarora', written on 4 January 1967,
Allen documents a car journey to California. Using the Uher tape
recorder Dylan gave him $600 to buy, he dictates his thoughts,
observations, memories, music on the radio and overheard conversations, and creates a sound poem, a collage and cut-up of
experience and analysis. Poems such as 'Beginning of a Poem of
These States', 'Hiway Poesy: L.A.–Albuquerque–Texas–Wichita',
'Wichita Vortex Sutra' and 'Iron Horse' are road poems, poetic ver-
sions of the American road movie. In these long poems, Ginsberg
mirrors Robert Frank's portraits of Americans and anticipates the
road photos of Garry Winogrand,[80] providing snapshots of people
and events as a portfolio-documentary of America.

As Greil Marcus notes, 'In 1967 the orderly assumptions and
good-natured disruptions that in the 1950s bordered real life were
melting down in riot and war; the civil rights movement, the great
wave of relief in a republic fulfilling its own promises, disappeared
into the Summer of Love, into the undertow of belief in a world
where everyone was his or her own Christ.'[81] Or Buddha, Messiah,
Shiva – Ginsberg, Leary and Kesey all played their part in creating
this underground yet dynamic cultural torque revolving around
Vietnam and peace protests, the Manson Family and the flower
children, 'All You Need is Love' and 'People Are Strange'.

The *San Francisco Oracle* announced 'A Gathering of the
Tribes for a Human Be-In' in Golden Gate Park's Polo Grounds

to start at 11 a.m. on 14 January. After Allen and Snyder prepared the area by sanctifying it with a Hindu *pradakshina* ritual, fuelled by White Lightning LSD cooked up by underground chemist Owsley Stanley and turkey sandwiches handed out by the Diggers, the 25,000-strong crowd listened to readings by Ram Dass, Snyder, McClure, Suzuki Roshi and Jerry Rubin. Leary urged everyone to 'Turn on, tune in, and drop out' – a slogan Allen was uneasy with, believing Leary had never really dropped out. The Hells Angels provided security, and Jefferson Airplane, the Grateful Dead, Moby Grape and Quicksilver Messenger Service the music. With a final blast from Snyder's conch at 5 p.m., Allen closed the Be-In chanting Om Sri Maitreya and asked everyone to take away any litter.

For months, Allen toured the country, reading at universities, organizing benefits; any money he made went into the COP coffers for yet more benefits, charities and hard-up poets. He even wrote to the CIA, asking for a $10 million grant – Richard Helms (Director of Central Intelligence) declined to reply. Allen pursued his interest in spirituality, studied with Snyder and travelled to New Mexico to witness Pueblo Indian initiation rites. It's not surprising that in the *Collected Poems* only seven date from 1967, three of them written in January.

In order to relax, Allen wanted to find a place out of the way but close enough to San Francisco or New York, something like Ferlinghetti's Bixby Canyon cabin. Barbara Rubin – maybe as part of a ruse to persuade Allen to start a family with her, something she had fantasized about and he had contemplated – found a 70-acre farm near Cherry Valley in upstate New York. The purchase went through the next year and Allen – being not at all practical with these things – asked his friend Gordon Ball to manage the farm.

Allen flew to Italy for the Festival dei Due Mondi, held in Spoleto on 4 July, and a few days later met Ezra Pound at a performance of The Magic Flute. On 9 July, Allen, Octavio Paz and

Desmond O'Grady got together for a drink. In the cafe, a plain-clothes officer arrested Allen. The local police questioned him about the obscene contents of his poems. On his release, the paparazzi took hundreds of photos and, fuelling Allen's ego, the story made headlines in the daily papers.

Allen then travelled to London where he planned to meet his father and stepmother. With Giuseppe Ungaretti, Auden, Spender and Olson, he read at the Queen Elizabeth Hall, went to a party with Mick Jagger and Marianne Faithfull, and to the recording of the Rolling Stones' 'We Love You' and 'Dandelion'. In the last two weeks of July, he participated in the Congress on the Dialectics of Liberation at The Roundhouse with David Cooper, R. D. Laing, Paul Goodman, Gregory Bateson, Herbert Marcuse and Stokely Carmichael. Iain Sinclair and Robert Klinkert made a 16mm colour-film documentary about Allen and recorded interviews published in *The Kodak Mantra Diaries*. After this, Allen travelled to Wales to stay with Tom Maschler. Inspired by the landscape and on LSD, he wrote 'Wales Visitation':

Crosslegged on a rock in dusk rain,
    rubber booted in soft grass, mind moveless,
    breath tremble sin white daisies by the roadside,
        Heaven breath and my own symmetric
        Airs wavering thru antlered green fern . . .[82]

Influenced by William Wordsworth's 'Tintern Abbey', Ginsberg envisions a mystical union with nature, a Wordsworthian pantheistic 'One' that is the Earth, the poet and the poem – what Wordsworth calls in 'The Preface to the Lyrical Ballads' a 'spontaneous overflow of powerful feelings'.

Joined by his father, Allen read at the ICA in London and Allen showed Louis and Edith around the city. They did similar things in Paris and in Rome (where Allen was once again arrested). From

Rome, they went to Venice and, after Louis and Edith left for home, Allen continued sightseeing between readings. On 23 September, Allen and his Italian translator Fernanda Pivano visited Ezra Pound and Olga Rudge at their house near Rapallo. In 1961, on hearing of the suicide of his old friend Ernest Hemingway, Pound had unwittingly echoed the opening lines of 'Howl' when he declared that 'American writers were all doomed, and the USA destroys all of them, especially the best of them.'[83] In the garden of the villa in Sant'Ambrogio, Pound sat taciturn as Allen sang mantras and played his harmonium.

Two days before Pound celebrated his 82nd birthday on 30 October, Olga arranged a lunch in the restaurant of the Pensione Cici in Venice with Allen. Peter Russell and Michael Reck were also there and would write about the meeting in the *Evergreen Review* as, 'A Conversation Between Ezra Pound and Allen Ginsberg'. In reality, the conversation was very one-sided. Allen bombarded Pound with questions and compared him to Prospero. Pound admitted, 'The worst mistake I made was that stupid, suburban prejudice of anti-Semitism', referring to his wartime radio broadcasts in which he proclaimed, 'That Jew in the White House . . . the kike and the unmitigated evil . . . the United States has been invaded by vermin.' Allen – used to such comments from Kerouac – replied that anti-Semitism was Pound's 'fuck-up' and asked if Pound would accept his blessing. After a pause, Pound replied, 'I do.'[84] According to Pound's biographer James J. Wilhelm, after lunch, Pound invited Allen to his Venice residence where Allen smoked pot, and played records by Dylan, Donovan and The Beatles.

On 15 November, Allen arrived back in New York but could not get into the apartment. When he did, he discovered the utilities disconnected, the telephone cut off and the apartment damaged. While high on methamphetamine, Peter had hallucinated that the apartment was on fire and smashed furniture and windows.

In early December, Allen took part in a march on the Whitehall Street induction centre to protest against President Lyndon B.

Ginsberg with his Italian translator, Fernanda Pivano, probably in Rapallo, near Genoa, at the time they were visiting Ezra Pound there, late summer 1967.

Johnson's escalation of the Vietnam War. Thousands of police surrounded the Draft Board building. The commanding officer allowed Dr Benjamin Spock, Susan Sontag, Allen and others to stage a sit-in on the steps, then arrested them. The American Civil Liberties Union defended the paediatrician, author and poet, and the charges were dropped.

On 1 December, Allen wrote his last poem of 1967 – 'War Profit Litany', dedicating it to Ezra Pound:

> These are the names of the companies that have made money
>   from this war
> nineteenhundredsixtyeight Annodomini fourthousandeighty
>   Hebraic
> These Corporations have profited by merchandizing skinburn-
>   ing phospho-
>   rus or shells fragmented to thousands of fleshpiercing
>   needles . . .[85]

Within two months, the National Liberation Front for South Vietnam and the People's Army of Vietnam would launch the Tet Offensive against the South Vietnam Army and American forces. The military operation shocked the American public and increased demonstrations against the war – Allen would be directly involved in the protests.

4

'The Most Brilliant Man in America', 1968–77

I want to be known as the most brilliant man in America[1]

Pin-up boy of conservative intellectuals, William F. Buckley Jr crosses his legs and turns a page of the yellow legal pad on his trademark clipboard. It is 7 May 1968, and Allen Ginsberg is appearing on Buckley's syndicated show *Firing Line* to discuss 'The Avant Garde'. Polite and professional, cunning and cutting, Buckley questions Ginsberg about hippies, obscenity, censorship, LSD, Vietnam, consciousness and America as police state. Allen has just finished reading his poem 'Wales Visitation', which Buckley likes; Allen then talks about China and delivers a rather Burroughs-like rap:

> In the sense of armored divisions, it seems to me, fear of the yellow life form virus taking over the planet. I don't think we're going to make it with the Chinese unless we display a certain amount of awareness of their existence on the planet and I think the cause of their paranoia is our paranoia. It's a nerve reflecting system, the two images are just reflecting each other building up to a barroom brawl.

Buckley sneers, 'If you keep this up I'll ask you to read more poetry.' The audience laughs. As Allen responds, Buckley, sensing weakness in his prey, moves in for the kill, eyes flashing wide while a supercilious grin spreads across his face, 'It's just that in politics you are a little bit naive.'[2] Allen glares, a look of hurt on his face soon replaced by anger, his dark eyes blazing with indignity. For a second, it looks as if he might lose his temper, throw one of his tantrums, but he reels in his ego, asks if Buckley knows the Krishna chant and, playing his harmonium, sings 'Hare Krishna'. Less than a year later, on the same show, Buckley half-jokingly threatened to smash Noam Chomsky in the face. Chomsky, calmer than Allen when faced with someone disputing his theories, replied coolly, firm in the knowledge and groundwork of his ideology. Despite his ego, Allen could be vulnerable and tentative in the spotlight of his fame. He wrote to Snyder, 'I keep straying on mental anger warpaths and then come back to milking the goats.'[3] Appropriately, Updike notes,

Celebrity is a mask that eats into the face. As soon as one is aware of being 'somebody', to be watched and listened to with extra interest, input ceases, and the performer goes blind and deaf in his overanimation. One can either see or be seen.[4]

In Newark on 12 July 1967, the arrest of a black cab driver by two white police officers had sparked six days of rioting in which 26 people died and hundreds were injured. Police arrested LeRoi Jones for illegal possession of firearms. Allen testified for the defence but, on 4 January 1968, the court sentenced Jones to three years. Allen sent documents relating to the case to *Playboy*, hoping to raise interest in what he saw as a perversion of justice, writing to Snyder, 'witnesses did testify to his being beaten and not having guns in trial. Just that all-white jury believed the cops.'[5] The year 1968 would be one of politics, a year of dissatisfaction with the peace movement, a year when Allen's fame reached its pinnacle – it began with a death and the end of an era.

Allen's address book bulged with contacts, people he had met – even fleetingly – from all over the world. In later years, his office Rolodex became so engorged with cards it barely turned. Some days, it felt as if every one of Allen's contacts was trying to call him. So, when the phone rang at 5 a.m. on 10 February, Allen was not expecting tragic news. On 3 February, after a wedding in San Miguel de Allende, Mexico, where, according to unconfirmed reports, he drank tequila and pulque and swallowed Seconal, Neal Cassady, wearing only a T-shirt and jeans, had walked along railway lines towards the town of Celaya and may have fallen, decided to sleep or passed out by the tracks. In the cold night air, exposure set in and triggered a coma. Discovered in the early morning and taken to hospital, Neal died on 4 February. The cause – according to the death certificate – was 'general congestion in all systems'.[6]

> After friendship fades from flesh forms—
>> heavy happiness hangs in heart,
>>> I could talk to you forever . . .[7]

'Elegy for Neal Cassady' contains the line, 'Sad, Jack in Lowell saw the phantom most . . .', but Kerouac wouldn't listen when Allen told him the news. His first ongoing adult sexual partner, Neal became Allen's muse, inspiring his more sexually explicit confessional poems; but Cassady also stoked Allen's suicidal tendencies, his – at times – pathetic neediness, and his exaggerated claims to the importance of his friends' writing. Four months after Neal's death, Allen wrote 'Please Master', a list poem, a necrophiliac plea for his sadistic partner to do whatever he wanted with the masochistic implorer, the poet as sex slave, as naive plaything. In August, Allen would visit Carolyn to see Neal's ashes:

> Delicate eyes that blinked blue Rockies all ash
> nipples, Ribs I touched w/ my thumb are ash
> mouth my tongue touched once or twice all ash . . .[8]

In her introduction to Neal's *Collected Letters: 1944–1967*, Carolyn Cassady – characteristically bitter – wrote, 'Only Jack and Allen considered him [Neal] a "writer"; the Beat elite disliked him.'[9]

To raise money for the COP and to fund the purchase of the Cherry Valley farm, Allen planned a gruelling reading tour throughout February and March. While on the road, he and others performed an exorcism at Senator Joseph McCarthy's grave to banish the anti-communist paranoia McCarthy had spread throughout America in the 1950s. Now in the psychedelic 1960s, Allen met with Robert Kennedy – three months before his assassination in Los Angeles – hoping the presidential candidate would consider his theories on drug legislature and the ecology. The 45-minute talk was convivial but all Allen left with was publicity and bragging rights.

With his reams of notes on drugs, censorship, the CIA, his journals and notebooks spread across the country, Allen decided to centralize his papers. Trilling suggested Columbia University's Rare Book and Manuscript Library, and the Special Collections Department accepted the boxes for safekeeping, opening them to researchers and students. Allen's accumulation of things as memories, hoarding of memorabilia, and his open-access archiving of texts relate directly to his poetics and his determination to be part of American literary heritage. The institutionalizing of his manuscripts, bus tickets, badges and flyers enacted a personal commodity fetishism. It is as if his hectic lifestyle made necessary the hypostatization of memory in things, of experience residing in objects, resulting in Allen appropriating the role of 'Allen Ginsberg', an apotheosis of the self.

Allen hoped Cherry Valley would provide a means of escaping 'Allen Ginsberg', become a place where he and others could relax and work; where Peter, by renovating the house, might overcome his addictions and psychiatric disorders. But a little craziness was never far away. As the VW bus carrying Allen from Newark Airport

With fellow-writers Herbert Huncke and Peter Orlovsky, *c.* 1968, at the Cherry Valley Farm in upstate New York.

neared the farmhouse at Cherry Valley at the start of May, a screaming Peter charged out wielding a machete; Allen remained calm and managed to mollify him. So much for escaping from New York.

Earlier in February, Allen had met with Abbie Hoffman and members of the Youth International Party (Yippies) to discuss organizing a Festival of Life during August's Democratic Party's National Convention in Chicago. Jerry Rubin of the National Mobilization Committee to End the War in Vietnam and activist-satirist Paul Krassner also became involved. Allen, wary of violence, agreed to take part but had doubts about some of the more radical groups, admitting to Snyder 'Yippie organization's in wrong hands sort of', and he worried about 'the undercurrents of violence everywhere'.[10]

In the last week of August, without permits to gather, protestors arrived in Lincoln Park, Chicago. Mayor Daley increased police presence dramatically, arming the officers with riot gear; National Guardsmen were held in reserve and troops called up from Fort

Hood, Texas. Burroughs, Genet, Mailer and Southern joined Allen to cover the occasion for *Esquire* magazine. In the days leading up to the nomination for the Democratic presidential candidate, 10,000 people took to the streets.

On 24 August, in the poem 'Going to Chicago', Allen wrote:

I am the Angel King sang the Angel King
as mobs in Ampitheaters, Streets, Colosseums Parks and offices
Scream in despair over Meat and Metal Microphone[11]

The next day, police surrounded Lincoln Park. Allen tried to pacify the more violent protestors and began a six-hour chant, his 'OM!' resonating through the park. Allen's passive demonstration had a short-term influence on the crowd and he experienced a sensation similar to that of his 'Blake visions' and nitrous-oxide experiments. When police closed down a music festival, protesters fought back, taking the riot into the streets. Hundreds were injured. On 28 August, the riots escalated. As Ginsberg asked, when the police state takes over, 'Who wants to be President of the / Garden of Eden?'[12]

At 3.30 p.m., police beat a young boy lowering an American flag at a rally in Grant Park. The crowd attacked the officers who responded with Mace and tear gas. Allen originally agreed to take part believing the festival would be a coming together of American 'breakthrough artists and manifesters of consciousness',[13] but viewed the violence as a missed opportunity and major setback for the peace movement. On 5 November, Richard Nixon won the presidential election by a close margin. Years later, Allen admitted Nixon's win and the prolongation of the Vietnam War may have come as a result of the left's refusal to support Hubert Humphrey's nomination.[14]

Allen spent the autumn with Barry Miles recording William Blake's *Songs of Innocence and Experience*. He first performed the songs, accompanied by musicians, in New York on 18 February

1969, and would continue to do so throughout his life to sell-out audiences. MGM released the album, *William Blake: Songs of Innocence and Experience, tuned by Allen Ginsberg* in 1970.

In late November, Peter crashed the station wagon into an oncoming car and Allen fractured four ribs and his hip. After a fortnight in hospital, he returned to the farm to enjoy the enforced retreat.

On 1 January 1969, he wrote:

A new year, no party tonite, forget
old loves, old words, old feelings.
Snow everywhere around the house,
I turned off the gas-light & came upstairs
alone to read . . .[15]

Once recovered, but walking with a cane, Allen read in Miami in February, Denver, San Francisco, Salt Lake City and Baltimore in March. In April, waking to find the left side of his face paralysed, Allen's doctor diagnosed Bell's palsy. Although ill, he went to Tucson to read at the University of Arizona. On 9 May, after a press conference, Allen questioned Bob Thomas about his article in the *Tucson Daily Citizen* regarding Allen's homosexuality. After the conference, Allen followed Thomas and, according to *Time* magazine, called him a 'motherfucker'. Thomas hit Allen twice in the mouth. 'Ah, those were only words I was speaking!' Allen said. Thomas replied, 'They may have been only words to you, Mr Ginsberg, but out here they are fighting words.'[16]

At 4.17 p.m. Eastern Daylight Time on 20 July, as Neil Armstrong stepped on to the moon, all at Cherry Valley gathered around a neighbour's television to watch. Allen recorded the event in the poem 'In a Moonlit Hermit's Cabin':

Voices calling "Houston to Moon"—Two "Americans" on the
    moon!

Beautiful view, bouncing the surface—"one quarter of the world
    denied these pix by their rulers"!
Setting up the flag![17]

Allen, Gordon Ball, Herbert Huncke, Julius and Peter Orlovsky
spent the summer on the farm installing a water pump, renovating
a barn and making the place more comfortable. Paranoid the
police would bust him for drugs, Allen asked his friends to keep
the farm 'as a refuge from chemical city conditions'.[18] His anxiety
increased daily – he owed the IRS $1,488.68, he worried about Peter,
about the livestock, about his manuscripts, about the state of the
world and about how he could possibly support all those living on
the farm.

As for Kerouac, glasses of Johnnie Walker Red Label whisky
might have helped him sleep but the Dexedrine pills he popped
caused insomnia. Late morning on 20 October, in the bungalow
in St Petersburg, Florida, where he lived with his mother
Gabrielle (Memere) and his wife of two years, Stella, Kerouac
sat in his rocking chair drinking beer and eating tuna from a
can while watching *The Galloping Gourmet*; suddenly, he collapsed with severe abdominal pains and vomited copiously.
Stella called emergency services. After lengthy surgery and
exhaustive blood transfusions, Jack died at 5.30 a.m. the next
day at St Anthony's Hospital. His death certificate recorded 'gas-
trointestinal hemorrhage, due to bleeding gastric varix from
cirrhosis of the liver, due to excessive ethanol intake over many
years'.[19] Allen took the call that evening. Shaken, he phoned
friends to tell them the news. By the end of his life, Kerouac was
looking much older than his 47 years, spent most of his time at
home or in local bars, and suffered from a hernia he taped in
place with a silver half-dollar; his abdominal pains and collapse
may have been exacerbated by a recent beating he took in a bar.
In the year leading up to his death, he became obsessed with

conspiracy theories; the last article he wrote, 'After Me, the Deluge', is a rambling rant against 1960s radicalism.[20]

That night, Allen made notes for 'Memory Gardens', an elegy for Kerouac:

> Can I go back in time & lay my head on a teenage
>> belly upstairs on 110th Street?
> or step off the iron car with Jack
>> at the blue-tiled Columbia sign?[21]

During a reading at Yale the next day, Allen prayed for Kerouac and read choruses from *Mexico City Blues*; then he, Corso, Peter and John Clellon Holmes drove to Lowell. The friends visited the funeral home, Gregory shot film of the corpse, while Allen caressed Kerouac's brow. Along with 100 or so mourners, they made their way to St Jean de Baptiste Church to celebrate mass. On 24 October, at Edson Cemetery, Allen threw a rose and the final handful of dirt on to Jack's coffin.[22]

> and that's the end of the dribble tongued
>> Poet who sounded the Kock-rup
>>> throughout the Northwest Passage . . .[23]

Allen read with his father in Miami at the close of the year but the police put a stop to the performance because of Allen's sexually provocative poems. He sued the authorities and the judge ordered that the authorities allow Allen and his father to finish the reading, which they did a week later.

Liver cancer claimed Charles Olson's life on 10 January 1970. At Beachbrook Cemetery, Gloucester, Massachusetts, Allen, Creeley, Wieners, Sanders, Ed Dorn and publisher Harvey Brown acted as pallbearers. Olson had recently finished *The Maximus Poems* and –

perhaps with the epic construction of Olson's magnum opus in mind – Allen craved time off from travelling to write, to realign the misapplication of his energies.

Politics had taken over from poetics; court appearances were becoming the new performance poetry. Allen continued research into CIA drug running and the government's clampdown on underground magazines and publishers. If Allen had been Rimbaud, he would have become 'somebody else' – 'Je est un autre . . .'[24] and disappeared – but he wasn't, he was the media darling of the counterculture, the instantly recognizable radical. In the next two years, he would complete only a dozen poems that made it into book collections. There may have been another reason for the dearth of poems; in autumn, on a flight to Bermuda after a short holiday in the Caribbean, Allen misplaced a manuscript of poems dating back to 1965.

As yet another tour finished in San Francisco, Allen travelled to New Haven to read along with Genet (in the country illegally) at a May Day benefit for Bobby Seale – the eighth man in the Chicago conspiracy trials and co-founder of the Black Panther Party – charged with the kidnap, torture and murder of Panther member and alleged FBI informant Alex Rackley a year earlier. Fearing violence, Allen took to the stage, chanting 'OM!' He later wrote the introduction to Genet's *May Day Speech* published by City Lights in December.

This was the height of what Thomas Pynchon called the 'anarcho-psychedelic' era.[25] The Panther rally occurred two days after the US invaded Cambodia, three days before the Ohio National Guard wounded nine students and shot to death four others at Kent State University. In the following weeks, there would be riots and demonstrations in New York, Washington and San Francisco. Allen responded with 'Anti-Vietnam War Peace Mobilization':

One hundred thousand bodies naked before an Iron Robot
Nixon's brain Presidential cranium case spying thru binoculars
from the Paranoia Smog Factory's East Wing.[26]

After taking psilocybin mushrooms in the autumn, Allen composed 'Ecologue' – a satirical state-of-the-nation address. Using
the farm landscape as a metaphor for America's political terrain,
Ginsberg looks at his role in the world and considers those outside
American law – Eldridge Cleaver, Timothy Leary and White Panther
leader John Sinclair. It is a clearing-house poem designed to simpli-
fy his life:

Get rid of that old tractor or fix it!
    Cardboard boxes rotten in garageside rain!
Old broken City desks under the appletree! Cleanum
        Up for firewood![27]

At the end of the year, the National Book Award for poetry committee tested Allen's radicalism when they asked him to be a judge.

Allen spent a quiet January and February of 1971 in the 10th Street
apartment, cataloguing recordings and working on the CIA, censorship and drug legislation files. With evidence of CIA complicity in
smuggling opium and heroin out of South East Asia, Allen researched
newspaper and government archives and visited columnists and sena-
tors to persuade them to publicize his findings. After a reading with
his father in Washington, DC, restless as usual, and not wanting to go
back to what was becoming the hellmouth of Cherry Valley, Allen
arranged a tour and Gordon Ball agreed to manage, record and tran-
scribe a number of readings for what would become *Allen Verbatim*.

While on the road, Allen wrote 'Milarepa Taste', a nineteen-word
poem in which he channels the ideas of the Tibetan yogic poet
Milarepa. Questioning his own physicality, the temporal body,

the illusory concept of ego and individual consciousness (again Rimbaud's 'Je est un autre . . .'), the breath of the 'I' escaping like smoke, he sees the interconnectivity of things and being, the saliva/soup referred to in the poems reifies the poetic thought processes by making fluid the abstractions of experience, connecting the mind directly with the world of objects, the weight of existence disappearing into the void. Allen's life at the time mirrored Milarepa's pronouncements 'If you are not content in yourselves, whatever you have will only benefit others' and 'If you do not suppress Ambition, desire for fame will lead to ruin and litigation'.[28]

The tour finished in California and Allen visited Kitkitdizze, Snyder's house near Nevada City. While there, despite breaking a finger, he assembled sixteen tape-recordings of readings and meditated for an hour every day using a sub-vocal mantra taught to him by Siddha Yoga founder Swami Muktananda.

On 4 July, the San Francisco Bay Prose Poets' Phalanx (including Allen, Kesey, Ferlinghetti and Anaïs Nin) published the *Declaration of Independence for Dr Timothy Leary* – Leary was on the run after escaping the California Men's Colony in San Luis Obispo with the help of the Weather Underground Organization. Allen included in the statement his theories on CIA drug running, underground press censorship, America's war in Southeast Asia, the criminal associations of the narcotics bureaus, and likened Leary to Whitman and Thoreau.

Since 26 March, the Bangladesh Liberation War had forced millions of refugees to flee into northeast India. In September, Allen flew to Calcutta to report on the tragedy. Conditions were appalling inside the makeshift monsoon-drenched camps, people slept under sodden cardboard and queued for food and medicine. On his return to New York, shocked at the conditions and disgusted with the government for spending billions of dollars bombing Cambodia, Laos and Vietnam, Allen wrote 'September on Jessore Road', a heartfelt protest song:

Border trucks flooded, food can't get past,
American Angel Machine   please come fast!
Where is Ambassador Bunker today?
Are his Helios machinegunning children at play?[29]

He visited John Lennon and Yoko Ono on 9 October, Lennon's
31st birthday. After Allen read an early draft of the poem, he,
Lennon, Ringo Starr and Phil Spector jammed for six hours, chanting mantras and singing Blake songs while Jonas Mekas filmed
them. Furthering his obsession with pop celebrities and his dream
of becoming a rock star, Allen persuaded Bob Dylan – increasingly
cynical about the methods and goals of a counterculture that
claimed him as a leader – to sit in on a jam session later in the year.
On 17 November, they went into the studio to record the
Dylan/Ginsberg collaboration 'Vomit Express', the title coming
from Lucien Carr's description of a plane journey to Puerto Rico.

On 5 January 1972, Allen played a blues poetry concert at St Mark's
Church. He worked hard on an album of these mostly improvised
tracks and, by the end of January, with a little help from Dylan,
recorded the songs, wrote liner notes and even designed the cover
for these 'blues chords with political *dharma* themes'.[30]

In late February, he travelled with Ferlinghetti to Australia for a
reading tour, stopping off to relax in Hawaii and Fiji. In Adelaide,
Allen asked four Aboriginal musicians to perform their oral poetry
and responded by singing Blake songs. The performance lasted
four hours, the musicians showing Allen how to strike songsticks
together to keep rhythm while reciting traditional migration and
funeral songs. Using these rhythms and the Aboriginal oral tradition, Allen composed 'Ayers Rock/Uluru Song' with creational and
apocalyptic haiku-like lines exploring the mythology of place: 'One
raindrop begins the universe. / When the raindrop dries, worlds
come to their end.'[31]

During the summer of 1971, Allen had spent a drunken evening in Berkeley with Chögyam Trungpa Rinpoche. The Tibetan Buddhist scholar advised Allen to shave off his trademark beard, pay attention to his breathing patterns and use improvisation in his poetry. Back in 1960, Kerouac had called Allen a 'hairy loss'[32] – no longer: Allen took Trungpa's advice, cut off his beard, trimmed his hair, swapped his dark work shirts for white ones and bought a suit. Unmasked, he could walk the streets of San Francisco – poet incognito. Maybe he should have seen signs of things to come when, at a benefit for his new guru in May, a drunken Trungpa interrupted Snyder's reading by banging a gong and smashing glasses. The next day, in a Buddhist taking-refuge ceremony Allen received the name Lion of Dharma.

He then visited Denver in honour of Neal Cassady, took LSD in Jackson Hole and met a Neal 'disciple' in Butte.[33] While on his travels, he worked on 'The Great Rememberer',[34] an introduction to Kerouac's *Visions of Cody*, which, he argues, is a 'consistent panegyric to heroism of mind, to the American Person that Whitman sought to adore' and a 'farewell to all our promises of America'. So, no longer the 'holy mess' he once thought.[35] In the essay, he associates the book's themes with contemporary issues. For Allen, Kerouac's twenty-year-old novel evokes Buddhism, the Vietnam War and Timothy Leary's legal problems. To paraphrase Stéphane Mallarmé, everything existed to end up in a book – a book of Allen's life.

That Ginsberg embraced Buddhism at the height of his fame showed an awareness of and concern with his overriding (some would say overblown) ego. His poetics, based on a 'stream of continuous perception', flows contra to the Buddhist 'notion that there is no Self'.[36] Ginsberg's poetry enacts a search for Self through the Self, a means of overcoming 'the illusions on which our desires are based' and a confrontation with 'the void beneath each object of desire'. With Cassady and Kerouac dead, Orlovsky sliding into mania, Allen was alone, only the illusion of his fame for company. Embracing Buddhism, he hoped to realize that the 'Self . . . is an illusion, an imposture'; something he also attempted using psychoanalysis. Still in fear of going mad like his mother and like his lover, Ginsberg hoped to 'undergo the process of "going to pieces without falling apart"', to escape his 'narcissistic/masochistic thoughts', Yet, as Slavoj Žižek argues in his thoughts on the separation between psychoanalysis and Buddhism, the no Self is a difficult state to achieve because of our drives, the life and death drives that go 'on even when the subject "has traversed the fantasy" and broken out of the illusory craving for the (lost) object of desire' – be it fame, Peter, and/or Naomi.[37]

After a hernia operation, Allen spent the summer at Cherry Valley, trying – with varying degrees of success – to meditate using Trungpa's techniques, and working on *The Fall of America*, a collection of poems written between September 1965 and November 1971. In early July, the Republican Party renominated Richard Nixon as presidential candidate. Allen flew down to Miami to take part in protests against this and the ongoing Vietnam War. The authorities tear-gassed the demonstrators and imprisoned Allen for two days. *Newsday* paid him to cover the event, and he wrote the essay 'Ah, Wake Up!' for the newspaper's 27 August edition. Following the convention, he spent the rest of the year on tour, recuperating the costs of recordings and running the farm. Alone over the holiday period at Cherry Valley, he worked on manuscripts and Buddhist theory. On 24 December, he wrote 'Xmas Gift':

"I invented a universe separate,
something like a Virgin"—
"Yes, the creature gives birth to itself,"
I quoted from Mescaline . . .[38]

On New Year's Day 1973, Allen composed 'Thoughts Sitting Breathing', taking as its form the six-syllabled mantra 'om ma ni pa dmi hum', in which each syllable represents one of the six realms of existence, each signifying a Buddhist deadly sin: *om* – pride; *ma* – jealousy; *ni* – lust; *pa* – prejudice; *dmi* – greed; and *hum* – anger; with Ginsberg in typical scatological form, writing:

> HŪM—I shit out my hate thru my asshole, My sphincter loosens the void,
> all hell's legions fall thru space, the Pentagon is destroyed . . .[39]

One of Ginsberg's more Swiftean poems, it portrays personal, public and political visions, at once excremental and experiential, a fusion of everyday complaints, a call for peace, and an attack on hypocrisy, violence and America's military-industrial complex. Written using Trungpa's breathing and sitting exercises, the poem attempts to banish materialism and ego, excise war and violence, and exorcize the demons of sexual desire, anger and frustration. It was also a farewell to Allen's habit of spending inordinate amounts of time chanting during so-called 'poetry' readings, Trungpa having persuaded him to stop singing the mantras and focus on his poetry.

On the farm in late January, Allen slipped in the snow and fractured his right leg. At the hospital, they diagnosed chronic hepatitis and hypertension. He had to wear a full cast and spend a month in bed at the farm. During the rest, he hoped to perfect his meditation techniques.

Allen watched the televised Senate Watergate Committee hearings on 17 May. The following year, at the acceptance speech for the National Book Award in Poetry for *The Fall of America*, Peter Orlovsky (standing in for a too-busy Ginsberg) would deliver Allen's summation of American political corruption:

Watergate is a froth on the swamp: impeachment of a living president does not remove the hundred billion power of the military nor the secret billion power of the police state apparatus. Any president who would try to curb power of the military-police would be ruined or murdered.[40]

Nominated by Kenneth Rexroth, the National Institute of Arts and Letters inducted Allen as a member. Kurt Vonnegut, also elected, remembered the day 'Allen Ginsberg and I both got elected to the National Institute of Arts and Letters . . . and *Newsweek* asked me how I felt about two such freaks getting into such an august organization. I said, "If we aren't establishment I don't know who is."'[41]

While in London for a poetry festival in August, Allen wrote 'What I'd Like To Do' – he would like to retire, build a hermitage, compose poems to the wind, masturbate in peace, read Dostoevsky's *Brothers Karamazov* and spend three years in solitude. A poignant wish list made more so by the last poem he would write, 'Things I'll Not Do (Nostalgias)', 24 years later. Allen returned home later in the month to the usual problems. The farm had a host of unpaid bills and Allen's correspondence had gone unanswered. He needed peace and quiet. He didn't quite manage the three years but, in the middle of September, began a three-month meditation retreat with Trungpa in Jackson Hole.

With the meditation, yoga and guidance he received from Trungpa, Allen felt relaxed and far from the madding farm, the endless legal cases. Trungpa planned to open the Naropa Institute in Boulder, Colorado – an independent university teaching Buddhism, psychology, arts and literature – and asked Allen to compile a list of writers, musicians and artists to teach in this 'academy of the future'.

Allen spent the rest of the year ensuring Cherry Valley would become Peter's property, drawing up plans for a house in north

California, and touring to finance the two projects. He also mourned the deaths of three influential people in his life – Pablo Neruda, who died on 23 September; W. H. Auden, on 29 September; and the Buddhist philosopher Alan Watts – one of Allen's 'wise elders' – on 16 November.[42]

In New York on 13 January 1974, Allen wrote 'Jaweh and Allah Battle' about the previous year's Yom Kippur War, voicing frustration at the centuries-old crisis (although he seemed oblivious to a crisis closer to home – Peter's ongoing mental deterioration). On the road again from February to May, Allen was busy raising money for the COP and other causes. He read with his father on 14 May at the Zen Center in San Francisco, then made his way to the Sierras to meet up with Peter and Gary Snyder. The three poets began felling trees and pouring concrete to assist the carpenters constructing the cabin – Bedrock Mortar – close to Snyder's Kitkitdizze. Allen envisioned a place for people to gather, talk, exchange ideas and relax – not having learnt the lesson that being who he was made those things an impossibility – Bedrock Mortar was destined to become Cherry Farm West. To raise funds for the project, Ginsberg sold his Jack Kerouac letters to Columbia.

The first Naropa Institute summer school ran from July to August in Boulder. The organisers expected to attract no more than 500 people, but over 1,000 arrived to enrol. The Naropa Institute – named after the eleventh-century Indian Buddhist yogi and founder of the *Kagyu* school of Tibetan Buddhism – attracted Anne Waldman, John Cage, Gary Snyder, Gregory Bateson, Ram Dass and Diane di Prima as instructors. Allen's seminars focused on spiritual poetics, the works of William Blake and William Carlos Williams. With Anne Waldman (poet and director of St Mark's Church Poetry Project) as co-director, Allen established The Jack Kerouac School for Disembodied Poetics – as he explained it,

'Disembodied,' because Kerouac was dead. His work is accepted in the Buddhist community as a great manifestation of poetic mind; true to the nature of mind as understood traditionally by Buddhist theories of spontaneous mind, how to achieve and how to use it.[43]

Allen's celebrity meant groupies and, at the age of 48, he could write:

—met you in the street you carried my package—
Put your hands down to my legs,
touch if it's there, the prick shaft delicate
hot in your rounded palm, soft thumb on cockhead—[44]

In Berkeley, on 18 September, Allen met with Ram Dass and Jerry Rubin. Rumours circulated that Timothy Leary, facing a 90-year sentence, had turned state's evidence against the Weathermen and other radical groups – the FBI codename for him was 'Charlie Thrush'.[45] Despite Leary's son believing the stories, Allen thought the government had conspired against the counterculture and made Leary the fall guy.

On his return to his East 10th Street apartment, the man who wanted 'to be known as the most brilliant man in America', who 'overthrew the CIA with a silent thought' and who 'wasn't afraid of God or Death after his 48th',[46] experienced a very down-to-earth New York moment. At 7 p.m. on Thursday 2 November, Allen left his apartment block, crossed the street, and walked past the pharmacy and the Chinese laundry. Some Puerto Rican teenagers were hanging out on the stoops. One of them stepped down and put his arm around Allen's throat, another grabbed his arm, kicking his legs away. Allen chanted 'Om Ah Hūm', clutching his woollen bag containing valuable manuscripts. The gang pulled him behind the metal door of a burnt-out store, took his fake snakeskin wallet containing $70, credit cards and Seiko watch, searched him for hidden cash, and threatened to kill him if he didn't shut up chanting (many others had felt the same way). Luckily, they didn't take his bag. When they left, Allen went to the local bodega to call the police. The *New York Times* published his poem about the event – 'Mugging' earned Allen $250.

On Christmas Eve, Allen had dinner with William S. Burroughs. After living abroad for nearly 25 years, Burroughs, now 60, had returned to New York in January and was living at 452 Broadway. Allen secured him a writer-in-residence position at CCNY and introduced him to James Grauerholz, who became Burroughs's friend, manager and literary executor.

Because of bronchitis, Allen spent the first weeks of 1975 in hospital in Amherst, Massachusetts, but continued to work on Naropa matters and the Leary case. Back in New York, he met Shelley Kraut and her husband Bob Rosenthal, who lived at 437 East 12th Street. Allen loved the building and rented two adjoining apartments there. He and Peter moved in in March, Shelley agreeing to help with Allen's towering paperwork.

In mid-March Allen read with Burroughs in Chicago – the first time they had appeared on stage together. In April, he found himself in hospital again, his Bell's palsy aggravated by a nervous reaction to antibiotics. On 20 May, with the final battle of the Vietnam War – the Mayaguez Incident – fresh in his mind, Allen wrote 'Hospital Window':

> . . . right eyebrow cheek
> mouth paralyzed—from taking the wrong medicine, sweated
> too much in the forehead helpless, covered my rage from
> gorge to prostate with grinding jaw and tightened anus
> not released the weeping screams of horror at robot
>   Mayaguez . . .[47]

The 'right eyebrow cheek mouth' paralysis, later diagnosed as Raymond's syndrome, afflicted Allen for the rest of his life. Ginsberg correlated his physical debilitation and collapse to the humbling of America; a quashing of the Western ego by the spiritual continuum of the East, New York – a synecdoche of America – made unstable by the shock of defeat, its buildings as intimate and vulnerable as the human body.

Allen taught 'The History of Poetry up until William Carlos Williams and Kerouac' at Naropa during the summer. The school created a strong poetic community of students and teachers. Ginsberg and Waldman invited poets Ted Berrigan, Dick Gallup and Jack Collom to complement Corso and Burroughs. After the summer session ended, and needing to relax, Allen visited the Rocky Mountain Dharma Center and then the Zen Center in San Francisco to study meditation and Buddhist texts.

On 30 October, Bob Dylan played the first show of the Rolling Thunder Revue in Plymouth, Massachusetts, and asked Allen to join the 25-date concert tour. While in Lowell, he and Dylan filmed a tribute to Jack Kerouac along the Merrimac River and at Kerouac's grave reading poems from *Mexico City Blues*. On 8 December, at Madison Square Garden, Allen read at a benefit for Rubin Carter, the jailed boxer and hero of Dylan's 'Hurricane'.

As his 50th birthday approached, Allen was a member of the National Institute of Arts and Letters, a Director of the Jack Kerouac School, and slowly moving from radical to respectable. On 12 January 1976, he admitted he could no longer consider himself Rimbaud, and he wrote in 'Reading French Poetry':

Poems rise in my brain
like Woolworth's 5 & 10¢ Store perfume
O my love with thin breasts
17 year old boy with smooth ass

O my father with white hands

specks on your feet & foul breath bespeak tumor . . .[48]

Allen was obsessed with Jonathan Robbins, a young poet who
wrote in the style of Poe and Baudelaire, and he portrayed
Robbins as Rimbaud to his own older Verlaine. Mixing references to the Song of Songs, his own problems with ageing and
his father's cancer, Allen finished the poem with a claim that all
of the above were 'very satisfactory subjects for Poetry'. In
January the following year, Allen and Robbins would spend two
weeks together reading Blake and tracing Edgar Allan Poe's biographical footsteps in Baltimore. For D. H. Lawrence, Poe's 'The
Conqueror Worm' is the 'American equivalent of a Blake
poem',[49] and Ginsberg's poetry resides within the interstices of
Lawrence's analysis of 'the rhythm of American art-activity . . .
(1) A disintegrating and sloughing of the old consciousness', and
'(2) The forming of a new consciousness underneath'.[50]
Although frustrated that his seduction techniques failed, Allen
found studying with Robbins intellectually stimulating and
thanked him by writing the long and ruminative poem 'Contest
of the Bards', a Romantic and romantic version of the Rimbaud
and Verlaine affair, reversing the dynamics so that it is the
younger poet who seduces the old 'boner' and is rewarded with
the answer to the mystery of poetry and 'our inner forms!'[51]

Despite growing concerns over his health – various operations
on hernias and escalating hypertension – Allen maintained a busy
schedule. His life demanded it, what with three properties, summers at Naropa, and a lengthening list of people and organizations
he sponsored through the COP. So, Brussels and Paris in late
January 1976, back to Washington, DC, to read with Burroughs on 9
February, and then into the studios to finally record the *First Blues*
album, before returning to Naropa to teach classes on Charles
Reznikoff and William Blake.

The Rolling Thunder Revue resumed and Allen joined it at Hughes Stadium, Colorado on 23 May. During the intermission, he read 'On Neal's Ashes' in front of 27,000 people. Two days later, at Salt Palace in Salt Lake City, he recited 'The Holy Ghost on the Nod' to over 10,000 fans.

Between 12 January and 26 February, Allen had written 'Don't Grow Old' charting the effects of his father's liver cancer:

He'll no more see Times Square
honkytonk movie marquees, bus stations at midnight
nor the orange sun ball
rising thru treetops east toward New York's skyline
His velvet armchair facing the window will be empty . . .[52]

On the morning of 8 July, Allen received a call informing him that his father had died. On the flight back to New York, somewhere over Lake Michigan, he wrote 'Father Death Blues'. He had to sell more letters to Columbia to help his stepmother Edith with the funeral costs and stood with her, head bowed, at the funeral service on 12 July at the B'Nai Israel Cemetery, New Jersey.

Allen used meditation and yoga to ease his mourning, strengthen his body after sickness, and to calm the stress brought on by snowballing correspondence, financial burdens and the demands of the school. It also helped him deal with his complicated relationship with Peter who had moved out of Allen's apartment but only as far as the one next door. Allen seemed incapable of allowing Peter a separate life. Although they went on Buddhist retreats together, their relationship, often strained, became poisonous and violent; friends found it difficult to gauge who was more dependent on whom.

After a three-month retreat with Trungpa in Land O' Lakes, northern Wisconsin, on 13 December, Ginsberg wrote 'For Creeley's Ear', using Creeley's trademark short lines. The emptiness of the page charts the heft of existence, the experience of feeling in the present, each word chiselled out of the page's white space rather than running over it. Rhythm is/as emotion, words searching for an answer within themselves and their relationship to others, foregrounding time and space (non)existent within the poem, for once, not culled from an actual event but a linguistic confrontation with poetry:

> The whole
> weight of
> everything
> too much
>
> my heart in
> the subway
> pounding
> subtly . . .[53]

Without the teaching of Creeley's 'ear' for enjambment, Ginsberg may have written the lines:

> The whole weight of everything too much
> my heart in the subway pounding subtly . . .

or even:

> The whole weight of everything too
> much my heart in the subway pounding   subtly . . .

as an opening line to a longer poem. A minimalist and abstract poem, it may have been written while Ginsberg had with one eye over his shoulder at the emerging Language poets.

Allen set out on another series of benefit readings in late January 1977. When in New York, he visited The Bunker, Burroughs's new

Sketch for Presspop figurine, designed by Archer Prewitt, sculpted by Kei Hinotani.

windowless apartment in a converted YMCA building at 222 Bowery. Just north across Houston Street, its doorway and entrance covered in graffiti, stood the legendary CBGB – home of New York punk. Allen told Snyder that 'Old fairies appreciate it', and wrote a poem about the scene, 'Punk Rock Your My Big Crybaby', claiming, '50 years old I wanna Go! With whips & chains & leather!'[54]

Spring and summer found Allen in Boulder working on school administration and curriculum. Students flocked to Allen's 'The

Literary History of the Beat Generation' focusing on the 1940s, and Allen fell in love with one of them, seventeen-year-old Bobby Meyers, who became another of Allen's 'straight hearts' delight[s]'.[55]

During the first few weeks of autumn, he returned to East 12th Street determined to find a publisher for his *Collected Poems* and to go through a mountain of paperwork. Ted Berrigan suggested that Bob Rosenthal – a fellow poet from Chicago whom Allen already knew – could help. Allen hired him and soon the position became permanent and full-time. Bob was indispensable and remained that way for the next twenty years.

Allen then embarked on a more extensive reading tour taking in Tulsa, Minneapolis, San Francisco, and attended an LSD conference in Santa Cruz. There he talked to the rather confused Timothy Leary – released from prison on 21 April 1976 – and finally met Dr Albert Hoffman. Allen moved on to Hawaii where he gave a reading and a lecture on *Vajrayana* meditation, comparing and contrasting the Tantric practice to the psychedelic effects of LSD. While there, he wrote 'What's Dead?' questioning the transience of life, fame, looks and the permanent mental shadows caused by his visions. Before he returned to New York, he worked with Dylan on *Renaldo and Clara*, the four-hour film of the Rolling Thunder Revue.

With Allen's assistance, Corso secured a grant from the California Arts Council and the Creative Arts Book Company published *As Ever: The Collected Correspondence of Allen Ginsberg and Neal Cassady* (1977). 'Grim Skeleton', another state-of-the-nation address, written on 16 December, concerns his paranoia, obsessions, his mugging three years earlier, the vicissitudes of fame, and what he hopes to write and experience:

> Is this Immortal history to tell tales of 20th Century to
> striplings

naked centuries hence? To get laid by some brutal queen who'll
beat my hairy buttocks punishment in a College Dorm? To
show my ass
to god? To grovel in magic tinsel & glitter on stinking powdered
pillows?
Agh! Who'll I read this to like a fool? Who'll applaud these lies[56]

5

'Many Prophets Have Failed', 1978–87

Many prophets have failed, their voices silent[1]

June 1978: a camera pans along a wire fence, past signs reading 'Warning', 'Prohibited', 'Danger'. Harsh light careens off the white water tower as members of the Rocky Flats Truth Force and the Satyagraha Affinity Group walk towards a makeshift teepee straddling train tracks servicing the Rocky Flats Nuclear Plant in Colorado. The plant produces plutonium triggers for w88 thermonuclear warheads, has a poor safety record, and contaminated topsoil. Drums and chants follow police officers as they approach Peter Orlovsky, who sits in the lotus position. He wears jeans, a white shirt, silver tie, his greying hair in a ponytail. Anne Waldman sits beside him, a hat screening her head from the sun, her right shoulder shawl-draped. Cut to a young boy holding a sign reading, 'We are Children. Save our Earth. No Nukes.' Allen, full beard grey at the edges, trademark glasses, wearing a pale yellow shirt:

> I turn the Wheel of Mind on your three hundred tons! Your
>   awful appellation enters mankind's ear! I embody your
>   ultimate powers![2]

Two motorcycle cops – white helmets, visors, guns on their hips – lead away Peter and Anne. More police arrest Allen and twelve other protestors. Found guilty of trespassing, the demonstrators win their appeal and the court throws out the charges. Earlier in May, Allen participated in an antinuclear movement march on the UN building in New York. Using this experience and the Rocky Flats protest, he wrote 'Nagasaki Days' and 'Plutonian Ode'.

City Lights published *Mind Breaths: Poems, 1972–77*, the sixth Pocket Poets edition of Ginsberg's poetry, on 1 January 1978. Allen remained loyal to Ferlinghetti despite pressure from larger publishers to sign with them. His notoriety as a counterculture icon meant media exposure and his poetry reached a large audience. The American literary establishment recognized this influence and the mutual absorption began. Charles Bernstein writes:

> if Ginsberg had astounding success at attracting media attention, this was not because he took stands in an effort to gain public exposure; his success in this realm is largely dependent on the authenticity of his way of life as much as his positions, a mode of authenticity that he takes, above all, from Whitman.[3]

On 22 February, wearing a tuxedo, Allen accepted a gold medal for distinction in literature from the National Arts Club. Later in October, the *New York Quarterly* held a dinner in his honour, and Brooklyn College invited him to substitute for John Ashbery as professor in the English department commencing March 1979.

Back in 1971, Allen had had lunch with C. L. Sulzberger, a journalist and member of the family who owned the *New York Times*. Allen tried to persuade him that he had proof of CIA involvement in drug running, but his claims were dismissed as paranoia. When reports surfaced in early 1978 confirming Allen's research, he was pleased to receive an apology from Sulzberger.

Allen spent until mid-March in Boulder, meditating and planning improvements to Bedrock Mortar – a new toilet seat seemed to be the main priority. After the Naropa summer session, he stayed at the cabin before embarking on a reading tour to pay off the building debts.

For three days from 30 November, the Entermedia Theater held the Nova Convention. Frank Zappa (standing in for Keith Richards), Patti Smith, Brion Gysin, Ed Sanders, John Cage, Laurie Anderson, Anne Waldman, Philip Glass and Terry Southern all took part in a tribute to William Burroughs, who opened and closed the proceedings. On the first night, Allen walked a block along 12th Street to 2nd Avenue to perform 'Punk Rock Your My Big Cry Baby' and – with Peter playing banjo and yodelling – 'Old Pond', 'Feeding Them Raspberries to Grow' and William Blake's 'The Nurses's Song'.

As the previous year ended with the publication of *As Ever: The Collected Correspondence of Allen Ginsberg & Neal Cassady*, so in December, at a party at the Gotham Book Mart, Allen, Peter, and friends celebrated City Lights' publication of Orlovsky's *Clean Asshole Poems and Smiling Vegetable Songs*.

Fifty poets, including Allen, performed at a Poetry Project benefit on New Year's Day 1979. Allen had transformed himself from Beatnik-hippie into Professor Ginsberg, wearing pink shirts, ties and tweed jackets. In Boulder, he moved into more permanent rented accommodation with Peter and Lafcadio but was happy to escape in mid-March to begin his three-month professorship in creative writing at Brooklyn College, a task he found difficult and exhausting, despite teaching for only two days a week:

> Hello Professor Ginsberg have some coffee,
> have some students, have some office hours
> Tuesdays & Thursdays, have a couple subway tokens
> in advance, have a box in the English department . . .[4]

He continued to give readings in New York, appearing with Ray Bremser, Huncke and Solomon at the Village Gate in April.

Allen arranged for Peter to read that night and it became apparent that his friends were more and more dependent on his generosity – Peter and his brothers required constant attention, while Corso and Huncke made demands on Allen's finances. If no money was forthcoming, Gregory stole Allen's books and sold them.

With Peter and Steven Taylor, Allen travelled to Europe for a reading tour in May, taking in Milan, Genoa, Spoleto and Rome before moving on to Paris and then London in June. Using Barry Miles's house in central London as a base, they visited Cambridge, Manchester, the Lake District, and read with Basil Bunting in Hexham, Northumberland. Before flying back to Boulder on 20 June, they made a quick trip to Rotterdam to see Pieter Bruegel the Elder's *Tower of Babel*.

After a brief return to Boulder to work on the Japanese translation of 'Plutonian Ode' with Nanao Sakaki, Allen flew to Rome to take part with Burroughs, Corso, Waldman, di Prima, Berrigan, Ferlinghetti, John Giorno and others in the First World Festival of Poetry in Ostia (the beach resort where Pier Paolo Pasolini had been murdered in November 1975). During Yevtushenko's reading, anarchists took the stage by force. Peter wrestled back the microphone and asked Allen to calm the audience with his 'AH' chant. He did so, quieting the troublemakers in the 20,000-strong audience.

After staying at Bedrock Mortar in September, Allen made a trip to Las Vegas where, rather than gambling to alleviate his money problems, he discovered that he and Peter had each been awarded $10,000 by the National Endowment for the Arts. Peter – much to everyone's amazement – gave his money to Trungpa's foundation, while Allen, back in New York by the end of September, used his to replenish COP funds. Flush with money, Allen thought others should receive similar funding and wrote to President Jimmy Carter on 26 October hinting (not very subtly) that he should award Allen a seat on the National Council on the Arts.

Allen, Peter and Steven Taylor travelled back to Europe. Again, while in London, they stayed at Barry Miles's apartment in the shadow of the Post Office Tower, which, in Patrick Keiller's film *London* (1992), the narrator claims stands as a monument to Rimbaud and Verlaine who lived nearby at 25 Langham Street. Allen fulfilled an ambition by visiting the village of Felpham. William Blake had lived there between 1800 and 1803, describing it as a place where 'Heaven opens here on all sides her golden Gates; her windows are not obstructed by vapours',[5] connecting Blake, in Allen's mind, directly with the 1960s, San Francisco and LSD.

As part of the One World Poetry Festival, Allen and Steven flew to the Netherlands and – after a fracas involving Gregory, a plate-glass window, a passport-control security guard and a brawl on the tour bus – moved on to Belgium and then Italy to join up with The Living Theatre. After visiting the Papal Basilica of Santa Maria Maggiore to see the art works, Allen, Peter, Steven and Gregory travelled to Germany to read at venues in Siegen, Heidelberg, Tübingen and Hamburg. While in Germany, Allen wrote a series of love poems – 'Some Love', 'Maybe Love' and 'Love Forgiven' – in which he confronts his attraction to straight men, his encroaching old age, loneliness and the stark knowledge that it is his fame that seduces young men:

> Now I come by myself
> In my hand a pot-bellied elf . . .[6]

Paul Roth, Hal Chase, Neal Cassady, Peter Orlovsky, Jonathan Robbins and Bobby Meyers – Allen's infatuation with (mostly) straight men continued throughout his life and, at 53, he worried that he was incapable of a permanent and stable sexual partnership. In Heidelberg, centre of German Romanticism, on 15 December, after a walk along the *Philosophenweg* – 'ambled and

presumably pissed on by Hegel, Hölderlin, and other worthies'[7] –
Allen wrote the following very *Sturm und Drang* poem:

> I haven't found an end
> I can fuck & defend
> & no more can depend
> on youth time to amend
> what old ages portend—
> Love's death, & body's end.[8]

Allen began the 1980s as he had spent most of the 1970s – on tour
and teaching. In Boston in February, he visited the photographer
Elsa Dorfman whose photojournal *Housebook* documents friends
and family who visited her home at 19 Flagg Street, Cambridge,
Massachusetts. Elsa Dorfman had photographed Ginsberg,
Creeley, Olson, Corso, Dylan and Orlovsky, and Allen copied her
method of writing details of people, date, place and circumstance
on the bottom white panel of her photographs. Elsa Dorfman
thinks *she* may have taken the idea from Diane Arbus or that
Raymond Foye may have suggested the idea to Allen.[9]

This constant travelling exacerbated Allen's hypertension. An
incident that had nothing to do with Allen – he had been in New
York preparing for the Rolling Thunder Review – heightened his
stress. In October 1975, at a ski lodge near Aspen, Chögyam Trungpa
had hosted a Halloween ball. At the party, the poet W. S. Merwin
and his wife Dana Naone danced, had a few drinks, and left early.
Trungpa, drunk with alcohol and power, summoned them back.
Merwin and Dana hid in their room while Trungpa's acolytes
smashed down the door. Merwin retaliated but Trungpa's security
dragged him and Dana from their room. Racially abused by
Trungpa, Dana asked someone to call the police but no one dared.
The guru's guards then forcibly stripped her and Merwin. The

Naropa authorities attempted to quash the scandal and Trungpa denied any wrongdoing, claiming it was part of his teaching methods. Ed Sanders, Tom Clark and Ed Dorn saw it differently, believing Trungpa's control and ego were signs of a messianic complex. Allen could have remained quiet but that was not his way. As Ed Sanders noted, Ginsberg 'was caught in the moil of its repercussions'.[10]

The incident – known as The Great Naropa Poetry Wars – pitched Allen, Anne Waldman and Trungpa against Ed Sanders, Tom Clark and Ed Dorn. In 1977, in his course 'Investigative Poetics', Ed Sanders's students had voted to investigate the scandal and Sanders went on to write a book about the subject, *The Party: A Chronological Perspective on a Confrontation at a Buddhist Seminary*. In February 1979, *Harper's* published Peter Marin's account of the scandal, 'Spiritual Obedience'. In an interview with Clark and Dorn, Allen unwisely commented on an event he had not witnessed, excusing Trungpa's behaviour: 'In the middle of that scene, [for Dana] to yell "call the police" – do you realize how vulgar that was? The wisdom of the East being unveiled, and she's going "call the police!" I mean, shit! Fuck that shit! Strip 'em naked, break down the door!' Allen asked Trungpa if the whole thing had been a mistake; Trungpa replied, 'Nope!'[11] Rather than the new Bauhaus or Black Mountain College, Naropa began to resemble Jim Jones's Peoples Temple whose members had committed mass suicide/murder on 18 November 1978. Allen wrote to Snyder on 27 December 1978 that Jonestown 'sent shudder through all populations unconsciously hooked on authority including my own *vajrayana* – "I got the fear!" as Burroughs character screamed 20 years ago.'[12] This 'fear' prompted a long letter to Merwin and Dana Naone on 10 March 1979, in which Allen apologized for his vanity, irritable and nasty arrogance, meanness, ineptness, and begged Merwin to return and teach at the school. Despite spending time with Trungpa at a retreat in the Canadian Rockies, Allen never reconciled the warring parties, nor did he arrive at an adequate answer for Trungpa's actions. Between 7 and 9 May 1980, he wrote:

> Trapped in the Guru's Chateau surrounded by 300 disciples
> I could go home to Cherry Valley, Manhattan, Nevada City
> to be a farmer forever, die in Lower East Side slums, die with no
>   lightbulbs in the forest . . .[13]

He escaped the scandal to teach at Evergreen State College in Washington State, taking a break for a plane trip on 3 June over the recently erupted Mount St Helens. After reading in New York and San Francisco, he returned to Naropa on 20 June to teach Shakespeare's *Tempest*, Aristotle's literary theory and Pound's poetics. After the course, Allen and Peter read at a festival in Bisbee, Arizona, and visited a hummingbird sanctuary. They then stayed with the cowboy poet Drum Hadley and took a road trip following the course of the Rio Grande to Taos where they read with Harold Littlebird, Nanao Sakaki and Hopi poet Michael Kabotie.

On 6 September, Gay Sunshine Press published Ginsberg and Orlovsky's *Straight Hearts' Delight: Love Poems and Selected Letters*, a celebration of 25 years together as lovers. Allen maintained the pretence that they were a couple; in reality, the relationship was fake, poisonous and detrimental to the mental health (and happiness) of both men. But that did not deter them leaving for Yugoslavia on 11 October, accompanied by Steven Taylor.

In Dubrovnik, at the Hotel Subrovka, unable to sleep, Allen sat in the lobby and wrote 'Birdbrain!' The poem attacks war, injustice, nuclear weapons, Ronald Reagan, and references Ginsberg's fame and state of mind, 'Birdbrain's afraid he's going to blow up the planet so he wrote this poem to be immortal.'[14] That evening, after a Beethoven recital, Allen composed 'Eroica', a quasi-Nietzschean call for humankind to find liberation and reconciliation in music. After travelling to Belgrade, Budapest and Vienna, the group took a trip into the Alps (190 years after Wordsworth) where Allen had a glimpse of the Sublime, thinking the 'panoramic vastness . . . amazing'.[15]

On 9 December, in Frankfurt, Allen heard the news that Mark David Chapman had shot and killed John Lennon outside the Dakota Building in New York City. A few days later, he recorded his thoughts in 'Capitol Air', written during the flight from Frankfurt to New York:

> Jesus Christ was spotless but was Crucified by the Mob
> Law & Order Herod's hired soldiers did the job
> Flowerpower's fine but innocence has got no Protection
> The man who shot John Lennon had a Hero-worshipper's
>   connection . . .[16]

In January 1981, Allen was suffering from flu, writing in his journal, worrying about his finances and where he might be living – his apartment building had been put up for sale and his landlord had disconnected the utilities. Allen's health troubled him throughout the year; he complained of overwork but refused to eat healthily and stop smoking.

On 2 March, a motorist discovered William S. Burroughs Jr passed out drunk in a ditch by the side of a Florida highway. Allen acted as a surrogate father to Billy – Burroughs Sr and Burroughs Jr had been estranged for a number of years – and Allen had helped him tackle his alcoholism and drug addiction. Billy, aged 33, died the next day of complications due to cirrhosis of the liver. Allen scattered the cremated remains near the Rocky Mountain Dharma Center.

During Naropa's spring term, Allen taught 'Literary History of the Beat Generation 1950–53'. While there, he wrote 'Industrial Waves' – reprising the rhythm and political themes of 'Capitol Air' – in support of the left-wing governments of Central America:

Freedom to fink out Nicaraguan liberty
Freedom to shove them into Soviet economy!
Freedom for Costa Rica to eat out military scenes
Freedom in Honduras for Contras & Marines![17]

The English punk group The Clash had similar political concerns. Released in December 1980, their triple album *Sandinista!* includes 'The Call Up' and 'Washington Bullets' with lyrics about the military draft, Nicaragua, the Bay of Pigs, China's rule over Tibet, and the Soviet Union's invasion of Afghanistan. Joe Strummer asked Allen to the band's seventeen-night residency at Bond's International Casino during May and June. One night, Allen appeared on stage to sing 'Capitol Air' with the band backing him. Later, in 1982, Allen sang on 'Ghetto Defendant', a track he co-wrote with Joe Strummer for the *Combat Rock* album.

In love once more, Allen wrote a poem to Brian Jackson, his new teaching assistant:

Tho' it hurt not much
a punishment such
as I asked to feel
back arched for the real
solid prick of control
a youth 19 years old
gave with deep grace . . .[18]

From as far back as 1955, Allen had known that his poems could be overly self-referential and egotistical. In 'Transcription of Organ Music', written on 8 September (the day he first met Gary Snyder), he had written, 'I am so lonely in my glory', and that he wanted 'people to bow as they see me and say he is gifted in poetry'.[19] Eileen Myles comments on this poem that the poet's body becomes a cyborg, continuous with the technology of the wired unwired room. There's a sci-fi spirituality to the construction of the poem – the outlets, the economic underpinnings of the capacity to use them and the psychosexual history of the poet and even his obscuring of the gender of who he 'gave' his cherry to – is remarkable and unforgettable.[20]

Allen had become that cyborg-double – Ginsborg – that simulacra materialized out of his own mediatized autobiography; driven by his constant search for a sexual partner, he had wired into the spiritual unconscious while seeking human touch.

While on a trip to the Rockies, Allen took mescaline for the first time in nearly a quarter of a century, and confronted himself with the reality of 'Allen Ginsberg': lazy, repetitive, pretentious and a fake, his life a 'Majestical jailhouse'.[21] Allen, always honest with those around him, struggled to see his true self under the instantly recognisable and regrown bardic beard.

After co-hosting the Dalai Lama's visit on 9 August, Allen travelled to Mexico City for an International Poetry Festival with Voznesensky, Jorge Luis Borges, Günter Grass, Octavio Paz and W. S. Merwin. On 14 November, he returned to Columbia University's McMillin Theater for a 25th anniversary reading of 'Howl'. Anne Waldman introduced him as a poet of 'postwar materialist paranoid doldrums'.[22] In addition to reading 'Howl', Allen sang Blake songs and read from his most recent poetry, including 'Ode to Failure':

O Failure I chant your terrifying name, accept me your 54 year
    old Prophet
epicking Eternal Flop! I join your Pantheon of mortal bards, &
    hasten this ode with high blood pressure . . .[23]

Ginsberg with the Russian poet Andrei Voznesensky in Mexico City, 1981.

The awareness of failure and fraud is apparent, yet vanity and fame overshadow the honest appraisal. The stare once fixed so doggedly inward slowly replaced by the outward appearance, the 1962 turning away from language almost complete. Allen had become an image of Allen. Barrett Watten argues 'for Ginsberg, the inadequacy of language to record states of consciousness suggests a focus on the *outside* of reference as a ground for poetry'. But even Allen's imagistic autobiography, his eye and ear for experience, lapses into a poetic autoeroticism. Watten again:

> A poetics of language is subsumed by the real-time presence of the poet, even as Ginsberg staged a powerful critique of the

mass media through his excessive and opaque incantations, as in his exorcism of the Pentagon.[24]

Despite reports of him leading Buddhist chants outside the Pentagon, at the time he had been in Italy socializing with Ezra Pound. Although he donated the poem 'Pentagon Exorcism' to be read aloud during the event (composed Milan, 29 September 1967), Ed Sanders performed the exorcism ritual and it was Abbie Hoffman's idea to levitate the building. Fifteen years on, and Allen's 'real-time presence' was as celebrity subsumed into – rather than critic of – mass media.

City Lights Books issued *Plutonian Ode and Other Poems: 1977–1980* on 1 January 1982. The collection won the *Los Angeles Times* Book Award, and was Allen's seventh and last publication in the Pocket Poets series. On 21 January, Allen and Peter flew to Nicaragua for a poetry festival. Yevtushenko, Ernesto Cardenal and Ginsberg wrote a manifesto, the 'Declaration of Three', condemning American support of the Contras. On 25 January, in the Intercontinental Bar, Managua, Allen composed 'The Little Fish Devours the Big Fish', a reggae-rhythmed satirical take on similar themes. In early February, he stopped off in Los Angeles to record 'Do the Meditation Rock' and 'Airplane Blues' with Steven Taylor and Bob Dylan, ruminating that while he drank 'Perrier at parties in Bel Air' governments manufactured 'Neutron Bomb Nerve Bacteria gas'.[25]

While at Naropa for the spring term, Allen organized the 25th Anniversary National Celebration of *On the Road*, inviting Burroughs, Corso, Orlovsky, Creeley, Huncke, Kesey, Leary, McClure, Waldman, Jan Kerouac and a host of other writers, artists and musicians. Allen enjoyed the ten-day event despite the crippling cost. During the conference, film producer Jerry Aronson asked Allen's permission to make a documentary of his life; with some reservations, Allen agreed.

In late August, Allen, Peter and Gregory toured northern Mexico. On a bus between Guasave and Los Mochis, Allen composed 'Going to the World of the Dead', a plea to the planet to eschew organized religion, to 'let go' claims on other countries and to share power. He suffered a kidney stone attack, his back hurt and, after the food he ate in Mexico, his blood pressure rocketed. He had to change his lifestyle, cut down on travelling, let others help him. Trungpa agreed to Allen's retirement from Naropa and they set a date for late 1983. Relieved, Allen packed his clothes and manuscripts to ship back to the East 12th Street apartment.

Hoping Charles Rothschild would nominate him for a MacArthur Foundation award, Allen stated in a letter written 13–14 November, 'I'm considered by some people in u.s. and Europe to be the greatest poet in the world; by others to be the most famous or celebrated.'[26] He then listed his successes, debts, health problems, and projects he wanted to finish before he died. Five days earlier, he had written 'Thoughts Sitting Breathing ii' in which he notes his reading material – *Rocky Mountain News*, *Newsweek*, a biography of Katherine Mansfield, John Addington Symonds' *The Greek Poets* – complains about high blood pressure and athlete's foot, worries about the cia, norad and nuclear submarines, and asks 'What way out of this Ego?'[27]

In Paris on 10 December, Allen took part in a unesco poetry festival organized by Jean-Jacques Lebel, in which a

score of poets from every corner of the globe will speak out through their poems against the never-resting forces of oppression and destruction, a platform from which the mingled voices of peace, poetry and liberty can declare War On War.[28]

He then took the train to Arthur Rimbaud's birthplace Charleville, where he participated in a conference on the poet, and visited Rimbaud's grave.

Allen, Steven Taylor and Simon Vinkenoog spent the first few days of 1983 recording 'September on Jessore Road', then travelled down the Dutch coast to Vlissingen (Flushing – from where, in 1592, the Dutch deported Christopher Marlowe for spying). Allen walked along the shore noting the detritus on the beach and wrote 'What the Sea Throws Up at Vlissingen'. On their return to the Vinkenoogs' house in Amsterdam, they found Peter in the throes of a manic phase, stripped to his underwear, obsessively cleaning the house and chanting under his breath. During a performance a few days later, Peter began to punch his own head. Back at the Vinkenoogs' house, he strummed his banjo all night and went out into the cold Amsterdam streets wearing only his shorts (eleven years earlier, Allen had written to Snyder, 'Peter . . . goes around hours outside impervious to cold in tee-shirt'[29]). Despite Allen's assurances that Peter sometimes acted this way, Vinkenoog called a doctor. Later, in the Milky Way concert hall, while the Mondrian String Quartet set up, Orlovsky destroyed his beloved banjo. Again, Vinkenoog called a doctor. A violent argument erupted, Peter shouting at Allen to leave him alone. The Amsterdam episodes were not new manifestations of Peter's troubled mind; for years, he had exhibited manic-depressive traits but Allen refused to recognize the signs and saw Peter's behaviour as part of the 'crazy wisdom' of Tibetan Buddhism rather than obvious indications of mental illness.

Allen, Peter and Steven travelled to Scandinavia and performed in Copenhagen, Stockholm and Helsinki, where they stayed with Kerouac's biographer Ann Charters. Allen discovered he was suffering from Peyronie's disease or *Induratio penis plastica*, fibrous growths in the soft tissue due to some injury or trauma to the penis. Despite his many male lovers, and the fact that he hadn't had sex with her in 30 years, Allen blamed Alene Lee.

In 'I'm a Prisoner of Allen Ginsberg', written in the Karmê Chöling Shambhala meditation retreat in Vermont on 4 April, Ginsberg invents an imaginary evil doppelgänger who treats him like a slave, forces him to answer correspondence, write poetry, look at bank statements, and who is:

> bald & panicky, with Pyronie's disease
> Cartilage stuff grown an inch inside
> > his cock root,
> non-malignant.[30]

Illness became a new theme in Ginsberg's poetry, the catalogue of ailments replacing the list of teenage boys he had slept with, the libido caught in a wrestling match with death, the ego jolted into reality by his body's meltdown. He wrote to Snyder that he wanted to 'retire a bit from the world',[31] and in 'Sunday Prayer', written on 25 September, his ears, back, hair, gums, kidney stones, blood pressure, cheek, eyes and cock signify senescence and death. Allen returned to Naropa in May. At 57, he had to take naps to maintain his energy.

Seriously in debt, Allen needed to consolidate his manuscripts and find a publisher for the *Collected Poems*. In the late 1970s and early '80s, Andrew Wylie and Victor Bockris had worked as a writing team, interviewing Burroughs, Dalí, Jagger and Warhol for many magazines including *Interview*. Bockris went on to write biographies of Lou Reed, Keith Richards and Patti Smith, while Wylie became a voracious literary agent, brokering a $100,000 advance for Miles's Ginsberg biography. Within a month of becoming Allen's agent, Wylie signed a deal with Harper and Row for the *Collected Poems*, two new books of poetry, an annotated version of *Howl* and two volumes of journals. The contract meant Allen received an advance regardless of sales, and had control over content and artwork. It also meant that he could minimize his debts and fund future projects.

On 5 October, Allen's mother appeared to him in a dream. He woke at 6.35 a.m. and made notes. In the poem constructed from the notes, Naomi inhabits a city of the dead and Ginsberg arrives looking for a place to live. He now has money enough to care for her. Naomi complains about her ill health; Allen wants redemption for agreeing to her lobotomy. He also feels guilty about Peter, Orlovsky's psychosis reminding Allen of Naomi, and he believes he cares for Peter in an overbearing manner to compensate for his mother's neglect. Ginsberg claimed 'White Shroud' was 'a sort of epilogue 25 years later to a long poem I once wrote, *Kaddish*'.[32] It is a thoughtful recollection of Naomi and an acknowledgement of Allen's inability to form permanent loving relationships.

New Year's Day 1984: Allen sits on a bench wearing a dark suit, burnt orange shirt and silver tie, harmonium on his lap. Behind him, Steven Taylor on guitar, Arthur Russell on cello, and Peter meditating. Allen performs a quick *namaste* and Steven counts '1, 2 . . . 1, 2, 3, 4', as the quartet perform 'Do the Meditation Rock' for Nam June Paik's video installation *Good Morning, Mr Orwell*, broadcast live by satellite throughout the world. George Plimpton, Peter Gabriel, Laurie Anderson, John Cage, Joseph Beuys and Philip Glass also participated. Although beset with technical difficulties, the show reached 25 million people.

At the end of January, Allen wrote 'Empire Air' while flying to a reading gig at the Rochester Institute of Technology:

> Rising above the used car lots & colored dumps of Long Island
> stubby white smokestreams drift North above th' Egyptic
>   Factory roof'd monolith
> into gray clouds, Conquer the world![33]

In this poem, Ginsberg questions his political ideals, his involvement in the peace process, and his, until now, unshakable belief that poetry can change the world. As Alain Badiou points out,

Thought only subtracts itself from the spirit of the age by means of a constant and delicate labour. It is easy to want to change the world – in youth this seems the least that one could do. It is more difficult to notice the fact that this very wish could end up as the material for the forms of perpetuation of this very world.[34]

Ginsberg's rebelliousness, his outsider status, was already assumed into the perpetuation of the American dream. In 1984, the Beats were about as dangerous and subversive as America's *Billboard* Hot 100, which boasted such radical acts as Paul McCartney and Michael Jackson, Yes, Kenny Loggins, Phil Collins, Lionel Richie and Wham! No wonder Allen doubted everything in his life – his relationships, his poetics and his Buddhism. Was he socialist or bourgeois? Buddhist or Jew? Poet or poetaster? The one thing he did know: he was afraid of dying alone.

In May, Allen and Steven flew to the Netherlands (Taylor insisted Peter stay in New York) before moving on to Brussels for the One World Poetry Festival. After a brief stop in Liverpool and a reading at the Albert Hall with Bunting, Pickard and Corso, Allen flew to Florida to teach at the Florida Atlantic Center for Arts with Robert Frank and Elvin Jones. The previous autumn, he had visited the photographer Berenice Abbott to discuss his photography, and had taken her advice to use 'universal panorama and maximum fine detail'.[35] Allen turned to Frank, Dorfman and Abbott whenever he needed technical tips and, once back in New York, he asked Raymond Foye to catalogue his photographs and create contact sheets from the negatives. Allen documented the people in the photographs and wrote short biographies for each. Brian Graham (a printer for Frank) printed a selection on 11 x 14 photographic paper, and Allen captioned and dated them. The following year, Foye would arrange the hugely popular and financially successful shows 'Hideous Human Angels' at the Holly

Solomon Gallery, NYC, and 'Memory Gardens' at the Middendorf Gallery, Washington.

1984: Bob Creeley sits at a desk, elbows on table, fingers entwined, a pen in the breast pocket of his white shirt, his head turned, angled and slightly lowered toward the camera, hair slicked back, beard grey and Elizabethan – troubadourish. Through tinted spectacles he stares at the camera, right eye keen and inquisitive, left dark and infinite as a full stop. A year later, Harry Smith, wearing what looks like a hand-me-down pair of Allen's glasses, oversized shirt, pours milk from a carton into a jam jar. He resembles the bastard offspring of Yoda and Brains from *Thunderbirds*. Thirty-two years earlier, William Burroughs stands beside a sphinx in the Egyptian wing of New York's Metropolitan Museum of Art, a tweed-jacketed spirit, a ghostly apparition of one of Howard Carter's ensorcelled archaeologists. Allen's portraits of Creeley, Smith and Burroughs are reflexive portraits of Allen Ginsberg, they are his memories, his desire to fix his fixations – poets, artists, lovers, friends, families. Move inward to the subjects' eyes and they become the I of Allen Ginsberg reflected in them. Writing about Walt Whitman in regards to photography, Geoff Dyer asserts that in '*Leaves [of Grass]* every thing is literally photographed . . . Nothing is poeticized', that 'Whitman created poems that, at times, read like extended captions in a huge, constantly evolving catalogue of photos'.[36] If so, then Ginsberg's photos contain captions that autobiographicize the poetry of his captured moment – like notes in his journals. Edward Weston (whom Allen had visited back in 1956), working on an illustrated edition of *Leaves of Grass* in 1941, had travelled by car across America photographing Whitmanesque sites on a journey prefiguring the Beats' road trips.[37] Aware of the history and techniques of photography, Ginsberg applied these discourses to his self-mythology. He photographed his own chorus.

Although 'retired', Allen agreed to help run Naropa's summer programme. Among other guests, Amiri Baraka (LeRoi Jones) taught classes on the Harlem Renaissance, Negritude, indigenisme and black modernism and Burroughs lectured on writing techniques, biological warfare and weapons. Diane di Prima celebrated her 50th birthday and Allen read 'White Shroud' at the birthday performance. While Allen proofread the *Collected Poems*, Barry Miles researched the biography, Bill Morgan collated the bibliography, and Gordon Ball worked on transcribing the mid-1950s journals.

Despite ill health, and domestic and office problems, Allen accepted an invitation to travel to China on an exchange programme – Chinese poets had visited the US in 1982. He flew out on 14 October with Snyder; Francine du Plessix Gray, Harrison Salisbury, William Least Heat-Moon, Leslie Marmon Silko, Toni Morrison and Maxine Hong Kingston were also in the group. Allen explored Beijing, and visited the Forbidden City and the Great Wall. From the capital, the delegation travelled to Xian to see the terracotta army, and then to Shanghai to visit the reconstructed Buddhist temples.

The rest of the party left on 6 November, and Allen stayed to travel alone, taking a three-day journey in a steamer down the Yangtze:

> Don't have to push my boat oars around a rocky corner
> in the Yangtze gorges, or pole my way downstream,
> from Yichang through the yellow industrial scum, or carry water
> buckets on a bamboo pole over my shoulder
> to a cabbage field near Wuxi—I'm famous . . .[38]

He had little time to himself, staying in official tourist hotels and escorted everywhere by bureaucrats, but he enjoyed himself when with other poets, eating pork dumplings, or taking photos with Snyder's Olympus camera. For the next two months, Allen

Buddha and Skull, a line drawing by Ginsberg, 1980s.

taught in various universities and wrote several poems, including 'I Love Old Whitman So', 'One Morning I Took a Walk in China' and 'Visiting Father & Friends' – in which he remembers Gregory healthy and humorous, Neal 'rosy-faced' and full of energy, and his father alive again.

Back in Shanghai by 2 December, and confined to his bed with bronchitis, he read *200 Selected Poems* by the ninth-century poet Bai Juyi. Once he felt stronger, he ventured out into the Shanghai streets to explore. A week later, he moved on to Nanking to visit the 600-year-old imperial tombs. On 20 December he sent a postcard to Tom Pickard and Joanna Voit in England, complaining that Voice of America radio played John Denver and not the Dead Kennedys or The Clash; the next night, in the Kunming Hotel, after a bout of vomiting brought on by a greasy chicken sandwich, Allen had another oneiric visitation from Naomi:

Her look at last so tranquil and true made me wonder
why I'd covered her so early with black shroud.
Had I been insane myself and hasty? I left the room.[39]

In 'Black Shroud' Ginsberg agonizes over his decision to agree to Naomi's lobotomy, asking why he hadn't sought advice from family members, and admitting he 'murdered' Naomi by – metaphorically – beheading her.

Published on 31 December, just after Allen returned from China, *Collected Poems, 1947–1980* garnered mixed reviews. *Time* magazine heralded 'Kaddish' as a masterpiece while relegating 'Howl' to a 'historical oddity'.[40] Allen, happy with the results, imagined the collection sharing shelf space with Whitman, Pound and Yeats.

News of Peter's violent behaviour tempered Allen's joy. While drunk and on drugs, Peter had wielded a machete in Allen's apartment, cut off all his hair, slashed himself with scissors, tried to stab

Bob Rosenthal and threatened Bob's sons. Around the time Allen was writing about 'beheading' his mother, Peter had threatened 'to sever his own head' and locked himself in his room.[41] A special police unit arrived to negotiate with him while film crews and reporters waited outside. Peter eventually emerged after running out of alcohol and the police forcibly escorted him to Bellevue Hospital. Peter spent two weeks under observation and he, his girl-friend Juanita, and Allen agreed to psychiatric counselling. The doctors suggested to Allen that he and Peter spend a year apart. 'What fun!' as Allen put it.[42]

At the end of January 1985, Allen found Peter holding a tyre iron, semi-naked, drunk, covered in blood and talking to himself. Peter attacked him, breaking Allen's glasses. Bob Rosenthal came to Allen's aid and called the police who questioned Peter but were unable to get any sense out of him. Allen had little option but to agree to Peter's return to Bellevue. When Allen arrived home from the hospital, he discovered that Peter had trashed a number of apartments in the building. The doctors prescribed Antabuse – an anti-alcohol medication – and, on his release, Peter went on retreat and rehab at the Karmê Chöling meditation retreat. But, over the next few months, Orlovsky's behaviour worsened as he stopped taking the medication and abandoned meditation.

Madness, sex and death had always been Allen's main subject-matter. Madness returned in the form of Peter's violent episodes. Friends advised Allen to end the pretence that the relationship was salvageable. He could still find sex in the shape of willing young men if he wanted to but, of his main poetic themes, death slowly became Ginsberg's literary obsession.

Allen had known Harry Smith since 1959 when he met him at a Thelonious Monk gig at the Five Spot. Harry drank a lot, took amphetamines, had a bad temper and nowhere to live. What else could Allen do but ask him to move in for a few weeks until he found somewhere more permanent? Harry did and then, within a week, a car backed into him and shattered his knee. He stayed for eight months; Allen likened him to the unwanted guest in *The Man Who Came to Dinner*. Harry hobbled around the kitchen on crutches, sat at the table making art out of his own faeces, growled at visitors and recorded sounds coming through Allen's kitchen window.

At the end of May, Allen visited Cherry Valley farmhouse for the last time. The farm had become too much of a drain on his finances. He threw himself into a heavy schedule of readings, meetings and appearances across the country; he had journals to edit, essays to write, letters to answer, and he was getting old, fat and grey. During the summer, he taught at Naropa, gave a class with Jerome Rothenberg on sound poetry and ethnopoetics and took part in a symposium on 'The Soul' with Burroughs and Mailer. On 6 August, he wrote to Lucien Carr complaining about negative reviews of the *Collected Poems* and compared his own life to that of T. S. Eliot. Charles Bernstein's comments that,

> the twentieth century poet he (Allen) ends up most resembling is not Bill Williams of Patterson but Tommy Eliot of St Louis. Resembles, but only in the sense of a reverse or polarized image: for Eliot became the poet as symbol of the closed, the repressed, the xenophobic, the authoritative; in short, of high culture in the worst sense; while Ginsberg became the symbol of the open, the uncloseted, the anti-authoritarian; indeed, of low culture in the best sense.[43]

After a three-week retreat in the Rockies, Allen worked with Barry Miles on the *Annotated Howl*, writing notes on people, places and events mentioned in the original poem.

In November, William H. Gass, William Gaddis, Louis Auchincloss, Arthur Miller, Harrison Salisbury, Susan Sontag

Ginsberg performing at Miami Bookfair International, 1985.

and Allen took part in a series of American-Soviet writers' conferences and readings, visiting Vilnius, Minsk, Leningrad and Moscow. While there, Ginsberg and Miller openly challenged Soviet censorship and the state's incarceration of dissident writers and artists. Allen extended his stay for a fortnight and visited the writers Bella Akhmadulina, Alexander S. Kushner and Yevgeny Rein. He required a visa to visit Tbilisi to meet the dissident filmmaker and artist Sergei Parajanov. At first, the authorities denied his application but eventually granted it for a single visit. Before flying back to New York, Allen performed at Alex Kozloff's new-wave jazz concert and gave a poetry reading at Moscow State Lomonosov University with Yevgeny Yevtushenko and Andrei Sergiev as translators.

Ernesto Cardenal asked Allen to take part in his second Rubén Darío Festival in Nicaragua at the end of January 1986. Frustrated that Ortega's Sandinista National Liberation Front was just as oppressive as other governments, Allen wrote 'You Don't Know It' in his hotel room in Managua in the early hours of 25 January. The poem compares the tragedies of Central America with Stalin's atrocities, decrying revolutionaries reneging on their promises. Back in New York, Allen, Arthur Miller and Günter Grass drafted a delegates' statement for PEN International condemning American intervention in Nicaragua, Allen writing to his old enemy Norman Podhoretz, 'Further push in the direction of right-wing terror tactics can only make matters worse, as it did in Vietnam.'[44]

On 15 March, Allen turned his attention away from the state of the union, poetics and fame, and wrote a humorous poem 'Sphincter' – his state-of-the-asshole poem:

a little blood, no polyps, occasionally
    a small hemorrhoid
active, eager receptive to phallus

coke bottle, candle, carrot
banana & fingers—[45]

As D. H. Lawrence noted, 'Heaven knows what we mean by reality
. . . Some insisting on the plumbing, and some on saving the world:
these being the two great American specialties.'[46]

Allen celebrated his sixtieth birthday on 3 June with a party at
the National Ukrainian Home restaurant on St Mark's and 2nd
Avenue. Bill Morgan and Bob Rosenthal presented Allen with *Best
Minds*, a tribute they edited with contributions by Burroughs,
Genet, Cage, Gysin, Ansen, Southern and others.

The young poet Chris Ide became Ginsberg's teaching assistant
during the summer session at Naropa (which had acquired accredi-
tation from the Western College Association) and lecturers
included Burroughs, Creeley, Rosenthal, Steven Taylor, Anne
Waldman, Joanne Kyger, Clark Coolidge, Anselm Hollo and Jim
Carroll.

Allen flew to Budapest in August, where he recorded a poetry
rock LP and a Hungarian version of 'Howl' – 'Üvöltés' – with the
Hobo Blues Band. At the Struga Festival in Yugoslavia, he
received a solid gold laurel wreath in honour of his lifetime
achievement in poetry. On 25 August, Allen, Steven Taylor and
the Pro Arte string quartet performed 'September on Jessore
Road'. Allen and Taylor then embarked on a reading tour taking
in Zagreb, Belgrade, Krakow and Warsaw where Allen, heeding
Robert Frank's advice, purchased a Leica camera. On 12
September, he wrote the apocalyptic poem 'Europe, Who
Knows?' about the recent Chernobyl disaster, imagining the end
of Europe, the prelude to a nuclear holocaust enshadowing the
world for over 40 years.

Allen won the Poetry Society Gold Medal Award and Harper
and Row published the *Annotated Howl* and *White Shroud Poems,
1980–85*, the first non-City Lights collection. In September, Allen

became Distinguished Professor in the English Department, a position that brought in much-needed cash (although he was shocked that half went on taxes and insurance). His classes were on Mondays between 2 and 4.30 p.m. Over the next ten years, Allen invited friends and colleagues to participate in the lecture series that started with the 'Literary History of the Beat Generation' in the spring term of 1987. Although he received grants for the events, the cost of inviting participants meant he had to pay out of his own pocket to get the writers he wanted.

Allen's doctor diagnosed a heart condition and advised him to curtail his travelling and cut down on his workload:

> You might grimace, a sharp breath from the solar plexus, chill
>   spreading
> from shoulderblades and down the arms,
> or you may wince, tingling twixt sphincter and scrotum a subtle
>   electric discharge.[47]

Tests also found evidence of reactive hyperglycaemia, meaning Allen had to cut out most carbohydrates. Peter (in and out of Bellevue) put pressure on Allen to sell his archives and semi-retire to Trungpa's recently established Shambhala centre in Nova Scotia, but Allen found it impossible to slow down, let alone retire.

In January 1987 Steven Taylor and others decorated Allen's apartment, painting the walls white and sanding the floorboards. The apartment smelled variously of cooking, incense, books, maturing mangoes; a sweet and musty aroma, inhaled by all who sat around the kitchen table drinking tea and coffee and looking out of Allen's kitchen window.

Allen's slow fade into the system was almost complete – he won the Wallace Stevens Award, a NEA Creative Writing Fellowship Grant and a Modern Language Association of America honorary membership. He read at Yale and took part in the St Mark's Poetry Project 20th anniversary celebrations, highlighting his broad appeal to both the establishment and new bohemia.

After a heart attack earlier in the year, on 4 April, at the age of 48, Chögyam Trungpa Rinpoche died in Halifax Infirmary, Nova Scotia. Allen took the message by phone, went to meditate, and returned home to share his grief with Peter. He dreamt of his teacher on 3 May, and woke at 2.30 a.m. to write the poem 'When the Light Appears'. Allen, Peter, Beverly Isis and Peter Hale (whom Ginsberg had met in Boulder), drove to the Karmê Chöling meditation centre in Vermont for Trungpa's cremation. On 28 May, Allen composed 'On Cremation of Chögyam Trungpa, Vidyadhara':

> I noticed my own heart beating, breath passing thru my nostrils
> my feet walking, eyes seeing, noticing smoke above the corpse-
> fir'd monument . . .[48]

After the ceremony, they headed back to New York. Orlovsky drove and seemed contemplative; he and Allen even wrote a poem together – 'Nanao' – the first in many years. But the calm did not last. Allen invited Peter to teach at Naropa that summer; the anti-psychiatrist R. D. Laing was also there. Both men got drunk; when Laing mimicked him, Peter attacked and bit Laing on the mouth, then smashed furniture and threw bottles damaging rare books. Police arrived and Allen tried to intervene but broke his little finger and hurt his knee, which, in November, he would have to have surgery on. Allen wrote to Peter a few days later: 'the aggression you get into has become too violent and dangerous to play with anymore. We will have to figure how to get out of this double bond.'[49] Allen explained to Peter that this had been going on for twenty years – but it had taken Allen this long to realize it.

During the Naropa summer session, Marianne Faithfull played Allen her *Strange Weather* CD. Impressed, Allen arranged to meet the producer and, in the autumn, Hal Willner began work on an album of Ginsberg's poetry. *The Lion for Real* contains seventeen tracks, including musical variations of 'Complaint of the Skeleton to Time', 'To Aunt Rose', 'The Shrouded Stranger', 'Hum Bom' and 'Ode to Failure'.

On 8 October, Allen wrote one of his most candid and humorous poems. Inspired by the closing lines of Robert Creeley's 'The Conspiracy', 'Personals Ad' takes the form of a lonely-hearts message in which Ginsberg states his age, profession, desires and influences, in an open-wound address to a potential lover:

> Find me here in New York alone with the Alone
> going to lady psychiatrist who says Make time in your life
> for someone you can call darling, honey, who holds you dear
> can get excited & lay his head on your heart in peace.[50]

With Trungpa dead, Burroughs in Lawrence, Kansas, and still trying to break the cycle of his co-dependency with Peter, Allen felt alone, ill and unloved. Where was the lover he so desired? Where was the family he wanted?

He still had his fame. He and Burroughs, feted by the likes of Madonna, Sean Penn, Chris Stein and Debbie Harry, spent time together while Bill was in town for the opening of an exhibition of his shotgun-splatter canvases and to promote his new novel *The Western Lands*. Despite warnings, Allen maintained his hectic pace, taking part in a Francophone Kerouac Convention in Quebec, a Buddhist Psychotherapy Conference and a consortium for PEN American Center. From the period between 31 October 1987 when he proclaimed himself (tongue wedged fully in cheek) 'King of the Universe',[51] and February 1988, only one poem – 'To Jacob Rabinowitz' – appears in the *Collected Poems*, showing how little time he had to write.

6

'An Urn of Ashes', 1988–97

Not myself except in an urn of ashes[1]

29 April 1988: Allen sits on his bed wearing a rust-coloured shirt, diagonal-striped tie – dark red, taupe, chestnut – and cream chinos. His trademark black-frame glasses have been replaced by large, clear urethane spectacles showing more of his drooping right eye and his twinkling and penetrative left; his beard and moustache are variant shades of silver, the dome of his head, bordered by darker grey hair, shining in the spotlights. The recording (for the Poet Vision documentary series) shows Allen reading a selection of poems; singing 'Father Death Blues' and 'Do the Meditation Rock' accompanied by Steven Taylor on guitar and vocal harmonies; reading Kurt Schwitters's 'Priimiititiii'; talking about his poetics, his father's death and Buddhism. Allen, avuncular, assured of his place in the pantheon of world poets, shows no signs of the once suicidal, depressive New Jersey boy; he is the counterculture's laureate, distinguished professor, and – despite protestations from his staff and doctors – an incorrigible workaholic. The apartment exudes a golden light and pencil-lead shadow, while Allen – approaching his 62nd birthday – resonates energy and eminence in turn.

From 5 to 28 January 1988 Allen, Steven Taylor and Robert Frank taught a course on 'Photographic Poetics' at Tel Aviv's Camera Obscura School of Art. With his Hebrew translator Natan Zach,

Allen read at Tel Aviv and Haifa universities and at the Jerusalem Cinematheque. While sightseeing in Jerusalem, Allen stayed in the Mount Zion Hotel with views of Gehenna, a valley surrounding the Old City, an ancient site of immolation, holocausts and burnt offerings. To Allen, the once hellish home of Moloch mirrored the landscape of prophetic poetry reaching from the Old Testament and the Mishnah through to Milton, Blake, Whitman and 'Howl':

> Moloch! Solitude! Filth! Ugliness! Ashcans and unobtainable dollars! Children screaming under the stairway! Boys sobbing in armies! Old men weeping in the parks![2]

Allen cried when he visited the Wailing Wall, and relatives of those 'boys sobbing in armies' listened to him read 'Jaweh and Allah Battle' at a 60,000-strong Peace Now Rally in Tel Aviv. He spent a few secretive days in Palestinian territories and, on his return to New York, supported Palestinian freedom of speech, presenting PEN with a dossier on the censorship and imprisonment of Palestinian writers. Like Genet, Allen supported the Palestinians in their struggle, both authors decrying the seemingly implacable ideological contradictions, but, where Genet saw America and not Israel as the real enemy,[3] Allen engaged the machinery of American democracy to publicize the problems.

During February, New York's Eye and Ear Theater staged 'Kaddish' with sets by Eric Fischl and music by Steven Taylor. Allen showed Philip Glass a passage from 'Wichita Vortex Sutra' he thought suitable for a Veteran's Theater Company benefit performance. This resulted in a full collaborative opera opening at the Lincoln Center. In June, the Hamburg State Opera premiered a multimedia jazz-opera version of *Cosmopolitan Greetings* with libretto by Ginsberg, sets, design and production by Robert Wilson.

The Federal Communications Commission (FCC), under pressure from right-wing politicians, initiated aggressive schemes against broadcasters to force them to suppress what it considered 'obscene' material and threatened to revoke licences if they did not comply. The cost of taking the FCC to court over this 'censorship' proved too expensive for independent broadcasters, so they postponed all airings of risky material (such as 'Howl') between 6 a.m. and midnight. Allen compiled a dossier on FCC decisions and lobbied to get the legislation reversed. With his help, Pacifica Radio, one of the stations warned against broadcasting 'offensive' material, won its appeal against the ban.

Between yet more readings and benefits, Allen visited Kerouac's hometown of Lowell, Massachusetts, on 25 June, where he and others dedicated the Jack Kerouac Commemorative in Eastern Canal Park, eight triangular marble columns intagliated with passages from Kerouac's work.

On 6 August, two blocks south of Allen's 12th Street apartment, police evicted homeless people living under makeshift shelters in Tompkins Square Park. The authorities argued that the park was home to drug pushers and addicts but the local people viewed the eviction as an attempt by Mayor Koch to gentrify the area. Allen witnessed police attacking innocent bystanders and later testified to the Civilian Complaint Review Board that he had watched mounted police officers beating a man. That night, Allen met Eric Drooker, future illustrator of *Illuminated Poems* (1996) and animation director for the 2010 film *Howl*.

From 18 October to 4 November, Allen visited Japan to attend the Watari Gallery exhibition of his photographs. He read with outsider-feminist-erotic poet Kazuko Shiraishi at the American Literature Society of Japan in Tokyo, spent hours in Akihabara shopping for electronic equipment, went to a Noh play and a butoh party, hiked in the area surrounding Matsumoto castle, attended an Osaka Anti-Nuke Rally, and gave benefit readings with Nanao Sakaki in support of a campaign to save the Okinawan Shiraho blue coral reef.

During the year, he read at the Smithsonian Institute, with Burroughs at Marquette University, at the San Francisco Jewish Community Center, and with Snyder at UC Davis. He taught at Brooklyn College and Naropa, presented the Olson Lectures at SUNY Buffalo, gave a seminar on 'Snapshot Poetics' at the Zen Mountain Monastery in Woodstock, and took part in the National Poetry Foundation discourse on 'Romantic Poets and the Absolute'. The inability to say no, the travelling, problems with his apartment tenancy, and Peter's increasing amphetamine use, all took a toll on Allen's health. He suffered from bronchitis in Israel and high blood pressure in Japan. In the poem 'May Days 1988', he complains about the 'smoking cough or flu', his 'body teeth brain elbow ache', the 'crooked creak at backbone bottom, dry nostrils, mottled ankle', and asks, 'How many more years . . . the ulcer in my cheek is't cancer?'[4]

During 1988, Allen wrote only three poems that saw publication. In 'Salutations to Fernando Pessoa', he light-heartedly dismisses Pessoa while acknowledging the anxiety of influence caused by reading other poets. If he exculpated Pessoa for his unwitting influence, he was less forgiving of two friends, sending letters – as honest and revealing as his best poems – to Harry Smith and Gregory Corso, outlining his frustration with their behaviour. The first, sent on 8 September, detailed Smith's debt of $4,752.23, accrued over a ten-week period. Allen chastised him for spending his daily stipend on items 'other than food', explained how future payments would be made, warned that their friendship was in danger, advised him to apply for Supplemental Security Income and Medicaid, and told Harry that he could not stay at the 12th Street apartment. In the second letter, to Gregory Corso written on 13 November, Allen admitted he loved him but was not willing to put up with his alcoholic tantrums, neediness and selfishness, and suggested Gregory undergo a detox programme. The letters show Allen's compassion, his charity under duress and the frustration he felt dealing with friends who drained his finances, tested his patience and sapped his ever-diminishing physical and emotional strength.

Recuperating from gall-bladder surgery, Allen spent the first weeks of 1989 working on his poetry and journals, subtitling photographs, annotating problematic entries he found in Barry Miles's biography, and catching up with correspondence – including an acerbic letter to the journalist Al Aronowitz, whom Allen accused of being egocentric, childish, masochistic and an ass-licker. All things, of course, that Allen was assuredly not. On 27 January, Allen felt well enough to read 'Kral Majales' at The Kitchen in support of Czechoslovakian artists against censorship.

Peter's behaviour became more erratic and violent; when drunk, he hammered his fists on Allen's wall and shouted obscenities. Worried for his safety and for that of others in the apartment, Allen obtained a restraining order on Orlovsky in the courts on 27 March.

The Ginsberg office moved in May to premises rented from Alene Lee on 14th Street and 2nd Avenue. It comprised an office for Bob Rosenthal, a side office with a new Macintosh Plus, and a separate room along the corridor where Jacqueline Gens archived the photographs. Jack Shuai, whom Allen met in China, came to stay in the 12th Street apartment, solving some of Allen's sexual demands, but the drugs Allen took for hypertension made it difficult for him to get an erection.

Despite his ill health, demands on his time and the continuing problems with Peter, Allen appeared happy. He inaugurated the Albert Hoffman Memorial Library in Los Angeles, and gave benefit readings for Hanuman Books, Gay Pride rallies, the AIDS Prevention Convention, St Mark's Bookshop, PEN Club's Salman Rushdie event, and the NYC Homesteaders and Squatters. With Professor Marie Buncombe, he taught 'African American Poetic Genius' at Brooklyn College, where he was now tenured. At Naropa Boulder and Halifax

'Steven Finbow, 14th Street Office, Winter 1988 – Best wishes from Manahatta' –
Ginsberg's caption for a photograph actually taken in 1989.

he taught 'Contemplative Poetics: Mind Forms/Poetic Forms'. He performed with Amiri Baraka, the False Prophets and The Fugs; chaired the Alumni Day at Brooklyn College with Tuli Kupferberg, Carl Solomon and Jackson Mac Low; hosted the Poetry Project Spring Symposium with Marjorie Perloff and Hugh Kenner; and won the San Francisco National Poetry Association Week Award for Distinguished Service to poetry and the Manhattan Borough President Dinkens' award for Arts Excellence 1989. Exhibitions of his photographs premiered in Los Angeles, Chicago, Austria, Poland and Germany. Most importantly, he won his court appeal against the FCC broadcast ban on 'indecent' language.

Allen also attended a NAMBLA (the North American Man/Boy Love Association) convention. Knowing Allen was not attracted to underage boys, his staff questioned his open affiliation with the controversial group. He countered that members should be able to publicize and promote their ideas and desires under the banner of free speech, that an open discussion of the age of consent was democratic. Despite his staff's misgivings, they helped draft an open letter explaining his affiliation: 'Most people like myself do not make carnal love to hairless boys and girls', he wrote, arguing that 'A dash of humor, common sense humanity and historical perspective would help discussion of NAMBLA's role',[5] portraying the organization as another victim of media and FBI witch hunts.

Philip Glass introduced Allen to Tibetan Lama Ngawang Gelek Rinpoche. Allen found Gelek's 'School of the Virtuous' less dogmatic than Trungpa's 'Crazy Wisdom' and enjoyed the company of his new guru, regularly visiting Jewel Heart headquarters in Ann Arbor to give poetry workshops and perform at benefits.

No poetry from 1989 made it into *Cosmopolitan Greetings* or the *Collected Poems*. A near two-year gap exists between 'May Days 1988' (1–3 May 1988) and 'Numbers in US File Cabinet (Death Waits to Be Executed)', written March 1990. Rather than write, Allen became involved in causes; he traded poetry and protest for appearances and awards, what Nicholson Baker's narrator in *The Anthologist* calls a 'misapplication of energies' and a 'a perversion of talent'.[6] Maybe he was resting on the golden laurel he received in Struga in 1986; maybe, as Baker's narrator asks and answers, 'What does it mean to be a great poet? It means that you wrote one or two great poems.'[7] Allen certainly had – 'Howl' (1955–6), 'Kaddish' (1959), 'White Shroud' (1983) – and would continue to do so with 'Death & Fame' (1997). Maybe he had written himself out, written too much in the sixties, 'the fluently tumbled profusion' of a twentieth-century Swinburne.[8] Yet even with the knowledge that his great poems secured him a position in the canon, he looked for reassurance. In a letter to Thom Gunn on 21 September, Allen thanked his fellow poet 'for the effort it took to write a formal essay, and the empathy with which you read my scribblings'.[9]

With the 14th Street office in full operation in January 1990, Allen was able to call on his staff to find substitute teachers for Brooklyn College, research various causes, write drafts of bios for his photography books, and type up poems on the Mac. This allowed Allen to fulfil engagements such as acting as keynote speaker at the Gay and Lesbian Writers Conference in San Francisco, perform a sold-out rendition of Blake's *Songs of Innocence and Experience* with Steven Taylor at St Marks Poetry Project, lecture on 'Photography and Poetics' at Rutgers University, host a PEN Gala Dinner as Vice President of the American PEN Center, and speak at the Earth Day Rally in Philadelphia. This constant activity could have been a shield against writing poetry – the more he had to do the less time he had to write. Although he took copious notes about what he saw and thought, he spent little time transposing them into poems. Being relatively happy meant that the poems shrank back into the shade, their natural habitat; Allen, blinded by the spotlight of appearances, promotion and publicity, failed to notice their deterioration.

Allen flew to Prague at the end of April. In southern Bohemia, he performed with Půlnoc ('Midnight') – made up of members of the avant-garde rock band The Plastic People of the Universe. With Waldman, Sakaki and Clausen, he gave a reading attended by Václav Havel in Prague, and – after reciting 'Return of Kral Majales' – presented the crown to the new king at the May Day celebration:

And I am the King of May with high blood pressure, diabetes, gout, Bell'spalsy, kidneystones & calm eyeglasses . . .[10]

Allen hoped to reclaim his notebook taken by the police on his previous visit, but the authorities could only uncover a Czech translation of a section of the journal. After appearing on radio and television, and lecturing on American Poetry at the Palacký University of Olomouc and Charles University, Allen flew back to New York where he was confronted by the ever-increasing problems of the Orlovsky family – Peter was in Bellevue after stealing his sister's inheritance, and Lafcadio in Kings Park Psychiatric Center after assaulting his mother.

With Steven Taylor in London in mid-June, Allen promoted the *Lion For Real* CD, then flew to Turkey to see Philip Glass. After visiting the Hittite Museum in Ankara, they took a boat trip along the Aegean coast to visit the oracular sites of Delphi and Didyma. Inspired by their Buddhism, the two men became firm friends and their artistic collaboration resulted in *Hydrogen Jukebox* – a 'millennial survey of what's up – what's on our minds, what's the pertinent American and Planet News?'[11] Allen and Philip travelled to Spoleto, Italy, for a performance of their opera, and Allen enjoyed being called 'Maestro' by opera fans and critics.[12] After readings in Paris and London, he returned to New York to find the office in disarray. The 14th Street premises' lease had expired, so Bob, Jacqueline and others were in the process of moving everything to a bigger and brighter location on Union Square.

Allen spent the summer at Naropa as Co-Director Emeritus before flying out to Seoul, South Korea, as American delegate in the 12th World Congress of Poets. He tried to raise interest in Korea's imprisoned poets but found the conference boring, only enjoying himself when travelling with Voznesensky and the Chinese poet Bei Dao. While there, he met the Zen monk and artist Jung Kwang and sampled *hoe*, raw fish 'sliced alive and head still gasping on the plate'.[13]

In France from 5 November for ten days, Allen promoted an exhibition held at Fnac stores (a French entertainment retail chain), his photographs on exhibit alongside those of Henri Cartier-Bresson, Man Ray and Berenice Abbott.

Alene Lee, one of the few women Allen considered a friend, his 'old love black lady',[14] was in hospital ravaged by cancer. Allen visited her on 1 January 1991 and again on the 11th, the day before she died – Alene and Allen had known each other for almost 40 years. Other friends and relatives from the past 50 years found their portraits in Twelvetrees Press's *Photographs* published in March. Photos of Peter showed how much he had changed since Allen first saw him in the *Nude with Onions* painting.

Operation Desert Storm began on 17 January, and Allen participated in demonstrations against the war. Eleven days before the US called a ceasefire, he gave a weeklong lecture series at the Virginia Military Institute in Lexington. On 11 June, he took to the streets again, walking through crowds celebrating the victorious military homecoming. He stopped to write a poem and asked, 'Will another hundred thousand desert deaths across the world be cause for the next rejoicing?'[15]

Allen won the court case against his landlord, allowing him and Peter to remain in their apartments. Unfortunately, the court ruled in favour of the claim for unpaid rent, and Allen had to pay $28,000, emptying his bank account. He had already arranged to sell his share of Bedrock Mortar, earmarking the money he received to pay Peter's rent once he was released from his rehabilitation at the Bath VA Medical Center, having spent the last six months there after trashing his apartment in a crack- and alcohol-fuelled rage.

Allen talked to Ed Sanders about the money Burroughs was making from selling his paintings. Maybe to see how Bill was doing it, in June, Allen visited and assisted Bill with his artwork as Burroughs was recuperating from triple-bypass heart surgery. Another old friend, Gary Snyder, agreed to teach for the first time at Naropa. Following the summer session, and attempting a reconciliation, Allen and Peter went on retreat for a month to the Rocky Mountain Dharma Center where Allen gave a talk on 'Shambhala Poetics in the Western Tradition – Working with Spontaneous Poetry'.

Because of the financial strain, and ignoring his high blood pressure and diabetes, Allen continued to tour. He taught at the Walt Whitman Birthplace Association, took part in a symposium on 'Art and Politics' at Kenyon College, and gave a keynote lecture at the Great Falls Preservation and Development Corporation 200th Anniversary in Paterson. In December, the MLA held a symposium on 'Kaddish' and Allen performed a rare recitation of the poem. He would try to attend any symposium, conference, even lecture that discussed his work. Although lured by the attention, he loathed negative criticism of his work, proclaiming that the critics did not know what they were talking about, that they had misunderstood his motives, his sources, his theories. To Allen, the academic world was as much an arena for spin, for self-mythologizing, as were his television and radio appearances, his live performances and his championing of causes.

On 27 November, Harry Smith, coughing blood, collapsed in the Hotel Chelsea. An ambulance arrived from St Vincent's hospital but the crew could not revive him. Allen visited the morgue to pay his respects and to meditate over Harry's bruised and bloodied body.

Constant travelling left Allen exhausted. Despite eating macrobiotic food and trying to de-stress through meditation, his body could not cope with the strain. After Burroughs's surgery, and Smith's death, Allen consulted his cousin Dr Joel Gaidemak, who suggested he have a full medical check-up. Along with liver trouble, doctors diagnosed congestive heart failure. Maybe he had seen it coming – on 16 September, he had written, 'Huffing puffing upstairs downstairs telephone / office mail checks secretary revolt . . .'.[16] The poem 'Not Dead Yet' is indicative of Allen's stubborn streak, but the latest health setback worried him and he agreed with Bob Rosenthal that it was time to start saying no.

Health problems persisted on a trip to Europe in January 1992, and Allen had to change his medications to control his blood pressure and diabetes. He managed to finish the tour, taking in Amsterdam, and dates in France and Italy. But the bronchitis he contracted worsened on his trip to Los Angeles to perform *Hydrogen Jukebox*. Doctors feared pneumonia would set in and weaken his heart:

Delighted to be alive this cloudy Thursday
February window open at the kitchen table,
Senior Citizen ready for next week's angiogram.[17]

The senior citizen – with his bus and subway pass – was, according to doctors, living on borrowed time.

Still, back in New York, he read at the launch of *The Portable Beat Reader* at St Mark's Poetry project with Sanders, Orlovsky, Huncke, Joyce Johnson and the editor of the volume, Ann Charters. After, a few of the writers went on to the Kiev, one of Allen's favourite restaurants. Although Allen had promised he would cut back on appointments, he flew to Amsterdam for a series of Jewel

Heart benefit readings with Waldman, then went on a weeklong retreat with Gelek Rinpoche.

In late March, Allen visited Burroughs to take part in a ceremonial Navajo sweat lodge purification in an attempt to exorcize Burroughs's 'Ugly Spirit'. Allen interviewed Bill, asking questions about *Naked Lunch*, the cut-up technique, and Bill's thoughts on Mailer, Salinger and Hemingway. After a trip to the cinema to see Cronenberg's *Naked Lunch*, they talked about the 'Ugly Spirit' Burroughs believed responsible for killing Joan.

Reading interviews with Ginsberg and Burroughs, it is surprising how much they repeat themselves, saying nothing new from about 1970 on. Yet their perceptions from the previous decades resonate through to the 2000s – drugs, ecology, control, power, war, sexuality, death. As Burroughs scholar Oliver Harris argues,

> You could say that further interpretation is simply not possible; but the cumulative effect of such texts, enhanced by repetition of words and phrases across several of them, is still clear enough; to invite us to infer a calculated relation between language and the genetic code, twin deterministic systems subject here to systematic scrambling by the use of chance procedures.[18]

The repetition and use of chance, in his poetics as well as in his interviews and prose, politicized Ginsberg's work – he ideologized his message, he promoted the work of others with a similar philosophy; he constantly repeated himself to get the message across. His linguistic apparatuses, frozen in a 1960s mantra, monopolized the arena of criticism to an extent that writing about the 'Beats' became parasitic or recombinant.

Allen stayed with Philip Glass in the composer's house in Nova Scotia, and then went on another retreat at Gampo Abbey in Pleasant Bay. Peter joined him there for the last few weeks of

August. After the retreat, even though friends were helping collate a selection of his letters and Allen planned to work with him on an 'Orlovsky Reader' for City Lights,[19] Peter fell back into his old ways and returned to Bellevue. Allen arranged for Corso to receive monthly payments from the Japanese artist Hiro Yamagata but was unable to find a way – without hands-on involvement – to keep Peter safe, sane and solvent.

At the end of the year, having promised to say no to appearances and faced with the real possibility that he could die, Allen travelled more and increased his poetic and photographic output. Because of this, Bob Rosenthal needed extra staff. In the summer, Peter Hale joined Bob and Jacqueline in the Union Square office, taking over Jacqueline's responsibilities when she left in 1994 and eventually succeeding Bob in running the Allen Ginsberg Trust. On one of Allen's more relaxed evenings in June, he and Peter Hale wrote 'Violent Collaborations', a song/poem; the two were 'stoned and trying to out gross out each other with those lines . . . both in stitches rolling around on his bed as each line came out'.[20]

Allen contributed an essay, 'Whitman's Influence: A Mountain Too Vast To Be Seen', to *The Teachers and Writers Guide to Walt Whitman*, another to *Tricycle: The Buddhist Review*, on 'Negative Capability: Kerouac's Buddhist Ethic', and wrote prefaces for Kerouac's *Pomes All Sizes* and Louis Ginsberg's *Collected Poems*. He lectured at the International Center for Photography; participated in the William Carlos Williams Conference; spent a week in residence at the National Poetry Foundation at the University of Maine; presented three lectures at the Santa Monica Writers' Conference; addressed the Walt Whitman Centenary Celebrations at Brooklyn College; appeared on Garrison Keillor's *A Prairie Home Companion Show* and *The Charlie Rose Show*; and chaired a colloquy, 'Exorcising Burroughs', with Bill in London. The French government awarded him the *Chevalier de l'Ordre des Artes et des Lettres*, the American Academy of Arts and Sciences elected him fellow, and St Martin's Press published Michael Schumacher's biography, *Dharma Lion*.

The last line of the last poem published while Ginsberg remained alive is from 'American Sentences', a compilation of fragmentary notes written between 1987 and 19 December 1992, based on his spontaneous observations in and of Tompkins Square Park: 'That grey-haired man in business suit and black turtleneck thinks he's still young.'[21] People around him hoped Allen would realize the irony.

Answering a request for a poem on Bill Clinton's inauguration on 20 January 1993, Allen sat up in bed on 17 January writing 'New Democracy Wish List'. The poem included lines on FCC censorship, decriminalization of marijuana, LSD, US backing of right-wing dictators, plus Allen's more health-centred personal concerns – ban smoking, promote alternative medicine, change to a vegetarian diet – mixed with calls for eco-technology, AIDS education and alternatives to fossil fuels. Allen wanted to see these things happen before he died; aware that the list was 'impractical',[22] he carried on, admitting, as he wrote a year earlier, that:

> If I don't get some rest I'll die faster
> If I sleep I'll lose my
>   chance for salvation—[23]

In February, a few weeks before Carl Solomon died from lung cancer, Allen visited, buying Solomon a milkshake and, after discussing their various illnesses with him, left his old friend a few painkillers. At the memorial for Solomon Allen sang the Prajnaparamita Sutra accompanied by Ed Sanders, Corso read new poems, and Allen finished with 'Howl'. Maybe this death forced Allen to consider his workaholism; the poetry output abated somewhat, and although he managed his teaching duties at Brooklyn College and Naropa he took six months' leave to concentrate on other matters and to recover from yet another bout of bronchitis.

Allen and Waldman left for Vienna on 7 September, to teach at the Schule für Dichtung, which offered a programme similar to that of the Jack Kerouac School of Disembodied Poetics but with better pay, travel and accommodation. Allen taught a class called 'Mind Writing Slogans' incorporating the 'first thought best thought' principle and using Kerouac's 'Essentials of Spontaneous Prose' as a basis for his lectures.

Exhausted but determined to fulfil his schedule, he moved on by train to Budapest, Belgrade, Bydgoszcz, Krakow, Łódź and Warsaw, before travelling to England where he read at the Cheltenham Festival. On his first trip to Ireland, he performed in Belfast and Dublin, recorded 'Hum Bom!' and 'Put Down Yr Cigarette Rag' for a television special at U2's studios, and visited Yeats's old home at Thoor Ballylee near Galway and his grave in St Columba's Church cemetery in Drumcliffe. Still suffering from bronchitis, he attended showings in Munich, Berlin and Prague of Jerry Aronson's *The Life and Times of Allen Ginsberg*, which had premiered at the Sundance Film Festival in January.

From Poland, he flew to Barcelona to meet Lucien Carr and they travelled to Madrid where Allen gave a reading. Lucien flew home, struggling with the flu and unable to keep up with the pace, while Allen left for Greece to stay with the wheelchair-bound Alan Ansen before departing for Tangier. To anyone keeping track, it must have looked as though Allen was cramming in all the places he had travelled to in the past.

It had been 32 years since he had last visited Tangier and he booked a $60-a-night room at the four-star Hotel Minzah and walked to the Villa Muniria where he had stayed on his previous trips in 1957 and 1961. Realizing that this would be the last time he would visit the place, that Peter was irrevocably lost to him and that his own death was close, Allen burst into tears. He paid $10 to stay in his old room for the day, looking out on the old palm tree under which he had photographed Burroughs, Ansen, Corso, Bowles, Kerouac, Sommerville and Orlovsky – the captioned photos now adorning the walls of international art galleries. On 22 December, after buying a sky-blue shirt, Allen walked down to the Socco Chico area to visit a cafe. Here – and this a subject rarely mentioned in Allen's journals and letters – he was racially abused: 'You look like a Jewish peoples you going to get killed, someday make you dead.'[24] The next day, Allen visited the 83-year-old Paul Bowles and the two writers reminisced – Jane Bowles and Peter Orlovsky foremost in their minds.

On 1 January 1994, to the tune of 'Here We Go 'Round the Mulberry Bush', Ginsberg wrote:

> I got old & shit in my pants
> > shit in my pants
> > shit in my pants
> I got old & shit in my pants
> > shit in my pants again . . .[25]

Even incontinence made Allen burst into song.

With Gelek Rinpoche, Allen spent the first ten days of January at a Vajrayogini Buddhist retreat in Michigan. Lee Hyla had composed music to 'Howl' and Allen performed with the Kronos Quartet in San Francisco and at Carnegie Hall, New York on 11 January. For a week from 20 January, he worked as Visiting Adjunct Professor teaching a 'Craft of Poetry' course at NYU. On 4 February, he travelled to Lawrence to celebrate Burroughs's 80th birthday. For the rest of the month, he lectured in California. In March, he gave a talk in Montreal, a benefit reading in Minneapolis, and starred in a video for the PBS TV series *United States of Poetry*. On 7 May, he took part in the annual St Mark's Poetry Project Symposium 'Investigative Poetics' with Sanders and Bernadette Mayer. For the year's Brooklyn College class, he taught 'The History of the Beat Generation' and helped organize an NYU Beat Conference in May.

Allen agreed to appear in an advertisement for the Gap clothing store – Burroughs and Warhol had also featured. The shoot paid $20,000, which he donated to the Jack Kerouac School. Microsoft would later use his image for twice the money and, once again, Naropa gained from Allen's generosity.

After the NYU Beat Conference, Allen set out on a promotional tour for his new collection of poems, *Cosmopolitan Greetings*. For its 20th anniversary, Naropa held a ten-day conference, 'Beats and Other Rebel Angels: A Tribute to Allen Ginsberg'. Allen read along with di Prima, Michael Ondaatje, Antler and Eileen Myles. Snyder, Creeley, Ferlinghetti, Kesey and Koch all taught at the school and helped dedicate and celebrate the opening of the Allen Ginsberg Library on 3 July.

Negotiations with Allen, Bill Morgan and Andrew Wylie resulted in Stanford University purchasing Ginsberg's archives of photos, artefacts, manuscripts – even laundry lists – for $1 million. Part of the negotiated deal included free accommodation for two weeks a year at Stanford so that Allen could look through his archives containing 174,061 items in hundreds of boxes, including over 24,000 pages of manuscripts, 19,000 pages of notebooks and journals, and 2,500 tapes. The sale helped Allen buy a loft space on East 13th Street in which he could house both home and office – in this way, someone would always be there in case of an emergency – and the building had an elevator, so he wouldn't get out of breath climbing stairs. Allen wrote to Snyder, 'With 1/3 left of my Stanford archive sale million, after Federal State Local Taxes, 1/10 to Bibliographer/ Archivist Bill Morgan for 14 years work . . . and 5% to Agent – I purchased a nice big loft . . .',[26] and he complained that he was 'back to square one' financially.[27]

In August, Allen and Gordon Ball went over proofs for *Journals Mid-Fifties: 1954–1958*; he performed at 'The Real Woodstock

Festival' with The Fugs; gave a benefit reading for Doctors Without Borders and, in September, one for the Abbie Hoffman Foundation in Long Beach. He read with old friends Creeley and John Wieners at UMASS, and gave more benefit readings for the Black Mountain Museum and the Karmê Chöling Meditation Center. On 6 September, the Rhino/WEA label released *Holy Soul Jelly Roll: Poems and Songs*, produced by Hal Willner, a four-disc CD collection of Ginsberg's music from the past 40 years.

Before flying to Paris at the end of November, he crammed in more invitations – lecturing at Swarthmore College and Penn University, and reading at Hot Springs Arkansas and Kent State University. In Paris, as the guest of *Le Nouvel Observateur*, he chaired a roundtable and had his portrait painted by George Condo. On 20 November, at a benefit at St Mark's, gospel singers and musicians backed Allen, Creeley, Jerome Rothenberg, Waldman and others while they recited verses for Sanders's project *The New Amazing Grace*. In early December, with Peter Hale to assist – Allen's heart had weakened significantly – he flew to London to read and sign books in a promotional tour for *Cosmopolitan Greetings* and then to Paris for the launch of bilingual editions of *White Shroud*, *Mind Breaths* and *Plutonian Ode*.

Allen began 1995 with a fresh attack on the FCC, neo-Conservative America, and the recently elected Speaker of the United States House of Representatives Newt Gingrich, defending the counter-culture and anyone threatened by the right-wing politician:

> Does that mean war on every boy with more than one earring
>   on the same ear?
> against every girl with a belly button ring? What about nose
>   piercing?
> a diamond in right nostril?[28]

In April, Allen would continue his defence of free speech with a long letter to Republican congressman Randy 'Duke' Cunningham, outlining his position on NEA funding cuts, FCC censorship and neo-con 'superpatriots'.[29]

Writing to Gary Snyder on 12 January, Allen described a dream in which he told Kerouac that 'he'd done enough work' and advised him to 'take it easy and maybe write one book every ten years and live to be 80 or 90 years old',[30] admitting to Snyder that 'I guess that's advice to me'. Yet between 9 and 13 February, he read with Carl Rakosi at Stanford University; went to Ann Arbor for a Jewel Heart benefit reading; appeared with Ray Bremser at the Village Vanguard; and on 28 February performed with Edie Brickell, Paul Simon, Natalie Merchant and Philip Glass at a benefit for Tibet at Carnegie Hall. But things caught up with him and he uncharacteristically cancelled a number of reading dates due to ill health, barely managing to take part in the United Kingdom Year of Literature and Writing Festival held in Dylan Thomas's hometown of Swansea. Before he arrived in Wales, Allen stopped off in Ireland and in Galway met the poet Michael Hartnett, whose poem 'Death of an Irishwoman' has 'Howl'-like anaphoric lines, and 'Kaddish'-esque surreal maternal memories:

> She was a summer dance at the crossroads.
> She was a cardgame where a nose was broken.
> She was a song that nobody sings.
> She was a house ransacked by soldiers.
> She was a language seldom spoken.
> She was a child's purse, full of useless things.[31]

Allen described him as 'a marvellous drunk thin dying poet'.[32] Hartnett died in a Dublin hospital on 13 October 1999, from alcoholic liver disease.

At the end of April, Allen took part in Leslie Fiedler's 80th birthday SUNY Buffalo discussion with Camille Paglia and Ishmael Reed. For five days at the beginning of May, he read chronologically through *Selected Poems, 1947–1995* (published by HarperCollins in 1996) at the Knitting Factory, performing two shows a day. After reading with Sakaki in Halifax, on 1 June, exhausted, Allen again fell ill – a blood clot formed on his heart and moved into his lungs, causing a painful embolism.

Only three days after being hospitalized, Allen felt well enough to attend 'The Writings of Jack Kerouac' conference at NYU. On 5 June he chaired a panel, 'Language, Voice, Beat and Energy of Kerouac's Poetry'. Weak and on medication (codeine) for the embolism 'the size of a Spanish olive',[33] he reclined on a couch before he went on stage to read on the final night, apparently looking 'thin and a bit green in the spotlight'.[34] A group of artists and poets – the UNbearables – protested and picketed some of the proceedings, claming the Beats, particularly Allen, had sold out and rolled over for corporate money.

Allen flew to Italy on 7 June for an exhibition of his photographs during the Venice Biennale. Exhausted by appearances and travelling, he stayed ten days with the artist Francesco Clemente in Amalfi where he relaxed on the beach and ate fresh pasta, fruit and vegetables. Before flying back to New York, Allen accompanied Clemente to the Château de Chenonceau for an exhibition of the artist's work, from where he wrote to Snyder after hearing the news of Leary's metastasizing cancer, 'I keep writing – journals and poems, much about physical aging or obvious deterioration of the body – with 2/3 of my heart working I have less physical energy approaching age 70 – tho I feel like 16 emotionally.'[35]

With Waldman, Allen flew to London in the third week of October for a performance with Tom Pickard, Alice Notley, Benjamin Zephaniah and Michael Horovitz to celebrate the 30th anniversary of the International Poetry Incarnation. Maybe aware that this was his

last reading in London, Allen told the audience biographical informa-
tion about the poems he read. Paul McCartney accompanied him on
'The Ballad of the Skeletons' and, for the finale, Allen invited the audience to join him in a rendition of Blake's 'The Nurse's Song'. (The
video for 'The Ballad of the Skeletons', directed by Gus Van Sant,
became a favourite with MTV viewers the following year.)

The Whitney Museum of American Art in New York opened
the 'Beat Culture and the New America: 1950–65' exhibition on 8
December. The show included paintings, sculptures, films, music,
books, magazines, notebooks, original manuscripts and sound
recordings by artists, writers and filmmakers associated with the
Beats. Allen – suffering from bronchitis – Sanders, Corso,
McClure, Steven Taylor and Ray Manzarek performed at the
museum on 10 December.

In 'Bowel Song', which he wrote on 2 January 1996, Ginsberg
discusses the congestive heart failure his doctors diagnosed
while he was hospitalized in Boston.

> Recovered from congestive heart failure,
> you took 7 hours last week to read the Sunday N.Y. Times
> Listen, your days are numbered, why waste the essence of your
>   clock . . .[36]

It may have taken Allen seven hours to read the newspaper,
but Bob Rosenthal and his staff still could not slow him down.
However many rest days they forced into his schedule, the more he
filled them with appointments. In early March, the French television company Canal Plus invited Allen, Corso and Huncke to
participate in a recording session with Ornette Coleman; as the
recording studio was in Harlem, Rosenthal agreed. Allen then flew
to Europe to give readings with Philip Glass in Paris and Prague
and to attend an opening of a photography show in Milan. In Paris

for the launch of the French translation of *Cosmopolitan Greetings*, Allen showed Peter Hale and Geoffrey Manaugh (a young poet he had befriended) his old haunts.

Allen heard the news of Leary's impending death from Steven Taylor. Leary spoke to Allen and Burroughs on the telephone but by 28 May was too ill from prostate cancer to respond to calls. On 31 May, Leary gained consciousness briefly, uttering 'Why not?' in various intonations to people in the room, before he died.

At Naropa, Allen lectured on 'English and American Lyric Poetry', Lewis Carroll, poetry and Buddhism, and writing from inside one's own death. With a life lived mostly in the spotlight, Allen constantly questioned who he was. While at Naropa, on 5 July, he provided answers to 'Multiple Identity Questionnaire':

I'm a jew? a nice jewish boy?
A flaky Buddhist, certainly
Gay in fact pederast? I'm exaggerating?[37]

In this poem and within his poetics, Ginsberg creates dialectical propositions in order to live in the interstices, in the margins between sexual preference, race, religion, fame and inconspicuousness, and by doing this he generates more reflexive questions.

In Los Angeles, Allen read at the opening of Burroughs's 'Ports of Entry' art exhibition at the County Museum, then visited Lawrence where he and Burroughs (recovering from a mild stroke) spent ten days taking photographs, recording interviews and editing Burroughs's essay 'Bureaucracy and Drugs'. While there, they heard the news that, on 8 August, Herbert Huncke had died at New York's Beth Israel Hospital. Three weeks later, Allen wrote:

Don't get angry with me
You might die tomorrow

I'm an empty hungry ghost
Any spare change I can borrow?[38]

Back in New York in September, Allen performed with Yehudi
Menuhin in Philip Glass's production of *Sunflower Sutra* at the
Lincoln Center. He reprised his readings of the *Selected Poems* and
performed 'Ballad of the Skeletons' backed by members of Sonic
Youth and other musicians for the Poetry Project's 30th anniver-
sary on 8 October.

For his Brooklyn College class at the end of the year, he taught
'Beginner's Blake'. In December, the National Jewish Book Council
gave him a Lifetime Award; and he celebrated the holiday period in
San Francisco performing at the Green Christmas Ball with Ralph
Carney, Orbital, The Lemonheads and Beck, in front of 14,000 peo-
ple, finishing the year on a ten-day retreat with Gelek Rinpoche at
Camp Copneconic in Michigan.

In 'Good Luck', a poem Allen wrote after entering hospital for a
hernia operation in Boston on 8 January 1997, he sets out his illnesses and contrasts them with his joy at being alive:

I'm lucky to have all five fingers on the right hand
Lucky peepee with little pain
Lucky bowels move . . .[39]

The day before, he had enjoyed sashimi at Teriyaki Boy, his local
Japanese restaurant on East 10th Street between 1st and 2nd Avenue.
To open the year, he wrote the playful yet acerbic 'Virtual Impunity
Blues', his excremental and sensual vision of President Clinton, the
CIA-Contra scandal, the FCC, American Family Values, the Pope, the
FBI and Waco, and the Chinese and Albanian governments.

With Patti Smith, Philip Glass, Michael Stipe and Natalie
Merchant, he performed a benefit reading for Tibet House at

Carnegie Hall in February. Apart from taking part in a poetry slam at NYU Loeb Center, Allen cancelled other readings, hoping to preserve his energy for a trip to Italy with Peter Orlovsky to see Nanda Pivano. Doctors ordered him to rest for a month and, on 22 February, after a burst of creativity, penning songs and short poems, he wrote 'Death & Fame'. He spent the next two weeks in hospital in Boston.

On 21 March, Bob Rosenthal found Allen at home in great pain. Bob called Allen's cousin Dr Joel Gaidemak and described the symptoms, then took Allen immediately to the nearby Beth Israel Hospital. In his private room, Allen wrote poems, received visitors, kept up with correspondence, and read *Mother Goose*. Doctors, baffled by the source of Allen's abdominal pain, performed a series of biopsies. Ginsberg's physician Dr Chain brought the results to Allen on the morning of 30 March. The tests revealed hepatitis c and cancer nodules in Allen's liver – too late for treatment, Dr Chain informed him he had three to six months to live.

After telling Bob Rosenthal, Peter Hale and Bill Morgan, Allen received visits from Peter Orlovsky and Anne Waldman, called Gelek Rinpoche for advice, then began the massive task of contacting friends. Allen decided he wanted to die naturally (apart from drugs to kill the pain) at home. Bob Rosenthal and Peter Hale worked tirelessly to turn the new apartment into a place where Allen could spend his last days. They rented a hospital bed, had artworks framed and hung on walls, and installed a recording studio for when Glass, McCartney or Dylan dropped by.

The day before leaving hospital on 2 April, Allen asked Peter Hale to type up a letter he had written to Bill Clinton, informing the president of his terminal cancer and asking for a medal or award for services to poetry – Peter thought Allen was joking, that it was a Burroughs-style routine, but Allen was serious – fame and death came together. In his last few days, with the help of Bob Rosenthal, Peter Hale and Bill Morgan, Allen edited and assembled the manuscript of *Death & Fame: Poems, 1993–1997*.

Peter Orlovsky moved into the loft to take care of Allen on Allen's return home. On 27 March, at 4 a.m., Ginsberg had written 'Dream', his last poem about his relationship with Peter. In it, he and Peter have a baby, one they had talked about having back in 1960, and Allen worries about Peter's ability to take care of a child, but – ever the optimist – is reassured by Peter's great compassion:

> Worried & pleased since it was true I slowly woke, still thinking
>   it'd happened, consciousness returned slowly 2:29 AM I was
>   awake
>   and there's no little mystic baby—naturally appeared, just
>   disappeared
>   A glow of happiness next morn, warm glow of pleasure half
>   the day.[40]

Allen enjoyed the new apartment, the bookshelves, paintings on the wall and his Buddhist shrine at one end of the room. He called friends, invited people over and stayed up late writing in his journal. On 3 April, with Bob Rosenthal and Peter Hale working in the office, Allen went to bed. A little later, Nanda Pivano called from Italy to say goodbye but Allen began to vomit and Peter Hale helped him into the bathroom. Feeling shaky but better, Allen returned to his bed where Peter Orlovsky watched over him.

Unfortunately, Orlovsky neglected to stay with Allen. He went out at some point during the night and bought a stolen bicycle that he left blocking the entrance to the loft. When Bob Rosenthal and Bill Morgan arrived on the morning of 4 April, they found Allen unconscious. Bob called the hospice and a doctor and nurse arrived. The doctor told Bob to contact whomever he needed to: Allen had had a stroke, lapsed into a coma, and would not last long. Allen's brother Eugene, friends, old lovers and relatives came to the loft. Jonas Mekas had been keeping a video diary of Allen's last days and filmed people paying their respects.

On 5 April at 2.39 a.m., Allen convulsed and stopped breathing. Gelek Rinpoche and others chanted until they felt Allen's spirit leave his body. Just before Allen died, Peter Hale symbolically touched a spoon to Allen's lips signifying his last meal and Bob Rosenthal recited the Sh'ma Yisrael. Everyone stood in the loft space in shock. Mekas continued to film while Peter Orlovsky and Gregory Corso took photographs of Allen's body. After everyone left, Bob Rosenthal closed the apartment. Allen's 'Chronological Addenda' – something he had been meticulously compiling since 1971 states '[April 4 suffered stroke early AM resulting in coma; died at home April 5 early AM in presence of close friends and teacher Gelek Rinpoche].'[41]

Written on 30 March, 'Things I'll Not Do (Nostalgias)', Ginsberg's last completed poem, the only one he was unable to revise before his death, is a list of farewells, reminiscences and regrets, a warm and (as always) honest reckoning of his life:

No more sweet summers with lovers, teaching Blake at Naropa
Mind Writing Slogans, new modern American Poetics,
    Williams
    Kerouac Reznikoff Rakosi Corso Creeley Orlovsky
Any visits to B'Nai Israel graves of Buba, Aunt Rose, Harry
    Meltzer and
    Aunt Clara, Father Louis
Not myself except in an urn of ashes[42]

There is no period, no final full stop.

7

See you later, Allen Ginsberg . . .

On 6 April, at the Jewel Heart Center, New York City, close friends and family attended a funeral service. Trungpa's Shambhala Center held a repeat ceremony on 7 April with Gregory Corso, Lou Reed and Kurt Vonnegut among the hundreds of mourners chanting mantras and singing Kaddish. Allen had asked to be cremated and his ashes divided and placed with his father's at B'Nai Israel cemetery, Elizabeth, New Jersey; scattered at Gelek Rinpoche's Jewel Heart Center in Ann Arbor; and interred at the Rocky Mountain Dharma Center.

Bob Rosenthal organized a public memorial on 14 May 1998 at the Cathedral of St John the Divine, a few blocks south of Columbia University, and asked Patti Smith, Ed Sanders, Natalie Merchant and Philip Glass to perform – thousands arrived to celebrate Allen's life and mourn his passing. More memorials took place around the world confirming Ginsberg as a truly international poet, although he once admitted, 'It's true I write about myself / Who else do I know so well?'[1]

After a long battle with lung cancer, Peter Orlovsky died at 11.30 a.m. on 30 May 2010, at the age of 76. The Karmê Chöling Meditation Center in Barnet, Vermont, held a Sukhavati funeral celebration for Peter on 2 June, attended by Peter and Allen's many friends. On 28 August 2010, Peter's ashes were interred with Allen's at the Shambhala Mountain Center near Red Feather Lakes, Colorado. Anne Waldman, Reed Bye, and members of the

Sketch for promotional packaging of Presspop figurine, designed by Archer Prewitt, sculpted by Kei Hinotani.

centre performed a traditional Mahayana Buddhist Sukhavati ceremony, burning images of Peter and Allen, reading prayers from the Tibetan Book of the Dead, Prajnaparamita Sutra, and Shelley's 'Ode to the West Wind'. Placed on a *stupa* in a meditation rest area, Peter's marker reads: 'Ocean of Generosity Peter Orlovsky, July 8, 1933–May 30, 2010. Train will tug my grave, my breath hueing gentil vapor between weel and track.'[2] Allen's marker reads, 'Dharma Lion Allen Ginsberg, June 3, 1926–April 5, 1997. My life work Poesy, transmitting that spontaneous awareness to Mankind.'[3] In July 2011, on a visit to the Mount of Olives in Jerusalem, Bob Rosenthal scattered a pinch of Allen's ashes into the wind.

Since Ginsberg's death, there has been an upsurge in Beat Generation publications and events. Books by Ginsberg published since 1997 include: *The Letters of Allen Ginsberg*; *The Book of Martyrdom and Artifice: First Journals and Poems, 1937–1952*; *Family*

Business: Selected Letters between a Father and Son; *Spontaneous Mind: Selected Interviews: 1958–1996*; *Deliberate Prose: Selected Essays, 1952–1995*; and *Jack Kerouac and Allen Ginsberg: The Letters*. Books published about Ginsberg include: *Allen Ginsberg's Buddhist Poetics* by Tony Trigilio; *American Scream: Allen Ginsberg's 'Howl' and the Making of the Beat Generation* by Jonah Raskin; *Beat Memories: The Photographs of Allen Ginsberg* by Sarah Greenough; *White Hand Society: The Psychedelic Partnership of Timothy Leary and Allen Ginsberg* by Peter H. Conners; and, of course, *The Typewriter Is Holy* and *I Celebrate Myself: The Somewhat Private Life of Allen Ginsberg*, both by Bill Morgan.

Ginsberg's music is available on iTunes, there is a graphic novel version of 'Howl' illustrated by Eric Drooker, and Ginsberg's IMDb listing grows by the day with the September 2010 highlight of the release of the movie *Howl*, based on events leading up to Ginsberg's writing of 'Howl', the Six Gallery performance and the subsequent obscenity trial. The film, directed and written by Rob Epstein and Jeffrey Friedman, with animation directed by Eric Drooker, and starring James Franco as Allen Ginsberg, premiered at the Sundance Festival in January 2010, opening in theatres in San Francisco and New York on 22 September.

Two weeks earlier, the Japanese design company Presspop had released a Ginsberg figurine designed by Sof' Boy creator Archer Prewitt, sculpted by Kei Hinotani. The six-inch (152-mm) doll wears a fabric cloth jacket with the three-fish-one-head logo on the back, an Uncle Sam top hat, beaded necklace, beard, trademark black-rimmed glasses, and carries a choice of book: *Plutonian Ode, Collected Poems, Howl and Other Poems* or *Kaddish and Other Poems*. The pack also contains a CD with unreleased recordings of 'Bricklayer's Lunch Hour', 'On Burroughs' Work', 'Wales Visitation', 'Manhattan May Day Midnight', 'After the Big Parade' and the song 'Capitol Air'. It is a limited edition of 1,000, officially approved by the Allen Ginsberg Estate.

James Franco as Allen Ginsberg, reading 'Howl', from the 2010 film of the same name directed by Rob Epstein and Jeffrey Friedman.

In a final twist to the Allen Ginsberg biography, music and film stars flocked to the film premiere of *Howl* at the ifc Center on 6th Avenue and West 3rd Street. A few blocks across town at St Mark's Poetry Project on 2nd Avenue and East 10th Street, Allen and Peter's friends Patti Smith, Philip Glass, Gordon Ball, Bob Rosenthal, Peter Hale, Hal Willner, Anne Waldman, Simon Pettet, Rosebud Pettet, Ed Sanders, Bill Morgan and Robert Frank were involved in Peter Orlovsky's memorial reading. What would Allen have done? Gone to the glitzy opening at Trump SoHo's Bar D'Eau, and mingled with other celebs while ogling the pretty male actors? Or would he have been with his friends on stage at the Poetry Project, reading, singing and playing harmonium? Bob Rosenthal and Peter Hale missed the opening-night screening but made it to the after-party – Peter Hale admits it was 'odd to have such a super celeb bash at the new Trump Hotel in Allen's honor, but there is some curious irony to enjoy in that'. From 'Death & Fame':

> Everyone knew they were part of "History" except the deceased who never knew exactly what was happening even when I was alive . . .[4]

References

Introduction

1 Lawrence Ferlinghetti, 'Allen Ginsberg Dying', *How to Paint Sunlight: Lyric Poems and Others (1997–2000)* (New York, 2001), p. 76.
2 Interview with Paul Auster, November 2010, available at www.goodreads.com, last accessed 13 February 2012.
3 Philip Roth, *The Facts: A Novelist's Autobiography* (New York, 1988), p. 8.
4 Roland Barthes, 'The Death of the Author', trans. Richard Howard, *Aspen*, 5 and 6 (Fall–Winter, 1967), box 3.
5 David Foster Wallace, 'Greatly Exaggerated', *A Supposedly Fun Thing I'll Never Do Again* (New York, 1997), pp. 138–45.
6 Mark Fisher, *Capitalist Realism: Is There No Alternative?* (Hants, 2009), p. 7.
7 Tiqqun, *Introduction to Civil War*, trans. Alexander R. Galloway and Jason E. Smith (Los Angeles, CA, 2010), p. 147.
8 Stephen Greenblatt, *Learning to Curse* (New York, 1990), p. 196.
9 Ed Sanders, *The Poetry and Life of Allen Ginsberg* (Woodstock, NY, 2000), p. 240.
10 Nicholson Baker, *U and I: A True Story* (New York, 1992), p. 7.
11 Don DeLillo, *Point Omega* (New York, 2010), p. 21.

1 'Hell on Earth', 1926–47

1 Allen Ginsberg, 'Two Sonnets', *Collected Poems, 1947–1997* [New York, 2006] (London, 2009), p. 13.
2 Allen Ginsberg, *The Book of Martyrdom and Artifice: First Journals and*

Poems, 1937–1952, ed. Juanita Lieberman-Plimpton and Bill Morgan
(New York, 2006), p. 8.

3 Ibid., p. 9.

4 Ginsberg, 'Kaddish', *Collected Poems*, p. 217.

5 Ibid., p. 223.

6 Michel Foucault, *Madness and Civilization*, trans. Richard Howard
(Oxford, 1989), p. 54.

7 Allen Ginsberg, *Deliberate Prose: Selected Essays, 1925–1995*, ed. Bill
Morgan (New York, 2000), p. 223.

8 Ginsberg, 'White Shroud', *Collected Poems*, p. 889.

9 Bill Morgan, *I Celebrate Myself: The Somewhat Private Life of Allen
Ginsberg* (New York, 2006), p. 10.

10 Barry Miles, *Ginsberg: A Biography* (London, 2000), p. 11.

11 Ginsberg, 'Drive All Blames into One', *Collected Poems*, p. 669.

12 Foucault, *Madness and Civilization*, p. 239.

13 Allen Ginsberg and Louis Ginsberg, *Family Business: Selected Letters
Between a Father and Son*, ed. Michael Schumacher (New York, 2001),
p. xxiv.

14 Ginsberg, *Martyrdom and Artifice*, p. 6.

15 Ibid., p. 4.

16 Ibid., p. 9.

17 Walt Whitman, *The Complete Poems*, ed. Francis Murphy (London,
2004), p. 696.

18 Ginsberg, 'Kaddish', *Collected Poems*, p. 222.

19 Ginsberg, *Martyrdom and Artifice*, pp. 14–15.

20 Ibid., p. 21.

21 'The Constitution of the Philolexian Society of Columbia University in
the City of New York', at www.columbia.edu, last accessed 13 February
2012.

22 Morgan, *I Celebrate Myself*, p. 37.

23 Miles, *Ginsberg*, p. 33.

24 Joanna Levin, *Bohemia in America, 1858–1920* (Stanford, CA, 2010), p. 20.

25 Ginsberg, *Deliberate Prose*, p. 208.

26 Paul Maher, *Kerouac: The Definitive Biography* (Lanham, MD, 2004),
pp. 112–14.

27 Jack Kerouac, *The Portable Jack Kerouac*, ed. Ann Charters (New York,
1995), p. 129.

28   Arthur Rimbaud, *Selected Poems and Letters*, trans. Jeremy Harding and John Sturrock (London, 2004), pp. 101–3.

29   William S. Burroughs, *Naked Lunch: 50th Anniversary Edition* (New York, 2009), p. 199.

30   D. H. Lawrence, *The Letters of D. H. Lawrence*, vol. II: 1913–1916, ed. George J. Zytaruk and James T. Boulton (Cambridge, 1979), p. 459.

31   Ginsberg, *Martyrdom and Artifice*, p. 52.

32   For a contemporary account, see Frank Adams, 'Columbia Student Kills Friend and Sinks Body in Hudson River', *New York Times* (17 August 1944).

33   Ginsberg and Ginsberg, *Family Business*, p. 5.

34   Ibid., p. 7.

35   Ginsberg, *Martyrdom and Artifice*, pp. 120–21. See also Ginsberg's poem 'The Last Voyage', pp. 401–9 for a poetic response to the 'New Vision' theories.

36   André Breton, *Manifestoes of Surrealism*, trans. Richard Seaver and Helen R. Lane (Ann Arbor, MI, 1969), p. 26.

37   See Ginsberg, *Deliberate Prose*, p. 371, and *Indian Journals* (New York, 1996), p. 75.

38   William S. Burroughs, *Junky: The Definitive Text*, ed. Oliver Harris (London, 2003), p. 4.

39   Ginsberg, *Martyrdom and Artifice*, pp. 419–27; Allen Ginsberg, *The Letters of Allen Ginsberg*, ed. Bill Morgan (New York, 2008), p. 15.

40   William Wordsworth, *The Major Works: Including The Prelude*, ed. Stephen Gill (Oxford, 2008), p. 597.

41   Ginsberg and Ginsberg, *Family Business*, p. 9.

42   Ginsberg, *Martyrdom and Artifice*, p. 433.

43   David Sandison and Graham Vickers, *Neal Cassady: The Fast Life of a Beat Hero* (Chicago, IL, 2006), p. 65.

44   Martin Heidegger, *Being and Time*, trans. John Macquarrie and Edward Robinson (New York, 1962), p. 253.

45   Ginsberg, *Martyrdom and Artifice*, p. 175.

46   Ginsberg, 'A Lover's Garden', *Collected Poems*, p. 759.

47   Ludwig Wittgenstein, *Tractatus Logico-philosophicus*, trans. D. F. Pears and B. F. McGuinness (Oxford, 2001), p. 22.

48   Neal Cassady, *Collected Letters, 1944–1967*, ed. Dave Moore (New York, 2004), p. 47.

49 Ginsberg, 'In Society', *Collected Poems*, p. 11.

50 Ginsberg, 'The Bricklayer's Lunch Hour', *Collected Poems*, p. 12.

51 Wittgenstein, *Tractatus Logico-philosophicus*, p. 68.

52 Morgan, *I Celebrate Myself*, p. 90.

53 Cassady, *Collected Letters*, p. 53.

54 Ginsberg and Ginsberg, *Family Business*, p. 15.

55 Ginsberg, 'Dakar Doldrums', *Collected Poems*, p. 763.

56 Foucault, *Madness and Civilization*, p. 9.

57 William S. Burroughs, *Exterminator!* (New York, 1973) p. 9.

2 'The Lost America of Love', 1948–57

1 Allen Ginsberg, 'A Supermarket in California', *Collected Poems, 1947–1997* [New York, 2006] (London, 2009), p. 144.

2 Jacques Derrida, *The Gift of Death*, trans. David Willis (Chicago, IL, 1995), pp. 70–71.

3 Neal Cassady, *Collected Letters, 1944–1967*, ed. Dave Moore (New York, 2004), p. 78.

4 Jack Kerouac, 'On the Road Again', *New Yorker* (22 June 1998), available at www.newyorker.com, last accessed 13 February 2012.

5 Jack Kerouac and Allen Ginsberg, *Jack Kerouac and Allen Ginsberg: The Letters*, ed. Bill Morgan and David Stanford (New York, 2010), p. 38.

6 Allen Ginsberg and Louis Ginsberg, *Family Business: Selected Letters Between a Father and Son*, ed. Michael Schumacher (New York, 2001), p. 19.

7 Cassady, *Collected Letters*, p. 82.

8 Ibid., p. 89–90.

9 Ginsberg, 'Vision 1948', *Collected Poems*, p. 16.

10 Allen Ginsberg, *Spontaneous Mind: Selected Interviews, 1958–1995*, ed. David Carter (New York, 2001), p. 42.

11 Martin Heidegger, *Being and Time*, trans. John Macquarrie and Edward Robinson (New York, 1962), pp. 387–8.

12 Ginsberg and Ginsberg, *Family Business*, p. 22.

13 Derrida, *The Gift of Death*, p. 68.

14 Allen Ginsberg, *The Book of Martyrdom and Artifice: First Journals and Poems, 1937–1952*, ed. Juanita Lieberman-Plimpton and Bill Morgan

(New York, 2006), p. 259.

15 Ginsberg, *Spontaneous Mind*, p. 64.

16 Ginsberg, *Martyrdom and Artifice*, p. 328.

17 Ibid.

18 Ibid., p. 327.

19 Kerouac and Ginsberg, *The Letters*, p. 125.

20 Ginsberg, 'The Archetype Poem', *Collected Poems*, p. 69.

21 Henry James, *The Ambassadors* [1903] (Oxford, 2008), p. 211.

22 William Carlos Williams, 'A Sort of a Song', *The Collected Poems of William Carlos Williams*, vol. II: *1939–1962*, ed. Christopher MacGowan (New York, 1991), p. 55.

23 Cassady, *Collected Letters*, p. 118.

24 Kerouac and Ginsberg, *The Letters*, p. 134.

25 James W. Grauerholz, 'The Death of Joan Vollmer Burroughs: What Really Happened?', American Studies Dept, University of Kansas (7 January 2002), prepared for the Fifth Congress of the Americas at Universidad de las Americas Puebla (18 October 2001).

26 Ginsberg, 'Walking home at night', *Collected Poems*, p. 78.

27 Kerouac and Ginsberg, *The Letters*, p. 141.

28 Ibid., p. 179.

29 Ginsberg, *Martyrdom and Artifice*, p. 349.

30 Ginsberg, 'A Ghost May Come', *Collected Poems*, p. 79.

31 William Carlos Williams, *Paterson,* revd edn (New York, 1992), p. 3.

32 Allen Ginsberg, *Howl: 50th Anniversary Edition* (New York, 2006), p. 13.

33 Cassady, *Collected Letters, 1944–1967*, p. 320.

34 Kerouac and Ginsberg, *The Letters*, p. 177.

35 Allen Ginsberg, *Empty Mirror* (New York, 1961)

36 Kerouac and Ginsberg, *The Letters*, p. 184.

37 Ginsberg, *Martyrdom and Artifice*, p. 352.

38 Friedrich Nietzsche, *Basic Writings of Nietzsche*, trans. Walter Kaufmann, (New York, 2000), p. 281.

39 Kerouac and Ginsberg, *The Letters*, p. 170.

40 Ginsberg, *Martyrdom and Artifice*, p. 515.

41 Kerouac and Ginsberg, *The Letters*, p. 185; ibid., p. 181.

42 Ginsberg, 'The Green Automobile', *Collected Poems*, p. 93.

43 William Burroughs, *Letters to Allen Ginsberg: 1953–1957* (New York, 1982) p. 5.

44 Kerouac and Ginsberg, *The Letters*, p. 205.

45 Burroughs, *Letters to Allen Ginsberg*, p. 27.

46 Ginsberg, 'Siesta in Xbalba', *Collected Poems*, p. 105.

47 Ibid., p. 110.

48 William S. Burroughs, *Cities of the Red Night* (New York, 1981), p. xvii.

49 Ginsberg, 'Love Poem on Theme by Whitman', *Collected Poems*, p. 123.

50 Allen Ginsberg, *Journals Early Fifties Early Sixties*, ed. Gordon Ball (New York, 1977), p. 76.

51 Kerouac and Ginsberg, *The Letters*, p. 238.

52 Blaise Cendrars, 'The Art of Fiction No. 38', *Paris Review*, 37 (Spring 1966), interview by Michel Manoll. This issue also contains 'Eleven Poems' by Blaise Cendrars; Ginsberg interviewed by Thomas Clark in 'The Art of Poetry No. 8'; a poem by Ginsberg 'Fragment 1957—The Names'; Ted Berrigan, 'Two Poems'; Joanne Kyger, 'Two Poems'; Charles Olson, 'Maximus from Dogtown—II'; and Gary Snyder, 'Three Poems'.

53 Kerouac and Ginsberg, *The Letters*, p. 249.

54 Allen Ginsberg, *The Letters of Allen Ginsberg*, ed. Bill Morgan (New York, 2008), p. 110.

55 Ginsberg, *Spontaneous Mind*, p. 322.

56 Kerouac and Ginsberg, *The Letters*, p. 254.

57 Ibid., p. 256.

58 Ginsberg, 'Blessed be the Muses', *Collected Poems*, p. 133.

59 Kerouac and Ginsberg, *The Letters*, p. 311.

60 Ginsberg, *Howl*, p. 26.

61 Ginsberg, *The Letters of Allen Ginsberg*, pp. 120–21.

62 Kerouac and Ginsberg, *The Letters*, p. 319.

63 Ibid., p. 320.

64 Christopher Smart, *Selected Poems* (London, 1991), p. 59.

65 Mick Sinclair, *San Francisco: A Cultural and Literary History* (Oxford, 2004) p. 185.

66 Philip Whalen, *The Collected Poems of Philip Whalen* (Lebanon, NH, 2007), p. 36.

67 Jack Kerouac, *The Dharma Bums* (New York, 1958), p. 7.

68 Charles Olson, 'Projective Verse', *Collected Prose*, ed. Donald Allen and Benjamin Friedlander (Berkeley, CA, 1997), p. 240.

69 Gilles Deleuze, *Essays Critical and Clinical*, trans. Daniel W. Smith and Michael A. Greco (London, 1998), pp. 56–8.

70 Gertrude Stein, *How to Write* (New York, 1975), p. 23.

71 Arthur Rimbaud, *Selected Poems and Letters*, trans. Jeremy Harding and John Sturrock (London, 2004), p. 61.

72 Antonin Artaud, *Artaud Anthology* (San Francisco, CA, 1965), p. 178. With thanks to Stephen Barber for bibliographic details – private correspondence 2 March 2011.

73 Stephen Greenblatt, *Learning to Curse* (New York, 1990), p. 206.

74 Fernando Pessoa, *The Book of Disquiet*, ed. and trans. Richard Zenith (London, 2002), p. 169.

75 Ginsberg, 'America', *Collected Poems*, p. 156.

76 Ginsberg and Ginsberg, *Family Business*, p. 50.

77 Ginsberg, *Howl*, p. 136.

78 Kerouac and Ginsberg, *The Letters*, p. 348.

79 Ted Morgan, *Literary Outlaw: The Life and Times of William S. Burroughs* (New York, 1988) p. 259.

80 Ginsberg and Ginsberg, *Family Business*, p. 70.

81 Kerouac and Ginsberg, *The Letters*, p. 368.

82 Ginsberg, 'Kaddish', *Collected Poems*, p. 234.

83 Ginsberg, 'At Apollinaire's Grave', *Collected Poems*, p. 188.

84 Kerouac and Ginsberg, *The Letters*, p. 378.

3 'Ugh!', 1958–67

1 Allen Ginsberg, 'Morning', *Collected Poems, 1947–1997* [New York, 2006] (London, 2009), p. 345.

2 Allen Ginsberg, *The Letters of Allen Ginsberg*, ed. Bill Morgan (New York, 2008), p. 175.

3 Ginsberg, 'The Names', *Collected Poems*, p. 187.

4 Ginsberg, *The Letters of Allen Ginsberg*, p. 173.

5 Ginsberg, 'American Change', *Collected Poems*, p. 194.

6 Jack Kerouac and Allen Ginsberg, *Jack Kerouac and Allen Ginsberg: The Letters*, ed. Bill Morgan and David Stanford (New York, 2010), p. 407.

7 William James, 'On Some Hegelisms', *Writings: 1878–1899* (New York, 1992), p. 679.

8 Ginsberg, 'Laughing Gas', *Collected Poems*, p. 198.

9 Ginsberg, *The Letters of Allen Ginsberg*, p. 171.

10 Geoff Dyer, *The Ongoing Moment* (London, 2005), pp. 168–9.

11 Norman Podhoretz, *The Norman Podhoretz Reader: A Selection of His Writings from the 1950s through the 1990s*, ed. Thomas L. Jeffers (New York, 2004), p. 38. Originally published as 'The Know-nothing Bohemians', *Partisan Review*, 25 (Spring 1958).

12 Allen Ginsberg, *Howl: 50th Anniversary Edition* (New York, 2006), p. 162.

13 Ginsberg, 'Lysergic Acid', *Collected Poems*, p. 242.

14 John Cheever, *The Journals* (London, 1991), p. 356.

15 Simon Critchley, *On Humour* (London, 2002), p. 100.

16 Don DeLillo, *Point Omega* (New York, 2010), p. 21.

17 Ibid., p. 22.

18 Ginsberg, 'To an Old Poet in Peru', *Collected Poems*, p. 249.

19 William Burroughs and Allen Ginsberg, *The Yage Letters Redux* [1963], ed. Oliver Harris (San Francisco, CA, 2004), p. 101.

20 Allen Ginsberg and Louis Ginsberg, *Family Business: Selected Letters Between a Father and Son*, ed. Michael Schumacher (New York, 2001), p. 136.

21 Peter Conners, *White Hand Society* (San Francisco, CA, 2010), p. 48.

22 Charles S. Grob, 'Psychiatric Research with Hallucinogens: What have we learned?' *The Psychotomimetic Model Yearbook for Ethnomedicine and the Study of Consciousness*, Issue 3 (1994). See http://www.druglibrary. org/schaffer/lsd/grob.htm.

23 Allen Ginsberg, *Journals Early Fifties Early Sixties*, ed. Gordon Ball (New York, 1977), p. 183.

24 Ibid., p. 191.

25 Ibid., p. 192.

26 Ginsberg, *The Letters of Allen Ginsberg*, p. 247.

27 Ginsberg, *Journals*, p. 219.

28 Ginsberg, 'This Form of Life Needs Sex', *Collected Poems*, p. 292.

29 Ginsberg, *Journals*, p. 270.

30 Ibid., p. 295.

31 Judith Butler, 'Who Owns Kafka?', *London Review of Books*, XXXIII/5 (3 March 2011), pp. 3–8.

32 D. H. Lawrence, *The Letters of D. H. Lawrence*, vol. IV: 1921–1924, ed. Warren Roberts, James T. Boulton, and Elizabeth Mansfield (Cambridge, 1987), p. 154.

33 Allen Ginsberg, *Indian Journals* (New York, 1996), pp. 7–8.

34 Ibid., p. 11.

35 Ibid., p. 38.

36 Ibid., p. 39.

37 See the letter to Monarch Notes regarding their 'Beat Literature' pamphlet in which Ginsberg corrects, 'Stein yes obviously influenced the dissociational improvisation of Kerouac', in Ginsberg, *The Letters of Allen Ginsberg*, p. 324.

38 André Breton, *Communicating Vessels*, trans. Mary Ann Caws and Geoffrey T. Harris (Lincoln, NE, 1990), p. 53.

39 Ginsberg, *Indian Journals*, p. 39.

40 Peter Conners, *White Hand Society* (San Francisco, CA, 2010), p. 158.

41 Stephen Greenblatt, *Learning to Curse* (New York, 1990), p. 214.

42 Robert Grenier, 'On Speech', *This*, 1 (1971), reprinted in *In the American Tree*, ed. Ron Silliman (Orono, ME, 1985), pp. 496–7.

43 See Barrett Watten, 'The Turn to Language and the 1960s', *Critical Inquiry*, 29 (Autumn 2002), pp. 139–83, for a discussion on Ginsberg, language poetry and the 1960s.

44 Ginsberg, *The Letters of Allen Ginsberg*, p. 273.

45 Ginsberg, *Indian Journals*, p. 112.

46 Ginsberg, *The Letters of Allen Ginsberg*, p. 274.

47 Ginsberg, *Indian Journals*, p. 143.

48 Walker Percy, *The Moviegoer* [1961] (New York, 1998), p. 13.

49 Ginsberg, 'Death News', *Collected Poems*, p. 305.

50 Ginsberg, *Indian Journals*, p. 210.

51 'Buddhists Find a Beatnik Spy', *New York Times* (5 June 1963); see online, posted 5 June 2009, at http://ginsbergblog.blogspot.com, last accessed 13 February 2012.

52 Ginsberg, 'Angkor Wat', *Collected Poems*, p. 323.

53 Stephen Barber, *Antonin Artaud: Terminal Curses* (Los Angeles, CA, 2008), pp. 119–20.

54 Kerouac and Ginsberg, *The Letters*, p. 473.

55 Neal Cassady, *The First Third* (San Francisco, CA, 1971).

56 Ginsberg, 'Morning', *Collected Poems*, p. 345.

57 Ginsberg, *The Letters of Allen Ginsberg*, p. 297.

58 Ibid., p. 297.

59 'The Boston Trial of *Naked Lunch*', *Evergreen Review*, IX/36 (June 1965).

60　Personal correspondence between the author and Miguel Grinberg, 10 August 2011.

61　Anne Luke, 'Youth Culture and the Politics of Youth in 1960s Cuba', unpublished PHD thesis, University of Wolverhampton, 2007.

62　Ginsberg, 'Message II', *Collected Poems*, p. 356.

63　Ginsberg and Ginsberg, *Family Business*, p. 247.

64　Ginsberg, *The Letters of Allen Ginsberg*, pp. 303–4.

65　Ginsberg, 'Kral Majales', *Collected Poems*, p. 361.

66　Ibid., p. 362.

67　Ginsberg, *The Letters of Allen Ginsberg*, p. 307.

68　Antonio Gramsci, *Prison Notebooks, Volume II,* trans. Joseph A. Buttigieg (New York, 2011), pp. 32–3.

69　Ginsberg, *The Letters of Allen Ginsberg*, p. 308.

70　Personal correspondence between the author and Anne Waldman, 7 September 2010.

71　Nicholson Baker, *The Anthologist* (London, 2009), p. 119.

72　See Tom Wolfe, *The Electric Kool-aid Acid Test* (New York, 1968) and Hunter S. Thompson, *Hell's Angels: The Strange and Terrible Saga of the Outlaw Motorcycle Gangs* (New York, 1966).

73　Allen Ginsberg, *Deliberate Prose: Selected Essays, 1925–1995*, ed. Bill Morgan (New York, 2000), p. 190.

74　Ibid.

75　Ginsberg, 'Wichita Vortex Sutra', *Collected Poems*, p. 410.

76　Norman Mailer, 'The White Negro', in *Advertisements for Myself* (Cambridge, MA, 1992), p. 339.

77　Ginsberg, *Deliberate Prose*, p. 67.

78　Ginsberg, 'Done, Finished with the Biggest Cock', *Collected Poems*, p. 474.

79　Ibid.

80　See Geoff Dyer's *The Ongoing Moment* (London, 2005), pp. 167–77.

81　Greil Marcus, *The Old, Weird America* (New York, 1997), p. 69.

82　Ginsberg,'Wales Visitation', *Collected Poems*, p. 490.

83　Quoted in James J. Wilhelm, *Ezra Pound: The Tragic Years, 1925–1972* (University Park, PA, 1994), p. 334.

84　Wilhelm, *Ezra Pound*, pp. 344–5.

85　Ginsberg, 'War Profit Litany', *Collected Poems*, p. 494.

4 'The Most Brilliant Man in America', 1968–77

1 Allen Ginsberg, 'Ego Confession', *Collected Poems, 1947–1997* [New York, 2006] (London, 2009), p. 631.

2 All quotes from transcript of *Firing Line: 'The Avant Garde'* (show 99), Hoover Institution *Firing Line* TV Program Collection, Stanford University.

3 Allen Ginsberg and Gary Snyder, *The Selected Letters of Allen Ginsberg and Gary Snyder*, ed. Bill Morgan (Berkeley, CA, 2009), p. 104.

4 John Updike, *Self-consciousness* (New York, 1989), pp. 252–3.

5 Ginsberg and Snyder, *Selected Letters*, pp. 100–101.

6 David Sandison and Graham Vickers, *Neal Cassady: The Fast Life of a Beat Hero* (Chicago, IL, 2006), p. 320.

7 Ginsberg, 'Elegy for Neal Cassady', *Collected Poems*, p. 497.

8 Ginsberg, 'On Neal's Ashes', *Collected Poems*, p. 513.

9 Neal Cassady, *Collected Letters, 1944–1967*, ed. Dave Moore (New York, 2004), p. xvii.

10 Ginsberg and Snyder, *Selected Letters*, p. 103.

11 Ginsberg, 'Going to Chicago', *Collected Poems*, p. 514.

12 Ginsberg, 'Grant Park: August 28, 1968', *Collected Poems*, p. 515.

13 Allen Ginsberg, *Spontaneous Mind: Selected Interviews 1958–1995*, ed. David Carter (New York, 2001), p. 180.

14 Ibid., p. 382.

15 Ginsberg, 'Car Crash', *Collected Poems*, p. 518.

16 *Time* (9 May 1969).

17 Ginsberg, 'In a Moonlit Hermit's Cabin', *Collected Poems*, p. 536.

18 Allen Ginsberg, *The Letters of Allen Ginsberg*, ed. Bill Morgan (New York, 2008), p. 345.

19 Paul Maher, *Kerouac: The Definitive Biography* (Lanham, MD, 2004), p. 274.

20 Jack Kerouac, 'After Me, the Deluge', *The Portable Jack Kerouac* (New York, 1995), pp. 573–80.

21 Ginsberg, 'Memory Gardens', *Collected Poems*, p. 541.

22 Maher, *Kerouac*, p. 476.

23 Ginsberg, 'Memory Gardens', *Collected Poems*, p. 542.

24 Arthur Rimbaud, *Selected Poems and Letters*, trans. Jeremy Harding and John Sturrock (London, 2004), p. 238.

25 Thomas Pynchon, *Vineland* (Boston, MA, 1990), p. 48.

26 Ginsberg, 'Anti-Vietnam War Peace Mobilization', *Collected Poems*, p. 549.

27 Ginsberg, 'Ecologue', *Collected Poems*, p. 559.

28 Gtsan-smyon He-ru-ka, Lobzang Jivaka and Walter Yeeling Evans-Wentz, *The Life of Milarepa: Tibet's Great Yogi*, ed. Lobzang Jivaka (London, 1962), pp. 158–9.

29 Ginsberg, 'September on Jessore Road', *Collected Poems*, p. 581.

30 Allen Ginsberg, *Deliberate Prose: Selected Essays, 1925–1995*, ed. Bill Morgan (New York, 2000), p. 195.

31 Ginsberg, 'Ayers Rock/Uluru Song', *Collected Poems*, p. 587.

32 Ginsberg, *Deliberate Prose*, p. 273.

33 Ginsberg and Snyder, *Selected Letters*, p. 141.

34 Ginsberg, *Deliberate Prose*, p. 348–57.

35 Ginsberg, *The Letters of Allen Ginsberg*, p. 81.

36 Slavoj Žižek, *The Parallax View* (Cambridge, MA, 2009), p. 384.

37 Slavoj Žižek, *Interrogating the Real*, ed. Rex Butler and Scott Stephens (New York, 2005), pp. 335–6. For an analysis of Ginsberg's Buddhism, see Tony Trigilio, *Allen Ginsberg's Buddhist Poetics* (Carbondale, IL, 2007).

38 Ginsberg, 'Xmas Gift', *Collected Poems*, p. 595.

39 Ginsberg, 'Thoughts Sitting Breathing', *Collected Poems*, p. 599.

40 Ginsberg, *Deliberate Prose*, pp. 19–20.

41 Kurt Vonnegut, *Conversations with Kurt Vonnegut*, ed. William Rodney Allen (Jackson, MS, 1988), p. 107.

42 Allen Ginsberg, *Spontaneous Mind: Selected Interviews 1958–1995*, ed. David Carter (New York, 2001), p. 453.

43 Ginsberg, *Deliberate Prose*, p. 371.

44 Ginsberg, 'Sweet Boy, Gimme Yr Ass', *Collected Poems*, p. 621.

45 John Higgs, *I Have America Surrounded: The Life of Timothy Leary* (Fort Lee, NJ, 2006), p. 230.

46 Ginsberg, 'Ego Confession', *Collected Poems*, p. 631.

47 Ginsberg, 'Hospital Window', *Collected Poems*, p. 642.

48 Ginsberg, 'Reading French Poetry', *Collected Poems*, p. 654.

49 D. H. Lawrence, *Studies in Classic American Literature* (London, 1971), p. 79.

50 Ibid., p. 70.

51 Ginsberg, 'Contest of Bards', *Collected Poems*, p. 687.

52 Ginsberg, 'Don't Grow Old', *Collected Poems*, p. 659.

53 Ginsberg, 'For Creeley's Ear', *Collected Poems*, p. 671.

54 Ginsberg and Snyder, *Selected Letters*, p. 199; Ginsberg, 'Punk Rock Your My Big Crybaby', *Collected Poems*, p. 691.

55 Ginsberg, 'Love Replied', *Collected Poems*, p. 693.

56 Ginsberg, 'Grim Skeleton', *Collected Poems*, p. 699.

5 'Many Prophets Have Failed', 1978–87

1 Allen Ginsberg, 'Ode to Failure', *Collected Poems, 1947–1997* [New York, 2006] (London, 2009), p. 745.

2 See variant lines in Ginsberg, 'Plutonian Ode', *Collected Poems*, p. 711.

3 Charles Bernstein, *My Way: Speeches and Poems* (Chicago, IL, 1999), p. 270. Also personal correspondence between author and Bernstein, 30 January 2011.

4 Ginsberg, 'Brooklyn College Brain', *Collected Poems*, p. 725

5 William Blake, *The Letters of William Blake*, ed. Geoffrey Keynes (New York, 1956), p. 51

6 Ginsberg, 'Maybe Love', *Collected Poems*, p. 731.

7 Allen Ginsberg and Gary Snyder, *The Selected Letters of Allen Ginsberg and Gary Snyder*, ed. Bill Morgan (Berkeley, CA, 2009), p. 220.

8 Ginsberg, 'Maybe Love', *Collected Poems*, p. 733.

9 Personal correspondence between the author and Elsa Dorfman, 21 September 2010.

10 Ed Sanders, *The Poetry and Life of Allen Ginsberg* (Woodstock, NY, 2000), p. 116.

11 All quotes from Tom Clark, *The Great Naropa Poetry Wars* (Santa Barbara, CA, 1980), p. 60.

12 Ginsberg and Snyder, *Selected Letters*, p. 207.

13 Ginsberg, 'Reflections at Lake Louise', *Collected Poems*, p. 742.

14 Ginsberg, 'Birdbrain' *Collected Poems*, p. 747.

15 Ginsberg and Snyder, *Selected Letters*, p. 226.

16 Ginsberg, 'Capitol Air', *Collected Poems*, p. 754.

17 Ginsberg, 'Industrial Waves', *Collected Poems*, p. 846.

18 Ginsberg, 'Love Comes', *Collected Poems*, p. 854.

19 Ginsberg, 'Transcription of Organ Music', *Collected Poems*, pp. 148–9.

20 Private correspondence from Eileen Myles to the author, 30 January 2011.

21 Ginsberg, 'Airplane Blues', *Collected Poems*, p. 860.

22 William A. Henry iii, 'Howl Becomes a Hoot', *Time* (7 December 1981).

23 Ginsberg, 'Ode to Failure', *Collected Poems*, p. 745.

24 Private correspondence from Barrett Watten to the author, 26 January 2011. See also Barrett Watten, 'The Turn to Language in the 1960s', *Critical Inquiry*, 29 (Autumn 2002), p. 182.

25 Ginsberg, 'Happening Now', *Collected Poems*, p. 868.

26 Allen Ginsberg, *The Letters of Allen Ginsberg*, ed. Bill Morgan (New York, 2008), p. 404.

27 Ginsberg, 'Thoughts Sitting Breathing ii', *Collected Poems*, p. 879.

28 *The UNESCO Courier: a window open on the world*, xxxv/11 (Paris, 1982), p. 3.

29 Ginsberg and Snyder, *Selected Letters*, p. 147.

30 Ginsberg, 'I'm a Prisoner of Allen Ginsberg', *Collected Poems*, p. 882.

31 Ginsberg and Snyder, *Selected Letters*, p. 252.

32 Ginsberg, *The Letters of Allen Ginsberg*, p. 414.

33 Ginsberg, 'Empire Air', *Collected Poems*, p. 893.

34 Alain Badiou, *On Beckett*, ed. Alberto Toscano and Nina Power (Manchester, 2003), p. 38.

35 Ginsberg, *The Letters of Allen Ginsberg*, p. 414.

36 Geoff Dyer, *The Ongoing Moment* (London, 2005), pp. 1–2.

37 Ibid., pp, 234–6.

38 Ginsberg, 'Reading Bai Juyi', *Collected Poems*, p. 905.

39 Ginsberg, 'Black Shroud', *Collected Poems*, p. 912.

40 R. Z. Shepard, 'Mainstreaming Allen Ginsberg', *Time* (4 February 1985).

41 Sanders, *The Poetry and Life of Allen Ginsberg*, p. 161.

42 Ginsberg and Snyder, *Selected Letters*, p. 262.

43 Charles Bernstein, *My Way*, p. 270. Also see personal correspondence between the author and Bernstein, 30 January 2011.

44 Ginsberg, *The Letters of Allen Ginsberg*, p. 418.

45 Ginsberg, 'Sphincter', *Collected Poems*, p. 950.

46 D. H. Lawrence, *Studies in Classic American Literature* (London, 1971). See Foreword.

47 Ginsberg, 'Graphic Winces', *Collected Poems*, p. 960.

48 Ginsberg, 'On Cremation of Chögyam Trungpa, Vidyadhara', *Collected*

Poems, p. 968.

49 Ginsberg, *The Letters of Allen Ginsberg*, p. 420.
50 Ginsberg, 'Personals Ad', *Collected Poems*, p. 970.
51 Ginsberg, 'Proclamation', *Collected Poems*, p. 971.

6 'An Urn of Ashes', 1988–97

1   Allen Ginsberg, 'Things I'll Not Do (Nostalgias)', *Collected Poems, 1947–1997* [New York, 2006] (London, 2009), p. 1161.
2   Ginsberg, 'Howl', *Collected Poems*, p. 139.
3   Edmund White, *Genet* (London, 1994), p. 642.
4   Ginsberg, 'May Days 1988', *Collected Poems*, pp. 979–81.
5   Allen Ginsberg, *Deliberate Prose: Selected Essays, 1925–1995*, ed. Bill Morgan (New York, 2000), pp. 170–72.
6   Nicholson Baker, *The Anthologist* (London, 2009), p. 121.
7   Ibid., p. 101.
8   Ibid., p. 182.
9   Allen Ginsberg, *The Letters of Allen Ginsberg*, ed. Bill Morgan (New York, 2008), p. 432.
10 Ginsberg, 'Return of Kral Majales', *Collected Poems*, p. 984.
11 Ginsberg, *Deliberate Prose*, p. 471.
12 Ed Sanders, *The Poetry and Life of Allen Ginsberg* (Woodstock, NY, 2000), p. 184.
13 Allen Ginsberg and Gary Snyder, *The Selected Letters of Allen Ginsberg and Gary Snyder*, ed. Bill Morgan (Berkeley, CA, 2009), p. 291.
14 Ibid., p. 292.
15 Ginsberg, 'After the Big Parade', *Collected Poems*, p. 1010.
16 Ginsberg, 'Not Dead Yet', *Collected Poems*, p. 1012.
17 Ginsberg, 'Lunchtime', *Collected Poems*, p. 1017.
18 Oliver Harris, '"Burroughs Is a Poet Too, Really": The Poetics of *Minutes to Go*', first published in *Edinburgh Review*, 114 (2005). Republished by RealityStudio, August 2010, at: http://realitystudio.org/scholarship/burroughs-is-a-poet-too-really-the-poetics-of-minutes-to-go/.
19 Ginsberg, *The Letters of Allen Ginsberg*, p. 436.
20 Private correspondence between the author and Peter Hale, 10 February 2011.

21 Ginsberg, 'American Sentences', *Collected Poems*, p. 1050.

22 Ginsberg and Snyder, *Selected Letters*, p. 298.

23 Ginsberg, 'After Lalon', *Collected Poems*, p. 1021.

24 Ginsberg, *The Letters of Allen Ginsberg*, p. 438.

25 Ginsberg, 'Here We Go 'Round the Mulberry Bush', *Collected Poems*, p. 1073.

26 Ginsberg and Snyder, *Selected Letters*, p. 313.

27 Dinitia Smith, 'How Allen Ginsberg Thinks His Thoughts', *New York Times* (8 October 1996).

28 Ginsberg, 'Newt Gingrich Declares War on "McGovernik Counterculture"', *Collected Poems*, p. 1082.

29 Ginsberg, *The Letters of Allen Ginsberg*, pp. 440–42.

30 Ibid., p. 439.

31 Michael Hartnett, *Collected Poems*, ed. Peter Fallon (Loughcrew, Ireland, 2001), p. 47.

32 Ginsberg and Snyder, *Selected Letters*, p. 309.

33 Sanders, *The Poetry and Life of Allen Ginsberg*, p. 207.

34 Edward Lewine, 'Conference on King of Beats, Punctuated by Counter Beats', *New York Times* (11 June 1995).

35 Ginsberg and Snyder, *Selected Letters*, p. 312.

36 Ginsberg, 'Bowel Song', *Collected Poems*, p. 1097.

37 Ginsberg, 'Multiple Identity Questionnaire', *Collected Poems*, p. 1103.

38 Ginsberg, 'Don't Get Angry with Me', *Collected Poems*, p. 1104.

39 Ginsberg, 'Good Luck', *Collected Poems*, p. 1121.

40 Ginsberg, 'Dream', *Collected Poems*, p. 1159.

41 Ginsberg, *Deliberate Prose*, p. 207.

42 Ginsberg, 'Things I'll Not Do (Nostalgias)', *Collected Poems*, p. 1161.

7 See you later, Allen Ginsberg . . .

The chapter title comes from Bob Dylan, *A Tree With Roots*, 4-CD Bootleg (White Bear, 2001), disc 2, track 24.

1 Allen Ginsberg, 'Objective Subject', *Collected Poems, 1947–1997* [New York, 2006] (London, 2009), p. 1137.

2 Peter Orlovsky, *Clean Asshole Poems and Smiling Vegetable Songs: Poems, 1957–1977* (San Francisco, CA, 1978), p. 42.

3 Ginsberg, 'Who', *Collected Poems*, p. 603.

4 Ginsberg, 'Death & Fame', *Collected Poems*, p. 1132.

Bibliography

Works by Ginsberg

Allen Verbatim, ed. Gordon Ball (New York, 1974)
The Book of Martyrdom and Artifice: First Journals and Poems, 1937–1952, ed.
    Juanita Lieberman-Plimpton and Bill Morgan (New York, 2006)
Collected Poems 1947–1997 [New York, 2006] (London, 2009)
Composed on the Tongue (Bolinas, CA, 1980)
Cosmopolitan Greetings (New York, 1994)
Death & Fame (New York, 1999)
Deliberate Prose: Selected Essays, 1925–1995, ed. Bill Morgan (New York, 2000)
Empty Mirror (New York, 1961)
The Fall of America (San Francisco, CA, 1972)
First Blues (New York, 1975)
The Gates of Wrath: Rhymed Poems, 1948–51 (Bolinas, CA, 1972)
Howl and Other Poems (San Francisco, CA, 1956)
Howl: 50th Anniversary Edition (New York, 2006)
Indian Journals (New York, 1996)
Journals Early Fifties Early Sixties, ed. Gordon Ball (New York, 1977)
Journals Mid-Fifties, ed. Gordon Ball (New York, 1994)
Kaddish and Other Poems (San Francisco, CA, 1961)
The Letters of Allen Ginsberg, ed. Bill Morgan (New York, 2008)
Mind Breaths (San Francisco, CA, 1978)
Planet News: 1961–1967 (San Francisco, CA, 1968)
Plutonian Ode: Poems 1977–1980 (San Francisco, CA, 1982)
Reality Sandwiches: 1953–60 (San Francisco, CA, 1963)
Spontaneous Mind: Selected Interviews, 1958–1995, ed. David Carter (New
    York, 2001)

White Shroud Poems (New York, 1986)

Ginsberg, Allen, and Neal Cassady, *As Ever* (Berkeley, CA, 1977)

—, and Eric Drooker, *Illuminated Poems* (New York, 1996)

—, and Louis Ginsberg, *Family Business: Selected Letters Between a Father and Son*, ed. Michael Schumacher (New York, 2001)

—, and Jack Kerouac, *Jack Kerouac and Allen Ginsberg: The Letters*, ed. Bill Morgan and David Stanford (New York, 2010)

—, and Peter Orlovsky, *Straight Hearts' Delight* (San Francisco, CA, 1980)

—, and Gary Snyder, *The Selected Letters of Allen Ginsberg and Gary Snyder*, ed. Bill Morgan (Berkeley, CA, 2009)

Select Bibliography

Amburn, Ellis, *Subterranean Kerouac: The Hidden Life of Jack Kerouac* (New York, 1998)

Artaud, Antonin, *Artaud Anthology* (San Francisco, CA, 1965)

Ashbery, John, *The Mooring of Starting Out: The First Five Books of Poetry* (New York, 1997)

Badiou, Alain, *On Beckett*, ed. Alberto Toscano and Nina Power (Manchester, 2003)

Baker, Deborah, *The Blue Hand: The Beats in India* (New York, 2008)

Baker, Nicholson, *The Anthologist* (London, 2009)

—, *U and I* (New York, 1992)

Baraka, Amiri, *The Autobiography of LeRoi Jones* (New York, 1984)

Barber, Stephen, *Antonin Artaud: Terminal Curses* (Los Angeles, CA, 2008)

Barthes, Roland, *Image Music Text*, trans. Stephen Heath (London, 1977)

Bernstein, Charles, *My Way: Speeches and Poems* (Chicago, IL, 1999)

Blake, William, *The Letters of William Blake*, ed. Geoffrey Keynes (New York, 1956)

Breton, André, *Communicating Vessels*, trans. Mary Ann Caws and Geoffrey T. Harris (Lincoln, NE, 1990)

—, *Manifestoes of Surrealism*, trans. Richard Seaver and Helen R. Lane (Ann Arbor, MI, 1969)

Burroughs, William S., *Burroughs Live: The Collected Interviews of William S. Burroughs, 1960–1997*, ed. Sylvère Lotringer (New York, 2001)

—, *Cities of the Red Night* (New York, 1981)

—, *Exterminator!* (New York, 1973)

—, *Junky: The Definitive Text*, ed. Oliver Harris (London, 2003)

—, *The Letters of William S. Burroughs*, vol. I: *1945–1959*, ed. Oliver Harris (New York, 1993)

—, *Letters to Allen Ginsberg: 1953–57* (New York, 1982)

—, *Naked Lunch: 50th Anniversary Edition* (New York, 2009)

—, and Allen Ginsberg, *The Yage Letters Redux* [1963], ed. Oliver Harris (San Francisco, CA, 2004)

—, and Jack Kerouac, *And the Hippos Were Boiled in Their Tanks* (New York, 2009)

Butler, Judith, *Gender Trouble* (New York, 2006)

Campbell, James, *This Is the Beat Generation* (Berkeley, CA, 1999)

Cassady, Carolyn, *Off the Road: My Years with Cassady, Kerouac, and Ginsberg* (New York, 1990)

Cassady, Neal, *Collected Letters, 1944–1967*, ed. Dave Moore (New York, 2004)

—, *The First Third* [expanded edn] (San Francisco, CA, 1981)

Caveney, Graham, *Screaming with Joy: The Life of Allen Ginsberg* (New York, 1999)

Charters, Ann, *Kerouac: A Biography* (San Francisco, CA, 1973)

—, ed., *The Portable Beat Reader* (New York, 1992)

—, ed., *The Portable Sixties Reader* (New York, 2003)

Cheever, John, *The Journals* (London, 1991)

Clark, Tom, *The Great Naropa Poetry Wars* (Santa Barbara, CA, 1980)

Conners, Peter, *White Hand Society* (San Francisco, CA, 2010)

Corso, Gregory, *An Accidental Autobiography: The Selected Letters of Gregory Corso*, ed. Bill Morgan (New York, 2003)

—, *Gasoline; The Vestal Lady on Brattle* (San Francisco, CA, 1976)

—, *Mindfield: New & Selected Poems* (New York, 1998)

Creeley, Robert, *The Collected Poems of Robert Creeley, 1945–1975* (Berkeley, CA, 1982)

Critchley, Simon, *On Humour* (Oxford, 2002)

Davidson, Michael, *The San Francisco Renaissance: Poetics and Community at Mid-century* (Cambridge, MA, 1989)

Deleuze, Gilles, *Essays Critical and Clinical*, trans. Daniel W. Smith and Michael A. Greco (London, 1998)

—, and Félix Guattari, *Anti-Oedipus*, trans. Robert Hurley, Mark Seam and Helen R. Lane (New York, 2009)

DeLillo, Don, *Point Omega*, (New York, 2010)

Derrida, Jacques, *Acts of Literature*, ed. Derek Attridge (New York, 1992)

—, *The Gift of Death*, trans. David Willis (Chicago, IL, 1995)

Di Prima, Diane, *Recollections of My Life as a Woman* (New York, 2001)

Dyer, Geoff, *The Ongoing Moment* (London, 2005)

Dylan, Bob, *Chronicles: Volume One* (New York, 2004)

Ferlinghetti, Lawrence, *How to Paint Sunlight: Lyric Poems and Others (1997–2000)* (New York, 2001)

Fisher, Mark, *Capitalist Realism: Is There No Alternative?* (Hants, 2009)

Foucault, Michel, *Madness and Civilization*, trans. Richard Howard (Oxford, 1989)

Geiger, John, *Nothing is True – Everything is Permitted: The Life of Brion Gysin* (New York, 2005)

Gifford, Barry, and Lawrence Lee, *Jack's Book* (New York, 1978)

Gramsci, Antonio, *Prison Notebooks, Volume II*, trans. Joseph A. Buttigieg (New York, 2011)

Greenblatt, Stephen, *Learning to Curse* (New York, 1990)

Hartnett, Michael, *Collected Poems*, ed. Peter Fallon (Winston-Salem, NC, 1994)

Heidegger, Martin, *Being and Time*, trans. John Macquarrie and Edward Robinson (New York, 1962)

Heims, Neil, *Allen Ginsberg* (New York, 2005)

He-ru-ka, Gtsan-smyon, Lobzang Jivaka, and Walter Yeeling Evans-Wentz, *The Life of Milarepa*: *Tibet's Great Yogi*, ed. Lobzang Jivaka (London, 1962)

Higgs, John, *I Have America Surrounded: The Life of Timothy Leary* (Fort Lee, NJ, 2006)

Hobbs, Stuart D., *The End of the American Avant Garde* (New York, 1997)

Holmes, John Clellon, *Go* (New York, 1952)

Huncke, Herbert, *The Evening Sun Turned Crimson* (Cherry Valley, NY, 1980)

—, *The Herbert Huncke Reader* (New York, 1997)

Hyde, Lewis, ed., *On the Poetry of Allen Ginsberg* (Ann Arbor, MI, 1984)

James, Henry, *The Ambassadors* [1903] (Oxford, 2008)

James, William, *Writings: 1878–1899* (New York, 1992)

Johnson, Joyce, *Minor Characters* (Boston, MA, 1983)

Johnson, Rob, *The Lost Years of William S. Burroughs* (College Station, TX, 2006)

Kashner, Sam, *When I Was Cool* (New York, 2004)

Kerouac, Jack, *The Beat Generation* (New York, 2005)

—, *Desolation Angels* (New York, 1965)

—, *The Dharma Bums* (New York, 1958)

—, *On the Road* (New York, 1957)

—, *The Portable Jack Kerouac*, ed. Ann Charters (New York, 1995)

—, *Pull My Daisy* (New York, 1961)

—, *Selected Letters: 1940–1956*, ed. Ann Charters (New York, 1995)

—, *Selected Letters: 1957–1969*, ed. Ann Charters (New York, 1999)

—, *Windblown World: The Journals of Jack Kerouac, 1947–1954* (New York, 2004)

Kramer, Jane, *Allen Ginsberg in America* (New York, 1969)

Kyger, Jane, *Strange Big Moon: The Japan and India Journals, 1960–1964* (Berkeley, CA, 2000)

Lawrence, D. H., *The Letters of D. H. Lawrence*, vol. II: *1913–1916*, ed. George J. Zytaruk and James T. Boulton (Cambridge, 1981)

—, *The Letters of D. H. Lawrence*, vol. IV: *1921–1924*, ed. Warren Roberts, James T. Boulton and Elizabeth Mansfield (Cambridge, 1987)

—, *Studies in Classic American Literature* (London, 1971)

Levin, Joanna, *Bohemia in America, 1858–1920* (Stanford, CA, 2010)

McClure, Michael, *Scratching the Beat Surface* (San Francisco, CA, 1982)

Maher, Paul, *Kerouac: The Definitive Biography* (Lanham, MD, 2004)

Mailer, Norman, *Advertisements for Myself* (Cambridge, MA, 1992)

—, *The Armies of the Night* (New York, 1968)

Marcus, Greil, *The Old, Weird America* (New York, 1997)

Miles, Barry, *The Beat Hotel* (New York, 2000)

—, *Ginsberg: A Biography* (London, 2000)

—, *William Burroughs: El Hombre Invisible* (New York, 1993)

Morgan, Bill, *The Beat Generation in New York* (San Francisco, CA, 1997)

—, *The Beat Generation in San Francisco* (San Francisco, CA, 2003)

—, *I Celebrate Myself: The Somewhat Private Life of Allen Ginsberg* (New York, 2006)

—, *The Response to Allen Ginsberg, 1926–1994* (Westport, CT, 1996)

—, *The Typewriter is Holy* (New York, 2010)

—, *The Works of Allen Ginsberg, 1941–1994* (Westport, CT, 1995)

—, and Nancy J. Peters, *Howl on Trial* (San Francisco, CA, 2006)

—, and Bob Rosenthal, *Best Minds: A Tribute to Allen Ginsberg* (New York, 1986)

Morgan, Ted, *Literary Outlaw: The Life and Times of William S. Burroughs* (New York, 1988)

Nietzsche, Friedrich, *Basic Writings of Nietzsche*, trans. Walter Kaufmann (New York, 2000)

Olson, Charles, *Collected Prose*, ed. Donald Allen and Benjamin Friedlander (Berkeley, CA, 1997)

Orlovsky, Peter, *Clean Asshole Poems and Smiling Vegetable Songs: Poems, 1957–1977* (San Francisco, CA, 1978)

Percy, Walker, *The Moviegoer* [1961] (New York, 1998)

Perloff, Marjorie, *Poetic License: Essays on Modernist and Postmodernist Lyric* (Evanston, IL, 1990)

Pessoa, Fernando, *The Book of Disquiet*, ed. and trans. Richard Zenith (London, 2002)

Plimpton, George, ed., *Beat Writers at Work* (New York, 1999)

Podhoretz, Norman, *Ex-friends* (New York, 1999)

—, *The Norman Podhoretz Reader*, ed. Thomas L. Jeffers (New York, 2004)

Pynchon, Thomas, *Vineland* (Boston, MA, 1990)

Raskin, Jonah, *American Scream* (Berkeley, CA, 2005)

Rimbaud, Arthur, *Selected Poems and Letters*, trans. Jeremy Harding and John Sturrock (London, 2004)

Roth, Philip, *The Facts: A Novelist's Autobiography* (New York, 1988)

Salewicz, Chris, *Redemption Song: The Ballad of Joe Strummer* (New York, 2006)

Sanders, Ed, *The Poetry and Life of Allen Ginsberg* (Woodstock, NY, 2000)

Sandison, David and Graham Vickers, *Neal Cassady: The Fast Life of a Beat Hero* (Chicago, IL, 2006)

Sargeant, Jack, *Naked Lens: Beat Cinema* (Berkeley, CA, 2008)

Schumacher, Michael, *Dharma Lion: A Critical Biography of Allen Ginsberg* (New York, 1992)

Shields, David, *Reality Hunger* (New York, 2010)

Shinder, Jason, ed., *The Poem That Changed America: 'Howl' Fifty Years Later* (New York, 2006)

Silliman, Ron, ed., *In the American Tree* (Orono, ME, 1985)

Sinclair, Mick, *San Francisco: A Cultural and Literary History* (Oxford, 2004)

Smart, Christopher, *Selected Poems* (London, 1991)

Snyder, Gary, *Passage Through India* (San Francisco, CA, 1983)

Stein, Gertrude, *How to Write* (New York, 1975)

Stevens, Jay, *Storming Heaven: LSD and the American Dream* (New York, 1987)

Stiles, Bradley J., *Emerson's Contemporaries and Kerouac's Crowd: A Problem of Self-location* (Cranbury, NJ, 2003)

Thompson, Hunter S., *Hell's Angels: The Strange and Terrible Saga of the Outlaw Motorcycle Gangs* (New York, 1966)

Tiqqun, *Introduction to Civil War*, trans. Alexander R. Galloway and Jason E. Smith (Los Angeles, CA, 2010)

Trigilio, Tony, *Allen Ginsberg's Buddhist Poetics* (Carbondale, IL, 2007)

Tyrell, John, *Naked Angels: The Lives and Literature of the Beat Generation* (New York, 1976)

Updike, John, *Self-consciousness* (New York, 1989)

Vonnegut, Kurt, *Conversations with Kurt Vonnegut*, ed. William Rodney Allen (Oxford, MS, 1988)

Waldman, Anne, and Marilyn Webb, eds, *Talking Poetics from Naropa Institute* (Boulder, CO, 1979), 2 vols

—, and Laura E. Wright, *Beats at Naropa: An Anthology* (Minneapolis, MN, 2009)

Watten, Barrett, *The Constructivist Moment: from Material Text to Cultural Poetics* (Middletown, CT, 2003)

Wallace, David Foster, *A Supposedly Fun Thing I'll Never Do Again* (New York, 1997)

Whalen, Philip, *The Collected Poems of Philip Whalen* (Lebanon, NH, 2007)

White, Edmund, *Genet* (London, 1994)

Whitman, Walt, *The Complete Poems*, ed. Francis Murphy (London, 2004)

Wilhelm, James J., *Ezra Pound: The Tragic Years, 1925–1972* (University Park, PA, 1994)

Williams, William Carlos, *Paterson*, revd edn (New York, 1992)

—, *The Collected Poems of William Carlos Williams*, vol. II: *1939–1962*, ed. Christopher MacGowan (New York, 1991)

Wittgenstein, Ludwig, *Tractatus Logico-Philosophicus*, trans. D. F. Pears and B. F. McGuinness (New York, 2001)

Wolfe, Tom, *The Electric Kool-aid Acid Test* (New York, 1968)

Wordsworth, William, *The Major Works: Including The Prelude*, ed. Stephen Gill, (Oxford, 2008)

Žižek, Slavoj, *Interrogating the Real*, ed. Rex Butler and Scott Stephens (New York, 2005)

—, *The Parallax View* (Cambridge, MA, 2009)

Acknowledgements

No biography of Allen Ginsberg would be possible without the pioneering work of Barry Miles, the critical precision of Michael Schumacher, and the breathtaking scope, compassion, and learning of Bill Morgan. To all these I owe more than I can succinctly put into words. Ed Sanders, another of Allen's excellent biographers wrote, 'perhaps a day-by-day bio, maybe 25,000 pages long, is what is required.' That would be something.

Firstly, Peter Hale at the Allen Ginsberg Trust for unfailingly answering questions, responding to requests for addresses, generous provision of images, and doing so with such good humour – thank you. Huge thanks to Bob Rosenthal for giving me the chance to work with him and Allen back in the late '80s and for answering recent enquiries despite working on his own Ginsberg biography – which I am very much looking forward to, knowing Bob's honesty and sense of humour. And to Jacqueline Gens, Vicky Stanbury, and Victoria Smart for similar reasons. To Stephen Barber for wealth of advice and first contacts. Anne Waldman, Charles Bernstein, Helen Weaver, Elsa Dorfman, Michael Rothenberg, Barrett Watten, Ron Silliman, Eileen Myles, Peter Conners, and Stewart Home for comments. Taylor Mignon for Japanese poetic connections. Andrew Sclanders of BeatBooks for image help beyond call of duty. Jed Birmingham for journals and Burroughs assistance – and to all at RealityStudio. This book would not be what it is without the editorial advice and first reading of drafts by Melissa Mann and Haidee Kruger – cheers and tjeers. Finally, to Victoria for putting up with my obsessions.

Photo Acknowledgements

The author and publishers wish to express their thanks to the below sources of illustrative material and/or permission to reproduce it:

Photos © Allen Ginsberg Estate: pp. 24, 27, 36, 40, 50, 52, 54, 57, 69, 81, 90, 98, 103, 121, 127, 170; collection of the author: p. 185; reprinted by permission of City Lights Books: pp. 65, 87; photo by Ernesto Fernández: p. 107; collection of the Ginsberg Trust: pp. 53, 91, 161; © Miguel Grinberg: p. 107; © MDCarchives: p. 174; © Archer Prewitt: pp. 11, 147, 208.